Face 2 Face

Observing, Interviewing, and Rapport Building Skills

WORKS OF FICTION
BY MIKE ROCHE

BLUE MONSTER

COINS of DEATH

KARMA!

PRAISE for Face 2 Face!

"**Face 2 Face** is the kind of book I wish had been available when I started my career. When it comes to learning how to enhance observations skills, read other people, and increase your rapport building, **Mike Roche's book is masterful**."

—Joe Navarro, author of the international best seller,
What Every Body is Saying

Acknowledgements

My life has been an ongoing learning process. I want to thank everyone that taught me the value of treating others, as I would like to be treated. I have to thank my wife and Carol Ellis for correcting and catching my woeful mistakes. At times, my brain would run faster than my slow fingers and the results were not good. Rob and Amy Siders and the rest of the creative team at 52 Novels turned my manuscript into a professional appearing novel. Who says that you cannot judge a book by its cover? Lynne Hansen designed the fantastic book cover.

Contents

Face 2 Face

Observing, Interviewing, and Rapport Building Skills

Mike Roche U.S. Secret Service Special Agent (Retired)

MikeRoche.com

Chapter 1
Reaction Time

If I were standing before you, I would make my first impression upon you in one tenth of a second. Try typing "First Impression" into Google and see how fast the response comes back after hitting the enter key. I'll save you the trouble. My search was received in .18 seconds. Just that quick.

Your mind works almost as fast as Google. Your first image of your conversational partner will be cemented within two to three seconds. If you are the client, it is difficult but not impossible to overcome that first three seconds. As quick as you can clap your hands in front of your face, bang, the decision of likeability or distaste is cast like an etching in granite. You had better hope it is not an etching in a tombstone.

If you have found this book in a bookstore, the cover has grabbed you, and if I am lucky, you will read the first three pages. Bang just that quick and the book goes in the shopping basket. Unless you did not like the book, and you tossed it back on the shelf, probably in the wrong section with the spine facing the wrong direction alongside the other misfit books.

Imagine an individual who is a college dropout that traveled to India in search of his spiritual Zen, and attributes LSD as one of the top experiences in his life. Now imagine the challenges that same individual would face in projecting a positive impression in a corporate boardroom or conquering an auditorium full of cynical journalists. Yet Steve Jobs, the founder of Apple Corporation, did just that.

Jobs, who was known as a control freak, who often displayed a brash and short-tempered attitude. Some described him as an ego-maniac. No one can deny that Steve Jobs had passion for the products developed by Apple. He enjoyed surrounding himself with smart people and ensured every element was correct and functional. Apple has changed all of our lives. The home computer, the Mac, the iPhone, the iPod and the iPad have revolutionized consumer electronics. Even if you do not own an Apple product, the consumer electronics that you do own are the result or response to Apple's competitive edge.

Steve Job's charisma was described by Guy L. "Bud" Tribble the Vice President of Software Technology at Apple, as a "Reality Distortion Field." His embracing of enthusiastic optimism and passion for the Apple products energized colleagues, journalists and devoted consumers. He made believers of the unbelievable.

When we expect to see the CEO of the largest publicly traded corporation in the world, you would anticipate a power ensemble with a suit, white shirt and red tie. The CEO would strut with confidence in his hard leather shoes to the podium and display an authoritative persona.

Jobs was none of that. Sauntering on stage, wearing his signature black mock turtleneck, Levi's 501 jeans and New Balance tennis shoes, Steve Jobs presented the opposite first impression that you would expect. He was confident yet portrayed humility, and perhaps that was why he appeared trustworthy as a spokesperson. The message was not about him, but Apple's new product.

With the anticipation of a magician, he was able to wow the audience with simplicity and easily conveyed comparisons. He mirrored the simple PowerPoint presentation. His body language conveyed his passion, using his hands as illustrators, like a painter uses his brush on the canvass. He had a subtle panache.

By the end of his product introduction demonstrations, everyone wanted one. When he pulled that first iPod out of his jeans pocket with the simple message of, "1000 songs in your pocket," everyone wanted one under the Christmas tree that year. His dress attire embraced the understated and simple but functional design of his products. Albert Einstein said, "Everything should be made as simple as possible, but not simpler."

I have observed former President Bill Clinton from afar and up close. As a young police officer, I patrolled around the Governor's mansion in Little Rock, Arkansas. Since 1992, my career with the Secret Service has often involved providing some level of protection to Bill Clinton as a candidate, as President, and as a former President. Despite what you think of his politics and ethical lapses, he has the innate ability to greet people and make them feel special.

Perhaps due to his humble beginnings, first in Hope and then Hot Springs, Arkansas, where he learned to relate to people from all socioeconomic backgrounds. He had an early interest in politics dating back to high school and continuing through college. His ability to develop rapport and display empathy towards his conversational partner was a foundation that he would utilize on his road to the White House. He optimized eye contact and used his disarming smile as leverage to ingratiate himself with strangers, as well as adversaries. Using his homespun demeanor and humility, he projected interest in his conversational partner, developing an immediate empathetic rapport with the individual.

People would repeatedly say that he made them feel like they were the only person in the room. He directed his interest and aligned his body with theirs. He locked his eyes on their eyes, flashed that smile, shook their hand, and nodded in interest. He talked with them and not to them. You do not have to agree with him, but Bill Clinton was one of the most powerful communicators I have witnessed.

I urge you to go to YouTube and watch videos of both Steve Jobs and President Bill Clinton. Watch their body language, demeanor, body inclination, and eye contact. Most of all, watch their ability to develop rapport with their audience or conversational recipient and what impression they made with the recipient of their interest.

To demonstrate how quickly the brain processes incoming stimuli, place yourself in this position. You are a police officer working the midnight shift. You have come on duty at 11:00PM, and you look at your watch as it approaches 6:00AM. You have less than an hour to quitting time. In thirty minutes, you can start easing toward the station. Of course, you yawn as you fight off the sleep monster. You think of the soft bedding and cool sheets calling your name.

The radio dispatching you to a disturbance at a bar interrupts your thoughts. Upon your arrival, you locate a drunk who tells you that he was thrown out of the bar, but did not mean any harm. He admits to having too much to drink.

You propose to him a simple solution that should be agreeable to all parties. You offer not to arrest the inebriated soul, as you know with all the paper work associated with an arrest, you will be late getting home. Instead, you will escort the intoxicated gentleman to Denny's for a little breakfast. He can sober up, and call his buddy to pick him up, and deliver him home. He readily agrees to this wonderful opportunity to avoid a ride in the backseat of a police car to the city jail.

He asks if he can first retrieve his hat from his car. Sure, no problem. You don't want a man to enter Denny's underdressed. First impressions count. As he reaches into his car, he pulls out the hat with his left hand, and in his right hand, you see a gun.

One morning, I found myself in that situation. The brain immediately observed, perceived, and reacted to the peril. Everything instantly slowed down. My mind had already processed that this man who had provided no earlier insight into these actions other than to say, "I meant no harm," was now posing an imminent danger.

My primary thought was that he would probably shoot me, but I intended to get off at least one shot. My intention was to take him with me, or make his identification unmistakable for the responding investigators. In one smooth motion, I unsnapped my holster, pulled my gun, and slid my finger into the trigger guard. My finger tightened around the trigger, as I raised my weapon. I would anticipate my shot by pulling on the trigger, as I raised the barrel towards the suspect. The goal was that as the barrel came up on the target, the hammer would be dropping and propelling the bullet toward my assailant.

My focus narrowed to his torso and the gun in his hand that was slowly turning toward me. The race was on, and he had a clear head start. My left arm was rising towards him in a defensive position, and my knees were bending slightly to lower my body. This would result in decreasing my silhouette and increasing my stability, as I had practiced hundreds of times.

A miraculous event occurred. Just as I had perceived a threat, his mind also perceived a danger to his future existence. Despite being impaired, he now recognized my intent. He immediately opened his hand and with his palm, propelled the gun towards the ground. He began the preliminary efforts to raise his hands in the surrender position. His buddy, who was on the far side of the car, also perceived the danger and dove for cover to reduce his exposure.

My mind now recognized the elimination of the threat, and I stopped the movement of my hand. I froze the action of my finger on the trigger. I turned the barrel away from the target and ordered the suspect to turn and assume a prone position. As soon as the trauma had become manageable, time resumed to normal. The gun turned out to be a starter pistol, and the impaired gentleman was merely showing me the reason for his ejection from the bar.

He displayed no body language to indicate a threat because in his mind, he was not a danger.

How long did this entire incident last? Two seconds at most. John Hinckley fired six rounds of .22 caliber ammunition towards President Reagan in less than two seconds. Four people were wounded. To take your hands from your lap and clap them in front of your face takes two seconds. Now you can see how quickly my brain processed, calculated, and reacted.

I recommend reading the thought provoking work of Malcolm Gladwell, *Blink, The Power of Thinking Without Thinking*. He closely examines the art of thin slicing and making snap judgments. Gladwell examines the decision making process that occurs during such events as heart attack triage, speed dating, and yes police shootings. Gut instincts do have their limits, but we often perceive more information than we think. You must understand when more careful analysis is warranted.

One day my wife brought to my attention a rabbit in our backyard. It was rare sighting. We watched in gratitude of the rare sight, when we observed almost as equal of a rarity. Two deer wondered into our backyard. The rabbit perceiving danger, reduced its profile, as it dropped its head into its body and pinned its ears back. The rabbit was a motionless ball of fur blending with the oak mulch.

The deer meanwhile were oblivious to the rabbit, but were nonetheless skittish. At some point, they heard some noise that alarmed them. In an instant, the first deer turned her head ninety degrees to look at the cause of the noise, as she ever so slightly dropped her rear legs preparing for a rapid departure. Once the alarm had dissipated, both deer resumed their normalcy and strolled away. The rabbit, now comfortable that the deer had left, returned his head and ears to the active position.

We are faced with rapid calculations by the brain on a constant basis. We decide if a person is a threat or an ally. As we are driving to work, our brain is making hundreds of calculations to anticipate the actions of other drivers and potential road hazards. Most of these occur subconsciously just as first impressions are also calculated in the subconscious of the brain.

"As if in slow motion, fire flashed from the shooters pistol. The plate glass exploded into fragments coming at me like glistening darts. A slug slammed into my chest, knocking me backward. Shards of glass pierced my skin. Fire burned in my chest. Someone screamed, the sound bouncing around my mind like an echo. Everything faded to black." An excerpt from Ken Cooper's, *Held Hostage: A Serial Bank Robbers's Road to Redemption.* This was a powerful description by Cooper, whose bank-robbing career came to a halt, after being stopped by a bullet fired by a sheriff's deputy. Notice his level of description of the observable events occurring and processed by the brain.

In his excellent book *The Gift of Fear*, Gavin DeBecker explains the process of perceiving danger. The brain is constantly inputting stimuli, perhaps information that you are not conscience of, such as a movement of a shadow. The brain will tell you to react, but the human brain, unlike an animal will quite often try to override the fear and suppress the fight, flight, or freeze trigger. As a result, those people have placed themselves in peril.

Think of looking for a pair of winter gloves from last season in your closet. If your closet is organized, you should be able to immediately enter the closet and retrieve the gloves. If your closet is in disarray, you now must start rooting through and thinking where you placed the gloves. The brain operates the same way. The less clutter, the quicker it reacts. Sometimes too much information can paralyze the brain as it analyzes the input and slows the response.

I watched several court cases fall apart, because the prosecutors wanted to impress the jury with an overabundance of data and information. The jurors were not PhD's and had difficulty with the sensory overload. Remember the simplicity of life. Stick with the Spark Notes version.

Chapter 2
First Impressions

A young good-looking young man wearing the uniform of a pilot for a major airline, walked with confidence into a bank. He strode up to the bank teller with a smile. He reached into his dark blue uniform jacket and extracted a personal check. If requested, he also had his airline identification. The young man presented a personal check drawn on another bank, and asked the teller if she would be so kind as to cash his check. The teller smiled, and conversed with the affable and dashing young pilot. She cashed the check for the non-customer without a second glance.

The young man was not a copilot for Pan Am Airlines. He was a sixteen-year-old conman named Frank Abagnale, Jr. and was responsible for passing 2.5 million dollars in worthless checks over a five-year time period. He also flew all over the world at the expense of Pan American. In addition, he also assumed the role of a college professor, a physician, an attorney, and a jail inspector. The book and movie, *Catch Me if You Can*, describes his unbelievable exploits.

Had he walked into the bank in street clothes, the bank would have thrown him out on the sidewalk. The costume and his demeanor made a positive first impression and established instant credibility. He was also a studious young man, who immersed himself into the assumed occupation to learn the lingo and the appropriate back-story.

As you walk into a men's clothing store, most sales associates immediately size you up in their mind. They will gladly point you to the proper section displaying your size of suits. Many times, they have analyzed you before you push your way through the doors. The same occurs in a ladies clothing store as well.

As I previously explained, the brain processes information in the bang of two hands clapping together. There are certain activities that you engage in that will allow for do-over's. If you fail a test, you can offset your grade on the next test. If your evaluation is poor, you can make alterations and work harder to achieve a better review. In first impressions, you get one. There are no second or third impressions. You may have an opportunity to counter a first bad impression, but it might be easier to climb the north face of Mt. Kilimanjaro.

People will banter about, "Don't judge a book by its cover." This is the difference between theory and reality. In theory that sounds nice and empathetic. Give them a second chance. The reality is that psychologically, that first impression has been anchored into your brain. We have all met people that we had a negative first impression and then over time, we changed our opinion. Many times, we do not alter our initial opinion.

One of my best friends started out with a negative first impression. He had a certain swagger and attitude that to me represented cockiness. I was turned off by my perception of his attitude. This was before I had any conversation with him. As time went on and I spent more time with him, we became close friends. In fact, he became my best man at my wedding. My first impression was not incorrect, but his other positive attributes and commonalities won me over in time.

Nalini Ambady, professor of psychology at Tufts University, has conducted a great deal of research into first impressions. She is probably one of the foremost experts in the field. In a 1993 study with Robert Rosenthal, Professor Ambady determined how quickly we could assess someone on the first impression.

They used three different video clips of thirteen teachers in ten second segments. Fifteen different characteristics were used to determine the rating of teachers on a scale from one to nine. These factors included empathy, likeable, dominant, confidence and others. The ratings were very similar between the nine judges. At the end of the semester, the students using the same criteria, rated the same teachers.

There was a significant correlation between the semester long judgments versus those exposed to the ten second video clips. Then they shortened the clips to five seconds and finally to two seconds. Unbelievably, there was still a significant correlation with the end of the semester ratings. What this extraordinary study revealed was that people exposed to a person for a mere two seconds did not differ significantly from those exposed to the person for an entire semester of weekly lectures.

In another study of first impressions, Dr. Frank Bernieri now a professor at Oregon State University, conducted a study while still at the University of Toledo. Professor Bernieri, along with a graduate student, provided training to interviewers. The trained interviewers interviewed ninety-eight individuals. After each interview of about fifteen minutes, the interviewer completed an evaluation. They wanted to determine if any individual traits would rule over others. The study was not able to determine any particular trait that could win over an interviewer.

They then showed fifteen second clips of the interviewees entering the room and shaking hands. They discovered that the original intent of the study was to learn whether interviewees coached in certain nonverbal gestures would do better in an interview. They did not.

However, later, an undergraduate student tested whether the initial handshake was important. One of Bernieri's students asked if the videotapes of these encounters could be used for another purpose. She had heard that "the handshake is everything" and wanted to test that old adage. She used a 15-second piece of video showing the candidate knocking on the door, shaking hands, and being greeted by the interviewer. The participants were asked to rate these applicants on the same criteria that the two trained interviewers had been using.

The results were surprising. What the researchers discovered was that in nine of the eleven categories that applicants were judged upon, they found that those brief glimpses mirrored the final evaluation of the ratings from the full interview. Bernieri told *The New Yorker*. "In fact, the strength of the correlation was extraordinary."

So, here we are back to the professors rating by Dr. Nalini Ambady. You can do all the evaluating you want, but those first few seconds of exposure will allow you to sink or swim. If you are applying for employment, an internship, or conducting a sales call, you must stand out. I am not talking about standing out like a clown at the rodeo. You must be memorable. You must make that personal connection. Your appearance, your stride, your posture, the tone of your greeting, your smile, and your handshake are essential elements. You can practice mock interviews and go through all kinds of tutoring and sales training. You might know your product inside and out and it may have a bearing as time goes on, but if you flop on the entrance, you may as well pick up your ball and go home.

You have to find a personal connection with the other person. I was preparing to conduct an applicant interview, and I entered the restroom and observed a person I thought could be an applicant. He was rolling a lint brush on his new suit and grooming. He looked at me and complimented me on the fact we were wearing matching shirts. He did a great job, despite not knowing if I was the interviewer. When I called him in from the lobby, he was carrying a briefcase and projected a great presence. It might have been empty, but it was something extra and added to his polished image.

I later found out this gentleman was not born polished. His parents moved from an impoverished country and worked blue-collar jobs. They instilled a good work ethic and integrity into this applicant. He came prepared. Not just his appearance, but knowledge of the job he was seeking. At the end, he asked if there was anything, he could do to enhance his performance. He wanted feedback. In my opinion, he hit it out of the park.

Attention spans have been shortened. In the age of twitter and texting, people want people to get to the point. Writers are taught to make every word count. Synopsis thinking. No one wants a long-winded diatribe. Twitter is based on completing thoughts in 140 characters or less.

You have heard of elevator pitches. You are focused on presenting your statement within thirty seconds. That is the length of one Super Bowl commercial. Just like those commercials, you can deliver a memorable commercial, or you can leave a bomb that everyone ignores.

When writing this book, I decided to get straight to the point. The introduction is at the back of the book. I find most people skip the introduction. They rarely start with a bang and delay the start.

Although attention spans have been Spark Noted, our memories can be long. Bad conduct can be forever engrained in the brain.

My daughter was the victim of a tailgater one afternoon. You have probably experienced the same situation where you cannot see the headlights of the car behind you because they are so close. The inconsiderate driver finally passed her and ran through a stop sign only to pull in a driveway a block from our house. A local service provider owned that home. Regardless of whom the driver was, their conduct spoke for the business in a negative light. My daughter may not be an immediate consumer of that product, but her parents would be. No bad deed goes unpunished.

On the other hand, you never know where your niceness will take you. Genuine niceness will make the recipient feel better and you will feel the benefit as well. There are certain people in our lives that make us beam with excitement. They just have that quality of likeability.

Your initial exposure to someone either through the telephone or in person will be transference of your current emotions. If you are carrying any baggage, throw it off the caboose like an old suitcase. If you had a disagreement at home, or with the boss, remember the person you are now dealing with had nothing, I mean nothing, to do with that. I cannot tell you how many politicians I have seen in a spirited debate with an adversary, only to step out to the crowd and morph into a smiling jovial person.

While we are on the topic of telephone contact, the fewer in-beweens the better. We have all played voice prompt bingo or I will transfer you hot potato. On the other hand, you are placed in "hold purgatory" listening to some obnoxious music.

Call yourself and see what the experience is like for your clients or customers. Most of all, how is the point person on the telephone greeting everyone. If you were in your customers' flip-flops, would you want to do business with yourself?

My daughters rented a cabin in the majestic mountains of North Carolina. The cabin was just as beautiful in person as the photos on the website. Unfortunately, they had a few uninvited guests. The four legged variety. My one daughter called and spoke with the owner of the management company to complain and obtain an immediate response. The broker was rude and dismissive. My wife called to coordinate a response while our daughters were sightseeing at the Biltmore Hotel. The broker was rude and deflective in her response. When you have to ask a subordinate if you are being rude, the chances are good that you are in fact being rude.

This broker could have been very nice in person. One would think she had some ability to interact with clients. Her demeanor on the telephone was terrible. She exacerbated a problem and refused to accept any responsibility or to apologize. She spoke poorly of the exterminator, and our daughters were forced to move to a hotel the last night. She made no attempt to diffuse the situation with an apology.

The administrative staff that greets your money train is the face and first impression of your business. They should take your name, ask you to have a seat and update you as to if the person you are visiting, has been notified or if there is a delay. Offer a refreshment. When your client gets across the threshold, ask them if they were treated properly. I believe it all goes back to training, and how you are prepared to treat those people that you first encounter. You need to stand in the other person's flip-flops.

Many years ago, when I was living in Miami, I had a scheduled appointment with an endodondist for a consultation. Soon after I left, my wife called and said their office had called and wanted to inform me they were running behind by thirty minutes. I was flabbergasted. I have sat in medical offices for hours, let alone thirty minutes, and no one ever cared about my time.

When I arrived, the staff was very upbeat and professional. As I was being called back to see the doctor, I complimented the staff and noticed several were reading positive attitude books. The doctor again apologized for the delay. When I told him how impressed I was with his staff, he waived the initial visit fee.

On the other hand, one dentist office I visited, had an obnoxious and rude office manager. I witnessed her instigate conflict with patients several times. Every time I walked into the office, there were new employees. The turnover was very high due to her toxicity.

Undercover Boss, is a television show that follows the CEO or executive of a major corporation. They leave the safe confines of the boardroom for a week and go undercover in the more menial jobs of their corporation. It is always an eye opener when they get in the trenches and see how hard their employees work. No show goes without the boss learning a great deal about the operations of their business from the bottom up, learning of the respect for the employee, and learning about themselves. I think it would help more leaders to step out of the cave and see what is going on in their own office. Call your office, and try sitting in the lobby from the viewpoint of your clients or customers.

Chapter 3
Initial Contact

How many times have you incurred the wrath of rude or un-caring staff or the unanswered phone message or emails? This is the face of the organization. The initial contact normally occurs through that initial phone call, email, website contact or person-to-person. Why would you not want you or your staff to be as professional as possible? The highest level of proficiency should be your goal.

Remember that the first impression happens in a split second. Very few do-over's. You had better present a good image. Have confidence in yourself and your product. Have you ever shopped at a big box store and made an inquiry of the sales staff. Their lack of knowledge made you wonder if they had been selling suspend-ers at the clown store the week before.

I recently had the occasion to visit the corporate offices of the Tampabay Lightning and on another day, the Outback Steakhouse Restaurants. I was so thoroughly impressed with the receptionists, that I complimented both of them as well as mentioning their positive image, as ambassadors for the company's they represent.

You never know where those positive interactions will lead you. I frequently gauge the pulse of the organization by the reception-ist. They interact with everyone in the company. I ask them how long they have worked there and how they like working with the company. Most of them are happy to be treated with some degree of recognition that they will willingly and honestly share their opinions. They may not spew hatred, but their body language and tone will convey their opinions.

The world is small. Chance meetings with folks, and how you treat them can lead to future networking opportunities or reestablish old bonds. Pulling over a speeder in Little Rock, Arkansas introduced me to the son of the receptionist of our family eye doctor in New York. At Ground Zero, I bumped into a high school classmate that I had not seen in twenty-five years. Among the thousands of runners at the Crescent City Classic in New Orleans, I bumped into a friend that I had not seen in years.

My wife and I became big fans of a noteworthy writer. I had seen on his website that he was having a book signing not too far away. I decided a signed copy of his book would make an excellent Christmas gift for my wife. When I reached the table, I presented the book and asked him to personalize the book to my beautiful wife. I also professed the professional respect I had for his abilities and presented my business card. I told him if I could ever be of assistance let me know. I had no expectation of any further contact with this author. I knew he had probably heard similar comments from others, but I wanted him to know that he captured the true spirit of being a cop.

About a week later, I received a surprising email from this author. He said he had run into a former intern through a friend. He asked the intern about me and was given the thumbs up seal of approval. Had I not treated her with respect and humility, she probably would have cast aspersions upon me. As a result of her endorsement, he asked me to lunch to discuss a topic. That lunch date evolved into him becoming one of my closest friends.

Focus on the initial interaction and realize the gravity of those first few seconds. Seize the moment, and realize you are setting the tone, and are enthusiastic about perhaps meeting your next best friend.

Smiles and yawns are contagious. So is a cough in church. Just by reading the word yawn, you could stimulate the response. If you do yawn, let the person know that you have had a long day or a longer night and assure them it is not due to them. Apologize. This will relieve the concern they are boring you.

You should be conscience of your body image and what image you present. Watch the sex appeal. Be careful of sensitivities and appearing as sex on a stick. In the Friday night hookup scene, this is ok. It is taboo in a business environment.

First impressions are difficult to overcome. Not impossible. When assigned to a task force, I was introduced to another member. His cubicle looked like a perpetual pep rally to the Oklahoma Sooners. No problem, my brother attended the school and I had grown up initially as a huge OU fan. The introducer was an avid Texas fan and Florida to a lesser degree. I too was a Florida fan. It became quickly apparent that the OU fan was upset at the outcome of the national championship game and was not taking the needling very well. It was perhaps due to the fact that the introducer was stirring the pot and mean spirited.

I realized that we had started on the wrong foot. I sent him an email to apologize for what probably appeared to be an orchestrated rally against OU. He denied there was ever a problem, but why take the chance.

One day, I received an email from an individual that referred to me by my last name. No Mr. attached or my first name. I was issued an order to follow the directions of the email. If this was from a supervisor, I would have been annoyed. This was from a younger employee. Others that viewed the email also had the same impression.

A subsequent exchange was not much better. I put a stop to it by requesting a telephone conference. I was all set to give this person an education on email decorum. It turned out he was just as nice as could be and additional emails were equally as nice. I had held my tongue. Whatever the reason, his initial impression by email was not good. Fortunately, he reversed the bad impression. This is not always an easy task in this hurry up world when folks are quickly moving on.

Chapter 4
Personal Attributes

The one tool I encourage people to use is an audio and video recorder. Set up the tripod or ask a devoted friend to record your entrance. Enjoy the stardom. Record for longer than a couple of minutes. Despite your efforts to relax and capture the real you, you will be aware of the camera and will try to alter your behavior. If you record yourself for thirty minutes, you will start to relax and any bad habits will start leaking out.

When reviewing the video, be honest. Athletes do this all the time to see what bad habits they have developed. Put yourself in the flip-flops of the HR person or the audience that will be forming that first impression.

Smile

Dr. Paul Ekman and other psychologists at the University of California Medical School at San Francisco, as well as Dr. Robert Zajonc, a psychologist at the University of Michigan, in their research, have attributed positive inner emotions stimulated by the creation of a smile across our face. There is not universal agreement with these theories, but in my unscientific study, I feel better when I smile, don't you?

As a kid, I attached valuable baseball cards to the spokes of my bike to make the sound of a motorcycle. Not everyone was destroying future investments. Researchers at Wayne State University examined photos of two hundred and fifty baseball players prior to 1950. They analyzed the smile or lack of smiles. Those that displayed no smile lived to 72.9 years old. Those with partial smiles lived to the age of 75. Players with big smiles lived on average to 79.9 years old. Coincidence? Perhaps.

When you flash a genuine smile at someone, the results are always positive. Studies widely reported without accreditation, conclude that people who smile frequently are seen as being more confident and successful, are more likely to strike up conversations with strangers if they are smiling, and bosses are more likely to promote people who smile a lot. The last one did not work for me. The bottom line is that smiles generate a positive response.

Remember the story we have all heard that it takes so many muscles to smile and a lot more to create a frown. The numbers of muscles used are all over the place, leading one to believe that no one really knows, but I know I feel better when I smile. Even when I am blue and someone is able to elicit a smile, I feel just a tad better for that moment. Smiles are usually reciprocated. The act of smiling releases the feel good endorphins from the brain, which leads to making us feel happier. Paul Ekman and University of Wisconsin neuroscientist Richard Davidson, used brain scans to show that smiling activates some parts of the brain associated with pleasure and happiness.

Dr. Ekman reported that a smile could be observed from 300 feet. I do not know if these people wore glasses or not, but I would agree that a smile is always recognizable. It is what we all want to see. No one wants to see a frown on a loved one's face or the boss.

Don't be a smile flooder. You want to avoid having the smile attached to your face like a plastic clown mask. When introduced to a new person, hold on to the release of the smile for just a second and then show the pearly whites. The polite politicians smile is better than no smile, but is quick evidence of insincerity. Smile like you mean it.

One day, my wife and I were greeted for a sales presentation. The individual greeting us was very professional and courteous. He was dressed in business attire. His face was devoid of a smile. Not once did his lips curl upward. Bad day? Who knows, but I noticed and so did my wife.

As we approach someone for the first time and smile, throw in an eyebrow flash or a quick wink. It is a bonding agent. I saw President Reagan do that frequently. He was quick with a smile, but he also enjoyed giving that wink. That immediately indicates, hey I like you and increases your likeability factor. You may not want to use it in a job interview or to a cop writing a speeding ticket.

Smiles are non-threatening and indicate that you pose no harm. When reading the book *Lost in Shangri-La: A True Story of Survival, Adventure, and the Most Incredible Rescue Mission of World War II*, written by Mitchell Zuckoff, I was intrigued by the interaction of the local Uwambo tribesmen in the remote jungle of Dutch New Guinea and the survivors of a C-47 plane crash. A potentially volatile situation was diffused with the greetings of smiles. We come in peace. John McCollom and Wimayik Wandik met half way, shook hands, and exchanged peaceful and submissive smiles. The Uwambo had never met a Caucasian prior to this smile filled meeting.

We all chuckle at a joke that we do not think is funny. We are being polite and sensitive to the feelings of others. Be aware that the nervous laugh can indicate insecurity and quickly become annoying.

Eye contact

When you first meet someone, make sure you address the person with your eyes. The eyes reflect that you have an interest in the recipient. Due to cultural differences, some people are reluctant to look you in the eye.

Avoid the stalker stare. People start getting nervous when eyes are locked on like heat seeking radar. A quick flash of the eyebrows will also invoke interest. Walk down a busy sidewalk and flash the eyebrows to strangers. Very few people will not respond in the same manner.

The optimum time frame to maintain eye contact is around seventy percent of the time. It shows interest, but allows the eyes to move around the room. When you are emphasizing a point look to the face and hold for a moment before looking away. If you tend to look down, many people will view that as a sign of low confidence. In certain situations, we will all look away. It usually indicates some level of discomfort or an effort to break the conversation string.

Focus your initial gaze on the golden triangle of the face. This is the region covering the eyes through the mouth. Try and distinguish the color of the eyes. Men are usually not as good in this department and will suffer from wandering eyes when face to face with a female. Be careful. Do not get caught, or you are sunk.

Handshake

The first thing is to stand and face the person you are shaking hands. Never remain sitting. It is a show of disrespect. Even if the person insists you remain sitting, make the effort to stand. If an event is in progress, you may be excused to shake while remaining in your seat. I watched one day when two superiors who failed to stand and face the issue with a handshake, exacerbated a disciplinary problem. They remained seated while the employee stood. The subordinate took that as a slight and added to the confrontation. It also provided him the strength to look down on his supervisors. They should have stood and provided equal standing.

Whenever possible, do not shake hands across the table. Stand and walk around to greet the person face to face. This will demonstrate the value you have meeting this person. Remain standing until they leave or assume a seat.

There is nothing like a firm handshake web to web. Do not grip the fingers. Plant the web between the thumb and pointing finger with the target's web. Practice with a friend and see how your grip is conveyed. I have felt all extremes. One person I know crushes the hand to the point that I have to shake off the tingling loss of feeling. Others have felt like a wilting rose.

This may sound sexist, but when a female provides a firm shake, I am immediately impressed. I am not alone. Studies support this concept. In a study at the University of Iowa, they found women with firmer handshakes, were gauged higher and surpassed men with similar shakes. This could be a result of the women separating themselves from the competition. They left a good first and lasting impression.

Adjust the grip as you grab the hand. Just do not get into a battle of manliness to overcome the death grip shake. Another subtle technique is a person that grabs your hand and either pulls your body towards them or attempts to give a slight roll of the hand to exert their dominance. Accept it for what it is.

The standard grip is extended with the thumbs pointed upward. I have witnessed the hand coming in with either the back of the hand dominant or the palm exposed upward. They cause pause to the recipient and requires the receiver to adjust. Neither situation is optimum.

The back of the handgrip is not conducive to rapport building. It signals that I am in control. If you are the recipient of a palm down dominant shaker, take it, step into their space and put your free hand over the top. This will take control away. The alternative is to disconnect and develop an immediate dislike for the dominant shaker. If you are coming in with the back of the hand up, you are diminishing any rapport building.

Do not be a lingerer. You know the one that will not release the grip. Two seconds in and out. Squeeze and release. The lingerers are viewed again as being dominating and the extra long grip could be viewed as creepy.

The two handed shake is employed by politicians or those that are close friends. That free hand envelopes the handshake like the topping on a sundae. Keep it simple and keep that free hand to yourself, unless it is a person you have already established rapport. If it is a first time shake and the two-handed grip came out, I would be cautious about their intentions.

I like to give a gentle pat of my free hand to the my friends forearm or elbow. Notice, I said friend. It is someone that I have familiarity with, but not to a point of a hug or not the right setting for a hug. I stay away from touching much higher than above the elbow. The further up the arm that the free hand touches, the more intimate the touch is perceived. If you touch the shoulder, you could be conveying dominance as opposed to equality.

There was one person I met, and my hand almost slipped out of his grip from the perspiration. This was in what I thought was a low stress environment to discuss an event setup. At the first opportunity, I headed to the washroom. My associate asked me later if I had experienced the slippery shake. I admitted I had. The next day, the same thing happened. Perhaps it was a medical condition. If you have this problem, see a doctor or carry a dew rag in your pocket. A little baby powder in the hand or a resin bag can also help.

If your hands are like snowballs, try to hit the bathroom and defrost them under some hot water. Warm hands are received in a more positive light.

If your hand is dirty, explain to your intended target why you will not shake their hand. Do not wipe your hands on your jeans and pretend they are sanitized. If you have just finished visiting the Colonel and have an empty bucket to show for your meal, wash your hands. If your hands are as dry and rough as the Sahara, squirt some lotion and soften them up.

In our germ-infested world, we are hypersensitive to catching the bubonic plague through handshakes. Many illnesses are passed through hand-to-hand combat. If you are shaking a lot of hands or have gripped someone that has already worked the room, keep your hands away from your mouth, nose, and eyes. Excuse yourself and wash the hands at the earliest opportunity. The hand sanitizer works, but can send a message that I think you are dirty and not good enough. Despite the fact, they probably want to do the same thing. In today's world, pump dispensers of antibacterial hand gel are abundant. At church, I witness the lay ministers taking a squirt prior to dispensing the communion wafers. Many politicians take a squirt outside the public eye for the same reason.

If you are sick, admit your affliction and keep your hands to yourself. The recipient will appreciate your honesty. If you insist on shaking and the person you have just shared germs with realizes you are sick, they will feel repulsed and want to go decontaminate their hands. The next time you meet again, their first thought will be to your previous germ infested meeting. Not a good way to start your second impression.

Hugs

As a society, we are now hugging more than ever. We are all among friends and the embrace is a welcome sign of affection. When we are greeting for the first time, the hug becomes kind of an awkward dance. Should I or should I not? Let the other person set the tone. If the greeter is someone that you have talked to and developed rapport via email of the phone, there is a basis for familiarity. Let the other person set the tone.

Man hugs or abrazos are reserved for men in more comfortable and familiar settings. It is a sign of affection between two friends. It involves a simultaneous handshake, hug, and back slap. Not seen in the boardroom unless two old friends are reconnecting.

Female to female is and always will be more acceptable. There are less rules with hugging among girls. The younger generation has really embraced, no pun intended, the world of hugging.

Male to female is a more tepid world and should always be established by the female. While meeting with a hotel sales manager for the first time, I extended my hand for a shake. She quickly dismissed the formal greeting and declared she was from the South and was a hugger. I quickly and warmly embraced her. We had already spoken on numerous occasions on the telephone and developed a deep rapport over common points of interest. I was going the safe route. She eased the transition with her openness.

Hugging can be great method to establish rapport. We enjoy the stimulation of touch. Do not linger unless you are consoling the recipient of the hug. Get in and get out. On first meetings, you can never go wrong with a handshake. Save hugs for future meetings, unless you have an established rapport.

Chapter 5
Stride, Posture and Extremities

The best way to determine your gait is to have your BFF (Best Friend Forever) watch or video your entrance. This is one of the most important aspects of the first impression. Stride with confidence. Even if you do not believe in yourself, it is ok to fake it. Pretend that you are about to deliver or receive the best news in your life and you are about to meet your next best friend. You never know where that meeting will lead. If you have some old videos, watch those to discover any bad habits. Flip through some old photo albums to see the pose you struck in different situations.

I walked behind a young lady in the student union at college one day. Her gait and her beauty caught my attention. We ended up sitting in the same booth with a mutual friend. That meeting turned into a marriage of over three decades.

On television, watch politicians enter rooms after their announcement. They walk with confidence. We have all seen the march. Not too fast or you seem too eager or perhaps a little desperate, but not too slow or you come across as lackadaisical.

One time, I was interviewing an individual who had allegedly made some inappropriate statements concerning the President. The case had garnered some media attention. I was suffering from Lyme's Disease at the time and walking was an effort. I marshaled all my energy and put on my best stride to display an air of confidence. At least I thought I had. The interviewee made no comments about my stride and the interview was successful. My sister-in-law who lives out of state caught the video feed. She noticed my tentative gait from a thousand miles away and pointed it out to my wife.

If you have a medical condition, you just have to do the best you can. Podiatry is a huge business and many people live in near constant pain. If you have some issue, be prepared to explain in a diminished manner the problem. No one wants to hear about your planter fasciitis or bunions in detail. Just a little hitch in your giddy up will do. The exception would be if you received turf toe while playing flag football, because the person you are meeting also plays in a flag football league. This now becomes a bonding moment.

Clicking heels can be a distraction. Just beware of the impact of your shoes. Some people have a heavy stride or because of the construction of the shoes, they sound like sledgehammers striking the floor. If the room has tile and sparse furnishings, you know it will sound like an echo in the Grand Canyon. Some floors or rooms tend to reproduce noise more than a carpeted room that would absorb the noise. You can place more emphasis on walking on the balls of your feet as opposed to the heal.

When you are walking with someone or in a group, maintain an equal position. Adjust your speed to theirs. If they are to one extreme or the other, slow down or speed up just a tad and hope they will mirror the mutual stride. If they do not, then deal with it. If you are out front, it portrays dominance. If you are a laggard, you cast an image of submission.

I observed two pedestrians out for an afternoon stroll. They were side by side. Their strides were in synchrony with each other. Their feet were striking the ground at the same time. It was if they were marching together in the band. If asked, they would not have realized their synchrony.

While escorting a former president, I was mirroring an enthusiastic stride of the dignitary. As I increased my speed, he followed the pace. He finally tapped me on the shoulder and asked to pick up the pace faster, because this was the only exercise he was going to receive on that day. I picked up the pace to a brisk walk and followed his direction.

Posture

I can still hear my mother telling me to stand straight, shoulders back and chest out. You do not want to grow up to be round shouldered. Moms know their business. To emphasize this point, while in school we would have to walk around balancing a book on our head. I do not know if that drill helped my posture, but it did help me to be mindful of my posture.

The straighter you position your body the better. Think of a yardstick against your spine. The straighter you stand the more confidence you project. If you tend to have rounded or slumped shoulders, you display a lack of confidence. Straighten up for the first minute of the meeting, until you can get past the initial barrier.

If you have a little excess in the midsection, try sucking it in back across the belt. It may not be possible, but the effort will help you stand taller. Men and people do this all the time when they meet someone attractive of the opposite sex. Similar to the peacock displaying their plume.

It is all about projection of an attitude. You have to walk in there as if you are the total package. Perception is reality. You also want to maintain congruence through the body. In other words, maintain your alignment so that you draw a straight line from the nose through the torso.

You have heard of the open stance and closed stance. Think of an autopsy cut down the middle of the body. Your entire body is screaming, "Look at me! I like you." I know the autopsy cuts are different for males and females, but the majority of the cut starts at the sternum. If you keep the middle line naked, you will project a more open accepting position of confidence.

Covering your neck with your hand, crossing your arms across the torso, or dropping your hands over your groin closes your body and sends the wrong signals. Leave yourself open to the viewers' eyes.

Extremities
Hands

Oh what to do with the hands. They do seem to get in the way at times. The most neutral position is at the sides along the hips. As you walk, you want them on the side and to swing naturally with the body's motion. You do not want them swinging like a seesaw or fixed to the side like the Irish Dancers on *Riverdance.*

After the initial greeting, the hands are really in the way. Keep them visible. No hiding the hands in the pockets digging out lint. It helps to have one hand occupied with a beverage or a folder. If you have a briefcase or a folder, keep it on the side so you are fronting an open position.

It is fine to use your hands as illustrators. Avoid looking look like you are conducting the Boston Philharmonic Orchestra.

In the Asian culture, excessive hand gestures are considered taboo. Be aware of your cultural surroundings. I grew up in a prominently Italian neighborhood and have travelled throughout the Middle East. The Mediterranean culture tends to rely heavily on the prominence of hand gestures as illustrators. As they say, when in Rome, do as the Romans do. One of my neighbors, Mrs. Leone was a very enthusiastic hand talker. She would say that if someone tied her hands, she would not be able to speak.

Use the hand to show interest in the conversation, kind of like stoking the fire. Imagine how your hands can encourage and stimulate conversation. You are saying this is interesting and you really want to hear the story.

Be cautious of displaying exaggerated hand movements. They project an impression of dominance. They are usually associated with someone that is controlling the conversation. You are flashing the sign that, "I am Important." It may not be conducive to rapport building, as your recipient becomes annoyed at your dominance. Mute your hand gestures and keep them in synchrony with your speech.

I was watching an interview, and the interviewee had some problems. They locked down. They clasped their hands together in the lap and froze their feet as if they were stuck in cement. They gave an occasional head nod. The overall body was stiff and stoic. The line of questioning was serious and they were confronted with possible deceptions. This person was trying to conceal the leakage of the body language, but instead broadcast the abnormal. Aldert Vrij's research indicates a correlation between decreased hand movements and those that are attempting to conceal deception.

Keeping your hands visible are always best. Keep them above the table when possible. The hands clasped together show that you are considering the input. If you maintain that position throughout the interaction, it signals inferiority. Move them around, but not to the point of distraction.

Arms

The arms are cemented to the hands. Where the hands go, so go the arms. Keep the arms from crossing the midsection. Keep them on the side in the neutral position flowing with your stride. Avoid placing your arms in front in a position known as the fig leaf. That is where the hands drop over the privies and cover them like fig leaf. The female gender assumes this position almost naturally when in social or formal setting in which they are not totally comfortable.

I have seen female politicians assume this posture. The stronger posture is the neutral default setting with arms at the side. It is very difficult to maintain that position for any period of time.

Try it yourself. Eventually, you want to put the arms and hand somewhere.

Avoid placing the arms behind the back. This is a position know as the royal or regal stance. It projects a dominant stance and sets the tone that you believe that your status is higher. Not a good way to start the first impression. You will see authority figures such as politicians, teachers, cops, and parents strike this pose.

Another strong dominant position is arms akimbo. This is the position in which you place your hands on your waist and the elbows point out away from the body. It is a territorial display and not conducive to the first impression. To soften this position, slide your hands down lower on the hips so not as much light is penetrating the gap of the elbow and the torso. Another alternative is only use a one arm akimbo, which has a softer approach.

Legs and Feet

Keep them pointed in the direction of the person or group of interest. Where your feet will normally point, is in your direction of interest. If the feet are pointing towards the door, guess what you are telling them, "I can't wait to get away from you and out of here." You can see this in a boring presentation or one that has lasted too long. Look at the feet of the attendees. They are screaming, "Let me out."

Try to keep the legs in a natural position. When you cross them, it displays a closed posture. After obtaining a level of comfort with the person, go ahead and cross if this makes you comfortable. This is especially true if they cross their legs first. Keep your hands from clasping the leg as if you are forming a sturdy fortress.

When standing and you cross one of your legs over the other, it shows a sign of relaxation and ease. The reason is that your body is not fully balanced. This is fine after you have time to interact. You do not want to portray the "Too Cool Cat" with your legs crossed at the moment of your first meeting. After you have had time to meet, then you can slip your leg over the other.

You do not want to fidget. Swinging or kicking the legs is not a sign of confidence. It might even reflect immaturity. You might not be aware of the jitters, but it reflects either impatience or nervousness. Neither is good for rapport building.

Chapter 6
Grooming

My wife and I were discussing a financial transaction with a business manager. She was attractive and her suit was well tailored. She had command of her subject matter, was well spoken and a nice delivery. Her problem was that one fingernail on each hand looked bedazzled and she had enough jewelry bling to stock a flea market jewelry stand. The extra adornments damaged the impression she was attempting to convey. It was a distraction.

When we prepared for our first date with a potential suitor, did we not try to look our best? As time goes on and we become more comfortable we tend to lose our edge. You know that comfy sweatshirt that is now frayed, or the suit that has become a victim of additional middle age bulk. Oh wait, I thought the cleaners shrunk that suit.

When I lived outside New Orleans, I would go for an evening run. The neighborhood was coming up on fifteen years old. As I huffed along, I noticed that many homes still had the original flowered wallpaper and paneling. As styles evolved, the residents comfortable in their environment had little motivation in embracing new styles.

I am not suggesting you must be a trendsetter, but merely a fashion conformist. I ask you to conduct a self-check inventory as you read the next couple of chapters. *Extreme Makeover* documented the gradual descent into obscurity that many never noticed. Plastic surgery is not necessary. Work with what you have. Look to a person that is respected for their sense in style or research the internet for current trends.

I do not want to insult anyone's intelligence, but it is shocking what you will see in business meetings. You do not want folks focused on your lack of style or fashion faux pas. Despite being the messenger, you are still part of the message. You do not want the recipient distracted by your presence but more focused on the message. So, here is the quick guide to appearance.

Hair

Hairstyles are constantly changing. Use your judgment or ask an opinion of an honest friend that will provide realistic feedback. As of this writing, for men the tussled and unkempt look is in. Who knows where it will be next year. Bald and shaved is in style, which replaces the need for cheap hairpieces, hair plugs or the comb over. Many times these instruments would become the focus of the first impression.

For females, remember to conduct a status update on your style. The big hair look was all the rage in the 80's and 90's but not so much today. Styles change and so too does your hair color. Gray starts to seep in or a gradual lightening and darkening can occur. Never ask a man how your hair looks. You will almost guarantee a poor assessment. Men do not always tell the truth when it comes to the matter of beauty. "Honey, does this dress make me look fat?"

Only your hair stylist knows for sure. If you suddenly change from a brunette, to a blonde, or gray, to auburn, it is a shock to the surprised recipient. The contact misses most of your initial message, as their thoughts are focused on your new hair color. The purple or pink streaks are great if you are joining a rock band from Seattle, but it does not transform well to the boardroom.

Hair bangs come and go and look good on some, while not so good on others. You be the judge or a good friend. You better not look like the sheepdog in which the hair is obscuring the eyes. The other item is not to have high maintenance hair. We have all seen the type where every few seconds, you are flipping the hair back with the chiropractic jerk, or using your hand as the grooming tool. It is very distracting and again becomes the focus replacing the message. Ladies sometimes like to play with their hair, such as twirling the fingers around a few strands of hair. This might work while flirting at happy hour but not so much at a business meeting.

Facial Hair

The conventional wisdom was no facial hair. Times have changed and standards have become more relaxed. Whatever facial hair you have should be well trimmed and as precise as possible. Long beards are a no go. Those little soul patches tend to minimize your standing. Most people still associate the patch as what the "Beatniks," would wear. They might be ok in some environments but in business, they undermine your standing.

The scruffy proverbial two or three day growth looks sexy. I personally hate the pain associated with removing two days let alone three days of growth. It looks good on the fashion models and lot of others. In the business world, people like clean or well trimmed facial grooming. I had an individual that was seeking employment. His beard shadow complimented his velvet sport coat for an appearance on the cover of GQ, but not making a good first impression trying to fit into the corporate culture

Another aspect of facial hair applies more for men. Avoid the uni-brow. Shave or wax between the eyes. If you have hairs waving hello from your nose or ears, trim them. The ears are tough to see in the mirror, but a set of tweezers will help find them.

I find people, present company included, like to play with facial hair. It is a pacifying gesture, but again it can become a distraction. Back in the day when I had a mustache, I always played with it. Even after I shaved it off, I still found myself stroking the missing mustache.

Ladies if you suffer from facial hair, you will have to embark on the time consuming and painful process of hair removal. That means either using the tweezers, waxing, or through costly electrolysis. If your face is manifesting a patch of whiskers, your hair follicles will be the talk of the post discussion. You must have them removed.

Hands

If your hands feel like a loofah sponge due to dryness or calluses, use a moisturizing cream. Chapped hands are more prone to holding on to unwanted bacteria. Ask a friend to shake your hand and offer an opinion.

Nails for men should be trimmed. If in doubt, get the clippers out. If you have just changed an engine in a '57 Chevy, get the nails and hands clean.

For ladies, I would avoid these far out designs or obnoxious colors on your fingernails. You can never go wrong with a clear coat, a conservative color or French nails. The same rules apply for the toenails.

Makeup

Remember Memi from the Drew Carey Show. Do not go down that road. Makeup should accentuate your beauty. Less is more. I met one female who was very pretty. She was model pretty, but she almost obscured her beauty with her mud caking of foundation. If you are not sure, look in a mirror, ask for some feedback or get a consultation. Many cosmetic counters will do this in hopes of selling their products or find a seminar.

Perfume

I worked for a while with a part-time co-worker. He was great worker, but you knew when he was working. It must be Tuesday.

He must have marinated himself in his cologne. There is also the female who if you give an embrace, they leave a remembrance of their scent for what seems like forever. Not the lasting memories you are striving to leave. Less perfume or cologne is better.

I remember a young woman that I was trying to impress. She had at one time said she loved Old Spice because that was the scent her father splashed on each morning. I promptly went out and purchased a bottle. It was good for that one splash. I never went out with her again nor did I use the Old Spice again.

Sometimes cologne or perfume can be viewed as an anchor. What that means is that they associate certain odors with good times. Such as their mother or father. Others may be viewed as a negative anchor associated with an ex-spouse and a nasty divorce. You cannot control their associations.

I can smell my wife's cologne in a crowded mall. It is not over-powering, but is pleasing to me. Perhaps to another, they would give a so-so response. Just a dab will do. Do not marinate.

Perspiration

I have one friend who merely looks up at the sun and profusely sweats. Others could run a half marathon in Miami Beach and hardly break a sweat. It is true that anxiety will increase perspiration. The polygraph uses perspiration as one measure of the baseline. I can tell you that few people can measure the subtle increase of the sweat glands.

If you are a sweater, make sure you are bathing and using ample deodorant. If you are prone to uncontrollable body odor, you might want to see a doctor. You should keep extra deodorant, cologne, and Febreeze with you. Body odor is one of the most repulsive scents known to the human nose.

While attending a multi-day seminar, one of the attendees was obviously not practicing good hygiene. Others in close proximity complained to others. The ring of odor expanded as the day went on and went into a second day. Most times, you would suspect this from a man, but in this instance, it was a well-proportioned and attractive female in her late twenties.

In December 1999, at a border crossing at Port Angeles, Washington, U.S. Customs Inspector Diana Dean observed an individual by the name of Ahmad Ressam. He was driving the last vehicle and it was quitting time.

Her antenna was raised because of his behavior. One glaring behavior was that despite the chill of the December wind on the Washington border, Ressam was sweating profusely. He was acting nervously and did not respond to her questions in a manner consistent with the truth.

It did not help that he provided his Costco card as identification. This led to the discovery of explosives in the trunk and the apprehension of a terrorist targeting the airport in Los Angeles. The sweating as it turned out was not a symptom of nervousness, but of a fever. The fever was eventually determined to be a result of malaria. Sometimes things are not as they seem.

Breath

Have you been close enough to the dragon's breath that made you feel you needed a Trojan warrior's shield? Is it from garlic or onions at the last meal, medication, or overdosing on vitamins. You can do the whole breathe into your hand and inhale. Another technique is to lick your hand and sniff. Crazy? I heard it from a doctor. In order to avoid being labeled weird, you might want to do this in private.

In your initial contact, you should not be so close that they can taste your breath. We have all been there when some odors are so strong they should have crime scene tape wrapped around the lips. Staying hydrated will help. Have the drink in your hand to wet your whistle. The scent of alcohol can also be offensive.

Smoker's breath is the kiss of death. As smoking has become more passé, you better have some heavy-duty mouth freshener. Remember smoke tends to adhere to your clothes as well. If you cannot shake the addiction, carry some Febreeze with you to spray on your clothes.

There was an establishment that I had stopped with friends a couple of times after work. This was before the ban on smoking in most places. This bar was like making your way through a curtain of secondhand smoke. As soon as I walked into the house and the draft went past my body, my wife immediately knew where I had been.

All I can say is floss, brush and rinse. Pop a mint or a piece of gum. Be careful on chewing the gum. Keep it for moisture not chomping like a cow.

Teeth

Check the grill before you go into the meeting. I knew one fellow that loved to eat poppy seed bagels. We would all giggle the rest of the day, because the black specks were captured between his teeth. Let us just say his hygiene was lacking.

With commercial teeth whiteners on the market, it is easy to eliminate the yellow hue. Pearly whites enhance the smile and make it more recognizable. Dental work quite often requires a home equity loan. Look and see for yourself.

If you have appearance problems, quite often you will unconsciously attempt to conceal your mouth. That happens by either covering with your hand or not being expressive with your mouth. Thus, the easily recognizable smile is banished or reduced. People do not like to listen as you talk through your hands.

Chapter 7
Exterior Façade

Physical attractiveness does form first impressions. Whether you like it or not, what you look like will in fact help form the first impressions. In a 1973 study by M. Clifford and E. Walster, they were able to determine that physical attractiveness had an effect on teacher expectations. They expected attractive students to have higher IQ's, greater potential, and higher parental involvement. Why not pay attention to your exterior façade. Men in particular will pay more attention to attractiveness than females. Professor Chris Boyatzis of Bucknell University, found a correlation between attractiveness and popularity. Look around the office. Who is the most popular? The frumpy dressed or the cover model for GQ or Cosmo? The better dressed will always make the better first impression. Females will always scrutinize your fashion attire more so than men.

Clothing

Dress for the occasion. I would always prefer to over dress. There is nothing worse than showing up underdressed. It has the effect of throwing a wet blanket over your confidence. You end up wasting time spinning a story, as to why you are in shorts rather than dress slacks. You can always blame it on the airlines charging you fifty bucks for your bag and then promptly sending it to Bangladesh, but it will still affect your poise.

One night after work, I was attending a wake for a fellow church member. The wake was in the church. I ditched my tie and almost left the sport coat behind. When I showed up, almost everyman had a coat and tie. I felt out of place. No one said a word, but I felt uncomfortable being the lone man without a necktie. I was just glad I tossed the jacket in the car and slipped it on before walking inside. It is easy to pull the tie and open the neck after you arrive, but impossible to add one that you do not have. If you are not sure, check some of the other voices you trust that may have previous experience.

Stay away from the fashion runways. It is nice to receive compliments concerning your dress, but do not become the "Thing" of the gathering. There was an office party at one of the offices I had worked and the entire talk of the party was concerning the attire of one of the spouse's. Let us just say her wardrobe was a little or a lot risqué. She was the "Thing," at the party. No one talked of anything else.

Look at your attire as you would the curb appeal for your house. You want to be warm and welcoming, but not ostentatious or gaudy. Does this dress make me look fat? I know more than a few men that could use the same advice. The poor sport coat that cannot button closed since the middle age spread. No it is not from the muscle mass you added from laying on the couch watching ESPN. Dark colors are more slimming as are vertical stripes. Horizontal stripes accentuate any girth and bright colors grab attention.

Cleavage is great for happy hour and speed dating, but not in a business environment. Men may glance then look at your face for fear of wondering eyes. Instead of focusing on the message, they are focused on not getting caught looking at the chest. If they do sneak a peek, their mind is on non-business enterprises. You do not need to be in a Victorian mode covering the neck. Just remember in business, conservative is better than sex appeal.

People often think we live in a democracy and believe they can wear anything they want. That may be true. However, your clothing can be directly attributed to income. When I am at home, I am a t-shirt and shorts or jeans kind of guy. At work, I dress professionally. I am not trying to make any statements one way or the other.

You do not have to shop at high-end specialty shops. If you have the money and enjoy those places, that is your prerogative. I buy my clothes in midlevel department stores. Examples are Macy's, Dillard's, JC Penney's, Joseph A. Banks and Kohl's. This is not an all-inclusive list. I have bought suits online at Lands End with good success. I have never paid more than $350 for a suit and many times less than $250, and no one at least to my face, has accused me of being a slob. End of the season clearances are great. If you cannot afford one, try shopping at a second hand store for lightly used clothing.

Try E-Bay. I have a friend that proudly displays Hugo Boss suits that he bought for a fraction of the cost on E-Bay. They may have come off a deceased coffin resident, but with a little Febreeze, no one is the wiser.

On the women's side, in addition to the previously mentioned department stores, Express, New York and Company, Banana Republic and The Limited are also in the stables of purveyors of decent clothes without breaking the bank. Never pay full retail. Wait for sales. Plato's Closet and others are consignment shops that have great bargains on light or never used fashions.

I like a good tie. I never spend more than twenty-five dollars on a tie and often less than twenty. I am selective. I feel the tie, and determine how it will knot and hang. You can always find ties at a significant markdown in many stores. A boss that I worked for always had nice ties that I complimented. I asked him where he made his acquisitions. He let me in on his secret and said he bought the ties at Steinmart and Marshall's.

A sharp tie will receive compliments, but you want to avoid the blinking billboard of being the center of attention. A ten-dollar tie usually looks like a ten-dollar tie. However, a fifty-dollar tie marked down to twenty looks like a good investment.

Men, stay away from what might look good at the club on Saturday night. Look at the successful people and executives within the company that you work for or are trying to gain employment. The three or four button suit with a wild tie and long tails will not work, unless you are some rocker or self-adulating sports star.

It never hurts to drive by the business and monitor what the employees are wearing. Never dress less than what you observe. If you are appearing for a job interview, it is always better to over dress than under dress. For men, a suit is always appropriate.

For women, slacks are fine as long as they are dressy and you are wearing a nice top. Hillary Clinton rarely wears a dress, but always looks professional. Dark colors are viewed as professional and thinning. Be aware that light colored slacks might reveal your style of under garments. Hemlines change over the years. You want to strive for being contemporary, but not flashing too much thigh.

Men, if your dress shirt is so thin that you can see the non-waxed chest hair, upgrade and get some starch to perk them up. A t-shirt underneath, helps to absorb the perspiration. One time, I was talking with a well-dressed businessman. When he raised his arms, he exposed tarnished perspiration stains on his seemingly good quality shirt. Yuck.

Jewelry

Get rid of the bling. Men should not wear necklaces displayed outside of their clothes. No more than one ring on either hand for a total of two ring sets. Pinkie rings went out with the Godfather. Ladies who sound like jingle bells with sixty-two bracelets may sound nice and look good for a girl's night out, but cut the bling in the business environment.

Men, you want an earring go for it. It is not uniformly accepted in business and therefore is a negative accoutrement. Ladies should wear earrings, but stay away from hoops large enough to do magic tricks. Ear studs surrounding the outer ring of the ear are not viewed in a professional manner.

Many folks enjoy wearing the rubber charity bracelets to show support for various causes. Be careful how proud you are and how many of these you put on your wrist.

Piercings

A quick word about piercings. According to Harris Poll, half of the adult population has pierced ears. Only 5 percent of adults have a piercing on their body, but not on their face. Two percent of adults have a piercing on their face, but not their ears. In other words if you have a piercing other than your ear and are visible, you are abnormal.

Shoes

They should have a shine and be in good condition. Shoes especially for females can enhance the outfit as an accessory. Be careful on the height of the heels. Look at the shoes and ask what image they represent. If you are not used to maneuvering in the high altitude heels, get some practice time under your belt.

Men can ruin the whole gig by wearing a nice suit or ensemble and then wear shoes that have not been shined since the Great War. Keep a brush handy to dance over the shoes to remove some of the grit and splatters. A good shoeshine is less than five bucks and lasts a long time with occasional brushings in between. Forgot your brush on a trip? Use the hotel towel.

Personally, I spend a good amount on shoes, but they last ten years and my feet are smiling after ten hours. I learned this the hard way. I spend good money on a mattress that I will sleep eight hours on, why be cheap on a pair of shoes that provide support to your feet and ultimately your spine. Happy feet, happy life.

Tattoos

Tattoos have been around for ages. They date back to the Neolithic period of 9500 BC. Previously reserved for bad boys, bikers, and sailors, a current popular trend is to indulge in "body art." I know one fellow who paid twenty thousand for his engravings. My thought was I could have bought a car for that amount. If it makes you happy, go for it, but understand there could be a downside.

In a January 2012, Harris Interactive conducted an online poll of 2,016 U.S. residents that showed 21% of the respondents had a tattoo. One quarter (25%) of those with a tattoo, said having the tattoo makes them feel more rebellious, and three in ten (30%) say the tattoo makes them feel sexy. One in five (21%) each say having the tattoo makes them feel attractive and strong.

As buyer's remorse has set in, recipients that have moved up the social ladder, or employer sanctions imposed, the business of tattoo removal is thriving. According to a *LA Times* article on August 9, 2009, Dr. Tattoff's tattoo removal clinic in Beverly Hills is looking to expand and is considering an IPO. They would not be the first.

Although an overwhelming majority of those with tattoos, 86% had no regrets, one-quarter of those without a tattoo (24%) say people with tattoos are more likely to do something most people would consider deviant compared to 12 percent of those with a tattoo who say the same.

The point is, if you have one, keep it under the tent. Yes, body art is becoming more accepted and popular. It may make you stand out in the singles bar, but with 1 in 4 people thinking you have deviant tendencies, it is not the best way to develop trust. If you have a tattoo of a snake creeping up the neckline from the collar, beware that it becomes a distraction to the initial impression.

If a perspective client has one and it is readily visible, by all means, compliment it as you would a Picasso hanging on the wall. Ask the significance and where they received the engraving. That is unless it is located someplace that is meant to be private and you received a momentary peek. If it is in an obvious location meant to publicly display the artwork and you have one, you can play, "I'll show you mine if you show me." Avoid the mine is bigger or better.

I know of a number of police departments that prohibit the display of tattoos. Other businesses may not openly provide that as a reason, but it could influence whether you get hired or not and could factor in if you ascend the corporate ladder. Marriott Corporation forbids the public display of tattoos by their employees. Some companies may not be as open about their dislike of tattoos.

Backpacks purses and fanny packs

Briefcases have become more passé and less functional. Messenger style bags and backpacks have become more commonplace because of the ability to carry laptops and the kitchen sink, while not making your arm feel like it just survived a power-lifting tournament.

Ladies bags have also grown in size. Many are now the size of Mary Poppin's bag that was large enough to conceal a pole lamp. Be aware of where you swing that thing.

When you are going into a meeting, leave as much behind as possible. If you have to bring the backpack, toss it under the table and have all your materials already extracted and ready to proceed. You should not have to hold up the proceedings by digging through the backpack looking for the necessary documents. Do not drop it in the seat next to you. It shows unnecessary ownership of that seat.

If you are still wearing a fanny pack from 1990's, then you need help. Everyone will be giggling under their breath at the doofus.

Chapter 8
Relating and Friends

Remember the movie *Erin Brockevich,* starring Julia Roberts? The movie closely portrayed the real life story of Erin who was working for a law firm. She was working as a clerk and self promoted herself to the position of paralegal and took an interest in what started as a minor case. The case evolved into a huge complex litigation. Erin vigorously and successfully advocated on behalf of over six hundred clients victimized from exposure to environmental toxins leaked into the groundwater from an industrial complex.

A great deal can be learned from Erin. She does not always work well with others, and her manner of dress could be described as a bit risqué. She was often offensive to coworkers. Her language was more suited for a construction site, as opposed to a law firm. She stood out from the herd and obviously did not care if she offended their egos.

What was impressive was her ability to relate to the clients. She treated them as human beings, not some ticket to prosperity. As a single mother of three, it would have been easy for her to lose the focus from the client to herself, as more attention was being paid to her campaign. She displayed genuine empathy and identified with the clients.

Likewise, the clients developed a strong bond for their lonely crusader. It was a relationship that was mutually beneficial. Erin heavily tipped the relationship in favor of those clients. That resulted in the clients placing their trust in her. The attorneys were viewed with apprehension and as being outsiders. She was the cohesive glue for the six hundred clients and the lawyers representing them.

Their faith and trust in Erin was rewarded in a judgment of $333 million dollars. Not everyone was satisfied with the payout. The lawyers take was forty percent. Erin received two million dollars as a bonus. Not bad for someone that just wanted to help some strangers' rail against big business.

All she wanted was a job and food on the table. She did not let her lack of education diminish her passion to drive the project to a very successful conclusion. It has turned her into an internationally recognized speaker and an advocate against environmental toxins.

Probably the number one person everyone would like to be friends with is Oprah Winfrey. Rooted in a dysfunctional background, she overcame the restraints of poverty to become one of the most wealthiest and powerful people in the world. Her net worth is estimated to be in excess of two billion dollars. Yet she presents herself as one of us. An endorsement by Oprah can launch a career into the stratosphere.

Oprah became relatable with her audience and fan base. She shared her vulnerabilities, she spoke in a conversational tone, and she was an empathetic listener. She is likeable. Oprah talks with her audience as if they are old friends gathering for an afternoon social. Like Oprah, isn't that what all of us would enjoy. We just want to be liked and have deep friendships.

Chapter 9
Name Calling

Everyone was born with one. Your mother did not say, "Hey you." Nor should you. The person's first name is the most recognizable word in the world to that person. When you are sitting in a conference and the speaker mentions someone with the same first name, your attention perks up. Depending on the forum, you might even get a little giddy-up in the heart rate, thinking you might be called upon. Police officers are conditioned to listen to their unit numbers. They can be carrying on a conversation with someone and immediately their ear goes to the speaker when their unit is called.

Never assume a person prefers the abbreviated version of their name. Michael is Mike or Robert is Bob. Some people really get bent out of shape using the shortened version. I will answer to either and although I have had a number of nicknames over the years, none bothered me. That being said, some people really dislike you evoking their childhood nickname. Queue in on how they introduce their name. Always go with the formal unless told otherwise. You can also ask what they prefer to be called.

I worked with one fellow who called everyone, "My Good Friend." The same for another who called every one, "Buddy." Make it a point to remember the person's name.

A professor I know had received an email from a student requesting an appeal of a grade. The student obviously did not proofread the email and sent it addressed to Dr. O'Ryan. Well Dr. O'Brien sent back a response that there was no Dr O'Ryan at that email address. The Professor then posted on his webpage that if you are requesting a grade appeal, make sure you get his name correct. We only have one name. Get it right.

I Bombs

Avoid the "I Bombs." It is fine to inject personal stories into conversation. The problem is when you use "I" as a pronoun, noun and verb. Every sentence is polluted with I. Give me a break. When in doubt shut up.

Name Dropping

Avoid name-dropping. One name association might provide credibility, but can very quickly be a slippery slope that leads to a splash into a bottomless lake. Sometimes in an effort to establish credibility, we want to associate ourselves with familiar people or those of a higher status. Like most vices that we rely upon, if kept in moderation, it is all right. The problem is when we start dropping names like snowflakes in a blizzard.

You have heard the type, I am friends with this person and that person, or when I was working with so and so. There is no problem when you say to a person, "Hey do you know Joey Bagofdonuts? We used to work together." Again, it could be a situation that Bagofdonuts is not well liked and can torpedo your opportunity. You can dip a toe into the water and ask if they know Joey. If they give a noncommittal, he is ok, then drop it and move on.

If they embrace Joey and say what a great guy he is and is the godparent to their kids, then attach yourself like Velcro to Joey. Keep it real. Your association should be verifiable and your conversational partner will probably check it out. A lot of people can meet the initial sniff test of appearing to be good folks, but those that are around them every day, may have a different viewpoint.

Chapter 10
Speech

Speak with clarity, diction, and vitality. What do you expect to accomplish if the person you are speaking to has difficulty understanding you. There are certain actors that you listen to closer because they are soft spoken in a general context. Russell Crowe, Keifer Sutherland, and Mark Wahlberg come to mind. On television, you turn on closed captioning and read along. When you speak to someone, do they need to turn on closed captioning?

In the book the *Blind Side*, then University of Mississippi coach Ed Orgeron, visits Michael Oher in an effort to convince him to play football at the school. According to the book, Oher did not understand much of what was said. Orgeron from Lafourche Parrish in Louisiana, has a thick and gravelly Cajun accent. Having lived there for four years, I do not have any problem with understanding the Cajun dialect, but for others it can be an obstacle to listening and comprehending the message.

I have witnessed college professors from different countries who struggle with their annunciation of English. After a period of time, the ears get tired trying to decipher what is being said and the students zone out after their attention span was drained to zero.

Each industry has a language of its own. The same goes for acronyms. Keep that in mind, as you want to be inclusive with those around you as opposed to alienating. The military needs a dictionary for all the acronyms. I find myself losing critical elements of the conversation as I attempt to decipher the letters they just dropped. Yes, I have stopped them and asked them what those initials mean.

When I say vitality, I am talking of the "E" word. Enthusiasm. Your speech should spew enthusiasm that can become infectious. The upbeat voice can make the recipients ears happier. Keep it in context. There are times when you need to mute the enthusiasm such as at a funeral. We have all experienced that someone that is a little too sappy for our taste.

The pace of your speech can be important. Record, listen and critique your voice. In Biloxi, Mississippi on business, several of my fast talking associates from New York entered a McDonalds for lunch. They went bonkers over the slow talking southern cashier. Perhaps having lived in the South for so long, I felt at home listening to the slow drawl. They were in a hurry up let's go mode and had no time for slow vowels.

James Earl Jones the actor, is noted for having such a rich, bold voice that he is the spokesperson for Verizon. He has starred in many movies including *Roots* and was the voice of Darth Vader in *Star Wars*. He has the perfect voice. At the age of five, his maternal grandparents adopted him. The event was so traumatic that he developed a severe stutter and eventually refused to speak aloud. He remained a functional mute as he entered high school.

Can you imagine a man with such an eloquent voice being a mute? In high school, his English teacher forced him out of his silence. The teacher insisted that Jones recite poetry each day in class. The millions of fans of James Earl Jones almost never heard his wonderful voice.

Volume adjust

The first time I testified in court, the defense attorney claimed that his client could not hear my commands as evidenced by my quiet and insecure voice. The judge was sympathetic to the coun-selor and he warned me that I was not talking loud enough. I won the case, but had to work on my voice projection. People who have to strain to hear you, will eventually get tired like any task you engage. Your focus of attention can only last so long before you become disinterested.

When I was in training for the Secret Service, our classroom was the worst learning environment I had been exposed to since elementary school. Despite the winter weather of January, the two window air conditioner units were always on. They were con-structing a building next door with the associated jackhammers and clanking of steel. Combine that with the projector fan and those of us in that zone, we really had to focus on the speaker. One of my classmates continually asked me, "What did he say?" to the point, it became an ongoing joke. Beware of other distractions and your volume control.

Keep in mind if you have a booming voice. I know of some people that even their whispers are loud. How far does your voice naturally project? Some people with hearing deficiencies will speak louder because they are unable to naturally monitor the voice level. Loud voiced folks are not the ones you want to be around when you are gossiping or sharing secrets. Other times, some people en-joy being the center of attention, like the barker at the carnival.

Chapter 11
Conversation

We all remember Joe Friday and just the facts. We have all been victims of Helpful Hal who has cornered us with a very long story about everything. Get to the point. Not as dry as Joe Friday, who could have made the dead at the morgue excited, but save the long stories. People's time is precious. In this hop to-it, text message in thirty words or less world, attention spans are short. Watch an old movie. Even the classics like *Casablanca,* are slow starters. Today a movie has five minutes to grab.

Everyone has a coworker or a neighbor that has enough wind to navigate a sailboat around the world. As soon as you see them, you are already coming up with plans to put a time limit on the conversation. You left something on the stove, or you need to make funeral arrangements for your long lost aunt. You do not want people to start running when they see you coming. Short stories and get to the point.

If you have a propensity to embellish or talk about what you do not know, you are swimming without a life preserver. One day while teaching a class, one person made an emphatic statement concerning flight regulations. I thought the information was incorrect, but was not confident enough to challenge the inaccuracy. He had apparently dismissed the fact that a pilot was sitting a few rows over. The pilot took him to school on his error and exposed the deception.

When I would interview people and they said, "Honestly," or "On my mother's grave," or "I am a religious person," my distrust meter started bouncing toward lie. If you are telling me the truth, you do not need to attach affirmations. That tells me that you do not think that I will believe you, so you need to convince me. This is not always the case. We all fall into speech habits both good and bad, and this may be one of them.

If people take the time to compliment you, respond in kind. Do not diminish their effort by dismissing it as nothing. If they compliment you on your scarf, your response should be, "Oh thank you for noticing, it was gift from so and so, or I bought it at such and such place." You do not want to say, "Oh this old thing or oh this." Along the same way if someone makes an inquiry as to say your health, respond back by thanking him or her for asking.

Chapter 12
Listening

"When people talk, listen completely. Most people never listen."
—Ernest Hemingway

This is one of the most overlooked aspects of interpersonal communications. Most of you have heard the saying that God gave us two ears and one mouth for a reason. In one study, physicians interrupted their patients after listening for only eighteen seconds. That is barely enough time to say hello and tell the good doctor that you think you might be dying.

I play a game when I meet a stranger and I see how little I can talk, but how much I can make them talk. One time I was talking to an ultrasound tech. I asked her how long she had been in the business and where she lived. I asked her what changes she has seen in her career and how she liked living in Florida. She never asked me one personal question, but with those few questions, I listened for twenty minutes.

I have seen people who spoke very little, asked a few questions and actively listened, who were thought by the recipients to be so very nice and charming, despite saying little. Active listening is the ability to show genuine interest in what the other person is saying. You nod every now and then, give a few uh hums, and ask a few clarifying questions to further stimulate the topic.

When your neighbor pulls up in a shiny new car and they start telling you about the car, you might add, "With that engine does it have much pickup?" "How did the dealership treat you?" Just listen to them bloviate about their great acquisition and great deal they received on the car. Remember, no one gets a bad deal on his or her car. At least in their opinion.

Yield the floor. Do not interrupt. We have all seen the talk show hosts that constantly interrupt their guests. I often wonder if they really want to hear the answer.

Like Mr. Magoo, avoid being a word hog. Balance the conversation. Actually, don't balance. Tilt it in their favor. Everyone loves a good story without all the details. You will enjoy this book with stories. Don't kill the story with "ALL" the details.

Show interest and avoid the "uh huh…yeah yeah," as you lean towards the door. If you have to leave, tell them you have to get on your way for an appointment. Avoid the professor's lecture. The type of conversation where you are holding court and overwhelming your listeners with your brilliance.

Be careful of the minefield of politics, religion and economics. Economics leads to politics. Jokes can be hilarious or bombs. Keep them short. For crying out loud, why are people still telling inappropriate jokes that are offensive? How many politicians and upper level managers have had their wings clipped from forwarding emails or text messages containing offensive jokes?

Joke telling is all in the timing and delivery. Some people have a knack. I have a friend Greg that has a wonderful delivery of jokes. Everyone gathers around him when he begins telling the jokes. While other people I have seen, fall as flat as a pancake dropped from the roof. Recognize your deficiencies and spare your audience.

Avoid the "that reminds me or oh yeah I remember" trap. Guilty. I myself often fell into this trap. I would like to think that I was telling a short story to enhance the conversation. I try to catch myself, but I fall short more times than not. Many people do not want to hear of the good old days and will start rolling their eyes.

Be careful not to hijack the conversation. I attended a writer's conference. One of the panels had three authors. One participant hijacked the panel and the audience's time. That goes along with the person that cannot wait their turn. They have something to say that is of such magnitude, they are like a boiler under too much pressure and the rivets have already started to pop. They remind me of the kid tugging on mom's skirt trying to get her attention.

We have all experienced the enthusiastic friend that asks if we saw the newest action or romance movie. Due to the demands of work and family, you have not been to a movie in six months. Your eager friend will save you the cost of the ticket. Even after you warn them, "Don't tell me what happened," they cannot help themselves and bloviate about the movie, while you drift off into happy land and tune them out.

Take an interest in your conversational partner's dialogue. Show a keen interest, and listen to what they feel is important. It will help anchor a friendship, and you may learn something along the way.

Chapter 13
Respect

A Los Angeles police officer assigned to a gang suppression unit was on patrol in the Watts neighborhood with his partner. They heard gunshots and then observed an individual fleeing on foot down an alley. The officer jumped out on foot and gave chase while radioing in his location, the suspected crime, and description of the suspect.

Responding officers immediately set up a perimeter in response to the radio broadcast. The idea was to box the suspect inside the area of containment. After the suspect was captured, he told the officer who had given the initial chase that he could have killed the officer. As it turns out, the suspect had dove through some hedges.

The officer with the adrenaline rushing through his body, provided updates through a radio broadcast. Unbeknownst to the officer, he ran past the shooter hiding in the bushes. Why did the shooter not kill the officer? After the shooter was located, he told the officers that it was due to the fact that the officer had always treated the suspect with respect.

I learned early on in my career, that ninety nine percent of the people I dealt with while working as a street cop, would responded positively to respect. There was always the one percent that would not respond. There was not much you could do for them. Many of those one percenter's who did not understand the concept of respect, landed up with a free ride to jail and did not pass go.

I know in the car business, they have customers that are referred to as tire kickers. In real estate, you have the open house lookie loos. They are looking for decorating ideas, curious, or dreaming. It is easy to dismiss these folks as not being serious. You do not want to spend a lot of time and resources with them. Always be nice and professional. The same with the tire kickers. You never know where it will lead. I spent a year shopping for a new car. One salesperson, was patient enough to be professional, and showed respect to me, and it led to four future sales.

My wife encountered a real estate agent accompanying a client on a walkthrough, while she was taking a walk in the neighborhood. She spoke briefly with the agent who presented his card.

Two weeks later when a dear friend of ours was on a househunting trip, their agent dropped the ball. The agent had ignored voicemails the night before and again was not available for contact the morning of their scheduled appointment. When our friend finally reached her after calling the agency, the agent was very curt and advised she never takes calls during her son's football game. That was where she was the night before and refused to take the calls. I am all about family, but when duty calls… Our friends had travelled from out of state and were now left high and dry. They were obviously serious buyers.

Our friend took the business card from my wife of the agent she had met the previous week. Deborah called the agent as a late inning replacement. In less than an hour, he was in the game. Our friends purchased a home and sold a home using the same agent. Think of the commissions the other agent lost because of poor planning and lack of respect. She should have reached out and confirmed the plans with her new client before the ball game.

Do not trash your competition. My mother would say if you cannot say anything nice do not say anything at all. I try, but I do tend to be opinionated. My mom would be disappointed in me.

She always adhered to that advice. Be very careful disparaging another employee, business, or competition. It can lead to nowhere but drama. At the very least it diminishes your standing with the person in front of you, who is wondering what you will say about them when they leave.

When a nurse asks me if I am allergic to anything, I usually say I am allergic to rude people. I would throw condescending people in the same pile. I absolutely cannot stand when someone does not treat someone with respect without cause. I cannot tell you how many times I listened to strap hanging political aides talking down to a hotel employee, a volunteer, or a cop because they thought they were somebody special and above the other person.

I have seen it in all professions from lawyers, to doctors, to business people, and to cops. I have seen federal agents look down on local cops. I have absolutely no use for disrespect. I witnessed one person who was newly appointed to his position talk down to an administrative person. I corrected that situation immediately. It goes back to respect. Treat others, as you would like to be treated. Stand in their flip-flops.

I observed one businessperson who had such utter disdain for people around them that their own staff would not sit near them on a plane trip. He was toxic. Like a toxic waste dump, the toxicity spreads and people do not like to live near toxic waste dumps.

A debate is sometimes good, but be cautious, as not to become too spirited. You do not want to be labeled as the "Awful Harry" that is always right. You can shout down most opposition, but you probably have not succeeded in changing their inner belief. What you have accomplished is alienated or at least damaged future associations.

Remember when people would hold open doors, and the benefactors said thank you to the door holder. Now the door holder is thought to be a door attendant, as ten people breeze past without uttering a syllable. Remember when you were driving down your street, and you accidentally cutoff another driver? They would hit their horn and you would wave your hand in omission of your mistake? Unlike the deviant driver who flashes the, "your number one" salute as the immediate reaction to a horn.

While driving through rush hour traffic in Washington, D.C., I was flashed the double middle finger salute by a driver behind me, as we both changed lanes at the same time vying for the same real estate on the road. I was sorry I encumbered his acceleration, but I was in front. Please forgive me for driving the speed limit. I would have waived an apology if he had just honked, despite not doing anything wrong.

An hour later that two fingered driver was very embarrassed when I asked him at his desk, how he was able to maintain control of his self guided missile, with both hands in the air and not on the steering wheel. He apologized because he was caught. He had no idea he had just flipped off someone that he knew. I enjoyed the last and best laugh.

Do you want to work for someone, purchase something from someone, or date someone that does not show you respect? How about repeat business to a doctor with a lousy bedside manner who does not value you as a person. You might have no choice working for a boss that disrespects you, but will probably not be an optimum producer. You may endure a disrespectful salesperson, and you may even make a purchase if you are desperate, but what are the chances of repeat business or a second date if the first date was with a selfish brat. Nada.

It all comes down the Golden Rule of treating others the same way you would like to be treated. It is really as simple as that.

Chapter 14
Enthusiasm and Dependability

I am not advocating that you bounce off the walls with the enthusiasm of Anthony Robbins. It is a start. Your performance is directly attributed to your attitude and energy. After working for the government for thirty years, I can tell you that as a whole, they do a poor job of enhancing attitude. It does not matter what agency, I found every federal agency suffered from an inherent lack of spirit de corps. There were a few exceptions.

That aside, you have to put that baggage in the trunk and drive on. Fake it. As Bob the Builder would say, "Yes we can." It is not always easy. Do it for yourself. Do it for your client. Do it for your family. I do it for my own self worth.

Speaking of yes, there were a few times that I employed this simple strategy of Dale Carnegie. Get them to become agreeable. If you are attempting to gain favor, it might be best if you start with a few questions that would demand a yes answer. If you get them to say yes a few times, they might be more likely to continue the trend. It will not guarantee a yes, but it will build a nest for a positive reaction.

Lou Holtz the former football coach had some simple guidelines for his athletes, "Do right." These are very simple words of wisdom. Avoid trouble and keep in mind, does this sound like a good idea. If it does not, avoid the temptation.

I know it is real easy to say that you should put your problems to the side. You are all stoked up about some problem at home or with the boss. Remember, the client did not cause that problem. Who cares how you do it. If it is the digital picture frame that reminds you of good times, positive self-talk, or "I be jammin" up-tempo music, find your own way to put on a happy face. Zig Ziglar says, "Get rid of the *stinkin thinkin*." You project what you are. A bad attitude is a guarantee for failure.

A positive attitude will compensate for a lack of intelligence, a lack of good looks, or a lack of a proper upbringing. Think of when you stop at the Greazy Spoon Café. You smell the grease before you walk in and have to burn your clothes after because now your car smells likes grease. The waiter is not well dressed and is doing as well as they can in life.

For the next hour, the server is giving you as good a service as you would receive at the five star eatery back home. He is hustling for tips and charging forward for a four-buck tip. I can forgive a lot of things when the right attitude is projected.

I recently experienced a similar experience. We had spent the night in Sarasota. We arrived in time for lunch at the Old Salty Dog and the next morning we had breakfast at the Holiday Inn Lido Beach overlooking the turquoise water of the Gulf of Mexico. The server at both locations did a great job and earned their twenty percent tip. For dinner, we went to a very well known restaurant. The food was excellent. The service, not so much.

The server seemed somewhat detached. Perhaps she had something on her mind. She never checked on the quality of our meal. We had to ask for refills and she splashed salad dressing on my wife and her water glass without an apology. Even a ten percent tip of the bill would have come out higher than the tip of either of the first two servers. Yet, they provided five star service.

Make people glad they have met you and leave them with a positive impression. Some people just make you feel better about yourself. You just enjoy being with them. Why not try to emulate them and return the favor to others. Be the daily caffeine for those around you.

Psychologist Edward Thorndike developed the "Halo Effect." In 1920, he noticed that military officers gave high grades in all categories of performance to soldiers who portrayed good posture and warm faces. This was in spite of their actual performance grades, which in some cases were not satisfactory. The Halo Effect transcends to today showing that upbeat people are likeable and viewed as intelligent and successful.

Dependability

You have to be dependable. Your word is your bond. If you say you will do something or be somewhere, you better hold true. I have been involved in quite a few charity events. It never ceases to amaze me when people volunteer for a particular effort and then come up with a pocketful of excuses as to why they could not or would not complete the task. Save them. No one wants to hear it.

My mindset was coming up with reasons why I had to accomplish this task. A pocketful of sunshine. The other motivation was that I did not want others thinking of me in a poor light. My image was important. As I sat there around the table as a low-level grunt for a fundraiser, the majority of people had not completed the requested tasks. It does not take much to separate you from the crowd. The desire to succeed, breeds enthusiasm that enhances your ability to come out on top.

At the Wyndham Hotel in Tampa, they strive to separate from the herd of other hotels. Two canisters of M&M's greet guests arriving at the front desk reception. One plain and one peanut. Go ahead and grab a handful. Their breakfast buffet enjoys a reputation for wonderful bacon. I have lost count of the number of people I have talked to, who have raved about those two seemingly small but significant items. They are striving to separate from the crowd.

In the nonprofit world, they have an iceberg theorem. Ten to twenty percent of the staff complete ninety percent of the preplanning or organizing work. The whole group will come together and show support for the event on game day.

I organized several different charity runs. I was the team leader for six of those events. For many of the volunteers, I kept getting the, "I'll help, I'll do this, let me know what I can do." The bottom line was when it came to crunch time, it was up to my family and me. It is for this reason that there is such a high level of burnout in nonprofits, despite the worthwhile cause. They are like roman candles going up in a brilliant fashion, only to burn out at the top of the arc.

When it comes to volunteering their time, people will focus the budgeting of time on the task that they are held accountable. Such as family commitments and work responsibilities. There were some people on game day that showed up like General MacArthur returning as the hero of the Philippines. They were there for the photo-ops, when others performed all the sweat and labor.

If a task is assigned and you think there are going to be problems or conflicts, get it out in the open up front. No one wants to hear on the due date that you were not dependable and could not deliver.

Success depends on others. You may be able to do most of the work on your own, but someone else is helping you. It might be your family sacrificing time, a supervisor that expressed their confidence and provided the opportunity, or perhaps your faith in God. There is always some help from others. Skip Holtz the son of Lou and the current coach of USF football said, "A turtle doesn't get on a fence post on their own."

Your enthusiasm and attitude could become dangerous and infect your client, patient, or customer. Think of your own attitude as you hang around the toxic office worker with a lousy attitude.

Most offices have someone that is miserable in their life. We all have our bad times. Life is not always good and sometimes we are spectators in our own life.

In some office cultures, there is that one person that hates his job and everything about it. Everything is wrong. Joe Navarro calls them, "wound collectors." Now, think how you feel around the energetic new puppy in the office that has to be kept on a leash to hold back their enthusiasm. Assume your target.

Chapter 15
Personal Space

As we entertain visitors in our homes or our office, the first impressions are so important. The skill of staging a house has become a cottage industry. With the downturn in the market, I believe it is an even more important aspect than in the past. It lifts the home above the competition. There was a time my wife and I dragged a poor real estate agent around to sixty homes in less than a week. There were some homes that when we pulled up in front of, I thought I was at 1313 Mockingbird Lane, the home of Herman Munster. To these homes, we were scared enough to remain in the car and continue driving. I was astonished at the conditions of many homes for sale. It is like trading in a car that is filthy inside and out. You will not get top dollar.

If you are expecting guests, straighten up and tidy the public area. There have been times when my desk looked like a bomb was detonated and the hazmat team should be called. In a matter of minutes, I can straighten the piles, and if I need to, throw some under the desk.

People will immediately decide if you are organized or disorganized just by examining your living or workspace. Sam Gosling, a professor of psychology at the University of Texas, and his researchers explore what our stuff says about us in his book, *Snoop*

What Your Stuff Says About You. He and his students explored personal space like urban archeologists deciding where the occupants fell on the Big Five personality traits.

Pets

I am a dog lover, but not everyone is. No one wants Hooch slobbering all over you or jumping on you. I have seen more than one dog wrap themselves around the leg of visitors and have a go of it. If you are anticipating guests, put Rover somewhere that he will not be an encumbrance. The barking from a bedroom is better than disrupting the visit. I am not talking about friends and relatives. I am talking about business related visitors.

If the tables are turned and the canine greeter to Wal-Mart meets you, bend down and present your hand for them to sniff. Ball up your hand in a fist in case the dog wants to chomp. I have the scars on my fingers to show what happens when you expose the fingers. Talk softly, pet them and hopefully the handler has restrained the dog. A lot of people have allergies to the feline and the canine.

Cats tend to be ambivalent toward new arrivals. Kitty enjoys curling around the leg of visitors like a snake. I have been at residences where Tabby jumped up on the table or kitchen counter. Not good. Put them in a bedroom.

Kids and Other Issues

If you have kids, tie them up and stuff them in the closet. No, don't do that! I have been blessed to have been a devoted parent and foster parent. I love kids, but at times, they can become a distraction.

If you are entertaining at home, your goal is to keep the children from disrupting the meeting. Speak frankly with the children and tell them it will be important to behave and mind their manners. Invest in some new surprises. Tell them that due to your confidence in their good behavior, you are going to reward them with a new coloring book, DVD or video game. You know what is age appropriate.

Children should be raised to understand manners and proper decorum, while guests are in the home. Unfortunately, not all parents are vigilant in this area. If your children are rambunctious and difficult to control during an important meeting, I suggest investing in a good babysitter, or a friend, or neighbor's house, where you can stash the kids.

Ill mannered and misbehaving children can torpedo your success with the person you are meeting. Well-behaved and polite children will embolden your positioning. Be honest and truthful in your evaluation. Do not make excuses for their conduct. It is what it is.

If you have pets or if you have humans, beware of scents and odors within your personal space. No one wants to smell last night's fried cod. A little air freshener or a scented candle does the trick. Real estate agents use a trick of putting an apple pie or a loaf of bread in the oven on a low temperature.

Smell is often overlooked, but it is engrained in our memory by association. Certain scents elicit memories from our past. Bread, apple pie, and cookies are usually sure bets. Some people swear by aromatherapy and the soothing response to lavender or other scents.

If you have music playing, try to find something that will not be offensive. I have a very eclectic interest in music. Some people love country, while others hate it. The same for hip-hop. Smooth jazz or new age is a happy medium. Think of Panera Bread with light classical. If you insist on country, ask if they mind it. Judge their response and make your decision.

It may be your castle, but if you are sharing, you really want to strive for common ground. If you are entertaining clients or co-workers, the following workday will be centered on the gossip of the gathering. The good and the bad.

Chapter 16
It's a Small World

You never know where a meeting of a new person will lead. Like the Disney ride, it is a Small World. I cannot tell you how many times I began talking to someone who knew someone that we had in common.

We have all heard of the six degrees of separation. This is the theory that six people separate everyone from another person.

Many years ago, my wife and I were in Hawaii on vacation. I observed a trio attempting to take photos with a China Men's Hat in the background. We stopped and offered to take a picture of all three together. They were happy with the opportunity and we engaged in some conversation. We learned one of the tourists attended high school in Little Rock, her brother was a deputy, and her father still lived there. Six months later I investigated a case in which her father was the victim. Who knew that someone I met four thousand miles away, would be the related to a victim of a crime that I would investigate. We identified the suspect and arrested him.

My children's high school counselor was meeting with me for the first time. She apologized for talking fast, because she was from New York. I started my inquiry and learned she attended the same high school that I had, and her husband ran cross-country with my brother. Her sister in-law was in the same class as my sister. You never know where we might bump into someone that has a connection.

While scratching through the debris from the World Trade Center, I was alerted to the fact that a New York City Police Officer across the conveyor belt, knew me. We were friends in high school and I had not seen him in twenty-five years. It is a small world.

Kindness

Generosity without the expectation of reward is a rare commodity. I have often taken the time to seek out a manager of a restaurant that I will probably never return to, just so I can praise one of his servers. Be generous, but sincere with praise.

When we became foster parents, our intention was to be helpful and generous of our family and provide a home to someone not as fortunate. I think our family benefitted more from the generosity of goodness and bestowing hope on the child.

Everyone wants a little love. Everyone likes to feel appreciated. Uplift others through genuine praise. Put a smile on their face. Think of yourself. We all enjoy a pat on the back accompanied with a warm smile.

Show your openness with a pleasant face and being approachable through body language. Most people are clueless about their projection. Are they projecting the Halo Effect or Devil Effect? Check the mirror or ask an honest reviewer.

Rejection

Everyone fears rejection. For the male species, remember the first time you picked up the telephone to ask a new acquaintance out on a date? In the old days before caller ID, I would call the number and then hang up after the first ring. Then I would wait a few minutes to call back, so they would not think it was me who had just called. When I heard the voice of the young lady, I would hang up. Now I had to wait at least an hour or maybe until the next day before I could make another attempt.

Why was I so terrified? I was horrified of hearing, "No." I did not mind running towards gunfire, but I was afraid of rejection over the telephone. Now the kids ask each other out over text messages. They also drop them the same way. Rejection is in the top ten of fears for most people. As a result, it is difficult to step out of your comfort zone.

We all want to be accepted. No one wants to be the subject of humiliation and ridicule. The acceptance by the tribe was essential for survival during the cave dwellers days. We were community dependent. That is less of a case today, but our basic need for acceptance is still strong. Dr. Steven Reiss in his groundbreaking research, identified acceptance as one of our sixteen basic motivational desires.

Adapting

Most people are satisfied with their own misery. It is their comfort zone. Change is uncomfortable and causes anxiety. Stretch yourself and experience different worlds. Seek insight into different worlds. So get on your way. As Dr. Seuss wrote in, *Oh the Places You'll Go*, "So be your name, Buxbaum or Bixby or Bray or Mordecai Ali Van Allen O'Shea, you're off to great places. Today is your day!"

You have to adapt to your surroundings. In the movie *New in Town*, actress Rene Zellweger is a prototypical professional business executive living the sophisticated cosmopolitan world of Miami. She is asked to take over the operations of a plant in Minnesota with a completely different set of norms and conduct. All of which is very foreign to her normal routine. Hostility grows, but as she learns to adapt, she becomes accepted by the local people and indulges in the local traditions of scrapbooking and tapioca pudding.

Then of course, there is *Sweet Home Alabama* with Reese Witherspoon, which is the opposite. The rural country girl ditches her background to become a socialite in New York, only to return to her roots and she is forced to readapt from a cosmopolitan life style to a simpler rural existence.

Humility

No bragging. You will look like a pompous jerk. There are certain accomplishments in life that we are proud of, but keep them in perspective. If someone were making the same claims to you, would you roll your eyes and think what a blowhard. My fish is bigger than your fish, or I have been there done that. Be humble and modest. Deflect acclaim and accolades, or share it with others on the team.

Passions

Explore people's passions. It is the key to the treasure chest. They relive the positive emotions associated with passion and release endorphins and feel better.

Men share success stories of work, finance, sports. Women share more stories that are personal or family related. Women are more open and forthcoming then men with emotions. Read the book *Men are from Mars and Women are from Venus*. We are different not just physically, but emotionally. Living as the lone man in my household, I learned to adapt and yes, even put the toilet seat down.

Chapter 17
Anchors of Life

Your perspective is based on your life experiences. Your decision making process is an outtake of your learned behaviors. Both the good and the bad. We all have panic irritators, an achilles heel, or pet peeves.

Life's experiences will mold our decision making process. How your parents interacted with each other. How your teachers and bosses interacted with you and others. How friends and lovers have interacted with you are inputted and stored in the cortex of your brain. It shapes how we interact with others.

Status

Some people cannot help but overvaluing their status. "I am a pediatric thoracic surgeon," instead of, "I am a doctor." "I am a Secret Service agent assigned to the President's detail," as opposed to, "I work for Homeland Security." Who cares? I am not impressed. Tell me you are a doctor and if I am interested, I will ask what type. I met a man, and he told me he was an attorney. I asked what field of law he practiced. He said he specialized in "Threshold Law." I started to answer for him, which was wrong, and then I stopped. His answer was that anyone that crossed the threshold of his door with a check in hand was his specialty.

I have observed folks who have come from a hardscrabble life that possess a bias towards the affluent. That is where people from more humble beginnings or lower socioeconomic positions in life carry a chip on their shoulder. They look at affluent people as having achieved their status due to favoritism or an unfair advantage.

I have witnessed the opposite as well. I have watched affluent people in various social gatherings that have displayed little regard for the lower class. Leona Helmsley, the famous hotelier, was well known for her inadequate treatment of servants and contractors. She earned the reputation as the Queen of Mean. This was despite her simple beginnings.

Stand in the other person's flip-flops. How would you want to be treated? Has that person individually caused you some sort of harm? If not, accept them for who they are. Do not judge them until you have had the appropriate time to interact with them. Some of the most genuine people I have met, fell on both sides of the track. They all deserved my respect.

The UPS driver was making a delivery to my house. These folks are usually under the gun to get their deliveries done quickly. I saw him pull-up and I walked out. As he bounded off the truck, I told him I would save him a few steps and how I appreciated his work. He thanked me and told me he made 150 deliveries per day. I found that very interesting and asked a few more questions. I did not take up much of his time, because I knew he had to move on. I showed value in his contribution to society and me.

I am saddened by the increased technology of the toll roads. I enjoyed stopping at the booth and saying hello. On busy days, I thanked the toll workers for their efforts. They all knew me by face. By exchanging a quick sentence or two, perhaps I made their morning, and I certainly benefitted from the pleasant exchange.

I was speaking with a hospital administrator. He said it did not matter who the person was or how much money they had in their pocket when they entered the hospital. The only thing that mattered, was once they were wearing a gown parted down the back, they were a patient in their hospital and deserved the best care possible.

Containing Adversity

I worked with one fellow who had twins born prematurely resulting in significant health issues. His medical bills the first year of their life was astronomical. Anytime I ever asked him to assist me on an assignment, he never hesitated. No one would have blamed him if he came to work with a horrible attitude, but he chose to focus on the job and separate his family problems from work. He was one of the most tenacious investigators and professional agents I ever had the privilege to work with. I admired his ability to separate home from work. At home, he was a dedicated father and husband.

I too had many health issues at home and it was a challenge to keep that from affecting my performance. I tended to my family's needs and tried to balance work and home the best that I could. I used a system of compartmentalizing those issues that could be worrisome to me, but I could do nothing about at that moment.

I visualized placing those worries in a box and tying the lid closed with a ribbon and bow. When my brother was diagnosed with lung cancer, I was in the midst of a long-term investigation that was coming to a close, as well as an upcoming dance competition for my daughters. Neither one of us realized the gravity of the situation. We knew it was terminal, but we had agreed that I would travel to see him in three weeks. We talked every week to monitor the situation. He sounded good and his spirits were high.

It was not until the plane arrived in Dallas, that I visually opened the box and faced the crises ahead. Neither my brother nor I had any idea that my brother would be dead in forty-eight hours. Although I thought of him often prior to my trip to visit him, I knew that I had other priorities that had to be handled before I could focus on his visit.

Rabbi Harold Kushner wrote an excellent book, *Why do Bad Things Happen to Good People*. Victimized by the death of his son, who suffered from a long-term illness, he chose to focus on the positive. The essence of the book, is that bad things do happen with little explanation and we have to treasure the time we spent during the good times and not dwell on the bad. We have to move on.

Going through a divorce is in many ways more devastating than a death of spouse. I have never observed anyone endure a divorce without significant impact on their lives. Many times that has bled over to the workplace. The pain is usually deep and has often been compared with enduring the death of a spouse.

I was talking to a businessperson one day in his office. I had spoke with him several times and was aware of his business and family. When we met in his office, we discussed his business, and how he had nurtured a small business into a larger successful international operation. Looking at photos of his kids, I made a comment about his family. For the next thirty minutes, I listened to him pour out pain from a divorce a year ago. Perhaps it was my ability to make him feel comfortable, but I also knew he was releasing the pain and betrayal he still felt a year later.

If I was a potential client, his confessional time might very well have dampened my enthusiasm for his product. If I had endured a divorce, he could have used his breakup as a bonding method. The trap to avoid is that the victims of divorce often do not recognize when to disengage and to move on. The pain of rejection is deep. I think most of us have all felt rejection at some point in our lives, but it is best to keep it out of the workplace.

It is similar to when someone asks you how you are doing. Most people really do not want to know how you are doing. Answer with brevity. Do not make people regret asking the question.

Chapter 18
Group Dynamics

The basic philosophy of group dynamics is that the gatherings tend to have a polarization effect. Ok, you have been invited to a housewarming party, or a retirement party, or a whatever party. When you arrive, are you an aggressive hunter, are you seeking out guests to meet, or are you curling up in the corner in the fetal position? Do not be like a framed piece of museum art. It looks good, but do not touch. You are wasting your time. Circulate.

I attended one party that had four distinctive interest groups. Co-workers, friends, neighbors that bordered the house and another set of neighbors associated with the children's bus stop. There was very little crossover. As a result, most group members retreated within the group to their territorial camps. They would leave the comfort zone for the central food and beverage station, and flea like mice with a block of cheese returning to their happy zone.

I worked for a boss that decided to indulge in an obligatory Christmas party. They were following a tradition established by their predecessor, who hosted an informal and warm gathering for employees to display his appreciation for a job well done. To ease the pain of having to interact with his subordinates, this new supervisor, invited his neighbors. I knew before I entered what would happen.

The neighbors congregated around the food in the kitchen and the employees would fill their plates and gravitate to the living room, so they could associate with people who shared commonality. There was nothing wrong with either group, it is just too difficult for most people to exit their comfort zone to engage and get to know people they will not see for another year.

Neither one of these hosts could have changed this dynamic, unless there were group activities. Using horseshoes or beer pong might force the group to assimilate.

I have been to some parties where the guest list was so diverse that there was automatic assimilation. Instead of attaching yourself like Velcro to an ally, you were forced to mingle.

If you walk into a party environment, meander around the established groups and listen to the conversations. If you hear a topic you know a little about, jump on that like a squirrel on a nut. Look at the feet of the folks in the group. If someone has his or her feet pointing out, that is the white space to fill. Those that have their feet pointed inward and shoulders squared to the group are displaying the most interest. Slide into the group and listen. When a pause occurs in the conversation, offer your two cents of brilliance. If the conversation falls off like a brick in a pond, you over valued your input. Just listen with your mouth shut, until you can slip out diplomatically.

As the focus of the conversation begins to trek downward, do not be afraid to offer your name, a smile and handshake to all participants. Point your torso and feet towards the persons of interest. Ask how they were selected to attend the gathering or their connection to the host. That will stimulate further conversation.

In social settings, I like to have a beverage in my hand. It keeps my hands occupied instead of shuffling them in my pockets. It presents a small defense barrier to hide behind. Most of all it keeps my mouth lubricated. No dry mouth. The downside is more trips to the bathroom.

Another fertile networking ground, is the restroom line or in the public lavatory. I have heard some stimulating conversation inside the tiled walls of the bathroom. Just make sure you wash your hands.

Do not be a scene-stealer. You know the type that is provided an opportunity to speak, and then hijacks the conversation with a long boring diatribe on their small corner of the world. You can just see everyone toe tapping with impatience, crossing their arms, and minds adrift. Stick with the short story version.

Monitor the exit migration from the party. If the hosts are starting to cleanup, that is a clue to start finding your way to the door. Be courteous. Some people have a day job. Do not overstay your welcome. Leave with the last wave or as soon as possible after. Offer to help clean up and leave a positive image.

When I meet people for the first time and receive a business card, I will always follow-up with an email. It was nice to meet you at XYZ and I hope to see you again. I try to personalize the note. Most times, they will respond in kind. On a few occasions, someone has beaten me to the email.

Having dealt a great deal with hotel sales staff, I have usually been impressed with their professionalism. On one occasion, I had met a new sales manager at an upscale hotel. We developed rapport with each other and exchanged cards. Before I could return to my office, my Blackberry received an anchoring email from the sales manager. It was a nice touch.

More than a few of my emails have been launched into cyberspace to never be heard from again. Perhaps they were not as enamored with me, as I had hoped. Do not go past anything other than the greeting. No selling. Otherwise, they will think you are using them and that is the only reason why you are hammering them. Even when the emails are not acknowledged, the recipient will probably remember your efforts.

Chapter 19
Scheduling and Organizing

When it comes time to schedule an appointment, make sure you cleared the deck. Look at your calendar and verify there are no conflicts and you have budgeted a time buffer. We expect to wait for a doctor's appointment, but most of us have experienced the frustration from the tardiness of the cable guy or the pizza delivery person. You want your client or customer to think that they are very important and deserving of your time.

Tardiness is unacceptable. Sure, every now and then, a piece of the space shuttle takes out your car in the driveway, or you stopped to assist a mother giving birth in the backseat of a taxi. Not every day and every meeting.

My time is precious. When you are late, that means you do not respect my time. For crying out loud arrive on time. I drove six hours for an appointment and the person I was to meet, was thirty minutes late for no apparent reason. I called them to tell them I was getting close and it was only then that they told me to put the brakes on and slow down.

In an article written for the Los Angeles Times, Dr. Anna B Reisman of Connecticut, lamented on the frustration of patients left to wallow in the waiting rooms of physicians across the country. She added that the lack of an apology by the staff and the doctor only added to dissatisfaction. It does not matter if it is the cable guy or a doctor, an apology is required for tardiness. I one time chastised a doctor for the defeatist attitude of their staff. The receptionist offered an excuse that a two-hour or more wait for a specialist, was acceptable. Sarasota Memorial Hospital will send a written apology to their emergency room patients who wait in excess of thirty minutes.

I have witnessed politicians routinely run behind schedule by an hour or more. Why have a schedule? I would rather be a half hour early than five minutes late. Allow for the bottleneck in traffic or weather. If the road kill monster grabs your car, then have the decency to call and say, hey I'm going to be late by thirty minutes, is that going to be ok, or do we need to reschedule? Do not underestimate the adjustment in time because then you are going to be late again.

I was standing in line at Heathrow Airport in London. I had been in town for three weeks and was looking forward to my return home in time for Christmas. I arrived three hours early for my scheduled flight home. The car company told me that I did not need to be there that early. I wanted no chance of being late. As I stood on line, I watched as countless tardy passengers were moved to the head of the line. My anger increased as time in the queue exceeded forty-five minutes. I thought I was waiting for the Space Mountain Ride at Disney. Not wanting to be the "Ugly American," I quietly fumed.

As I made my way to the front, I was once again stopped and leapfrogged, I quietly protested. I was told by the greeter that perhaps these people had overslept, or a car accident delayed them. My response was that I was being penalized for being early and they were rewarded for being late. The polite official informed me that they might miss the plane. I explained that perhaps the next time they would arrive early. They moved me along, which at this point was mute.

Be mindful that there is a social order to queuing up. Mark Changizi, an evolutionary neurobiologist, has studied the behavior of the violating social orders of those standing in line. The frustration due to a lack of conformity can reach critical mass and have unintended consequences to include violence. Three years of our life is consumed standing in line.

The same social order for conformity in line, also applies to tardiness. Not many people enjoy waiting for a person who shows little regard for their time. Build in extra time.

Have all the necessary paperwork ready to go. An attorney, I had retained for some estate matters was supposed to have the paperwork already for my signature. I sat their chatting about this and that while the printer spewed one page at time. I did not mind, because I was able to engage in some meaningful dialogue, but if I was pressed for time, I would have been annoyed.

I can tell you that on more than one occasion, real estate agents were not prepared when I met with them. They should have had corresponding maps for each property so they are easy to find, or preprogrammed into their GPS. Time is money. Why would you not be prepared? As a buyer with limited time, an unorganized agent is infuriating. I may not say anything, but I am seething as my time is being wasted.

If you are picking someone up, have your car clean and gassed up. I have had both situations, where they had no gas and the car was filthy. Always keep the other persons needs before yours. Do not assume that if you skip lunch that everyone else does as well. Schedule meals. I had one real estate agent show us two properties and wanted to stop for lunch at 10:30AM. McDonalds was still serving breakfast. Another real estate agent we worked with kept a cooler with drinks and snacks in the trunk for in between snacking. I have been in business meeting where they called out for a delivery of food. Sometime around noon is the lunch hour. Not at two or three in the afternoon.

Please pay attention to your driving. One time I thought I was in a demolition derby that scared me to death. More than one driver honked and waived the finger at us and it was not the thumbs up sign.

Chapter 20
Bias and Prejudice

Do not sit there and belittle yourself by saying you are not biased or that you are not prejudiced. We all are. The idea is to put aside those preconceived notions and try not to prejudge someone. It is very difficult. Stereotypes do not always fit.

Jo-Ellan Dimitrius, the famed jury selection expert, who was on the O.J. Simpson defense team, said that due to her extensive interviewing of jury candidates that she has become biased and, "… tend to expect that the wealthy will be tougher on crime than the poor; that men with long beards will be less conservative than those who are clean-shaven; and that young people will respect authority less than older people do." Jo-Ellen makes every attempt to put aside preconceptions of people. We are all victims of our experience. Just like Dimetrius, it is difficult to put aside our biases, but we owe it to our conversational partner.

Omari Hardwick graduated from high school as a standout athlete. He eventually became a starting defensive back on the football teams at Furman and the University of Georgia. While delivering crushing blows on Saturdays to opposing wide receivers, he was also a member of the Athens Theater Company. His hopes of an NFL career were dashed by injury and he refocused his passion into acting. He honed his acting skills on the stages of New

York and Los Angeles. In 2003 and 2004, he finished in the top five in the U.S. National Poetry Slam competition. Many of you have seen him starring in the television series *Dark Blue* and the move *A-Team*. Who would have pictured a bruising football player as a thespian and poet?

As a young patrol officer, I patrolled the streets of various impoverished neighborhoods. Over the years, I worked in areas of all socioeconomic classes. As a cop, I can tell you that some of my preconceived notions painted both upper, as well as lower class neighborhoods with certain ingrained biases. One thing I learned, was that regardless of what color skin they had, or what type of house they lived in, when they dialed 911, they needed my help and wanted to be treated with respect.

When I was reassigned to the street crimes unit, I grew my hair longer and grew a beard to blend and look less obvious. One day, while as a student on the campus of the university that I was attending, I was attempting to obtain a parking pass for my wife, who was also a student. The Chief of the Public Safety Office displayed an obvious dislike for me. This was despite not engaging in any actions to warrant such treatment. Finally, a female officer essentially pushed him to the side, gave me a smile and defused the situation. Had I been clean-cut or had I been in uniform, would he have treated me differently? Who knows?

One night, I was being dangled as bait in a high crime neighborhood. I walked along the street posing as a visually impaired man waiting to become a victim of a robbery. I do not recommend this as a hobby. One carload of young men, who had almost certainly faced bias in their time, quickly turned to me and made fun of my impairment. The last surprise of the same night occurred when a well-known pimp with a violent history, displayed compassion and assisted me with directions. The entire squad was surprised by this display of civility. By the way, I survived the night without being robbed.

A study conducted by Kelly Brownell of Yale University, uncovered obese bias in an unusual vocation. He conducted a study of health care professionals who specialized in treating obese patients. Now, one would think they would be very sensitive to the issues and concerns of patients suffering from weight negativity and self esteem challenges. Think again.

The surprise, was that their data supported an anti-fat bias by those practitioners for both attitude and stereotype. If there was any hope, the study found that they did show more compassion then the general public.

The Centers for Integrated Health Research at The Cooper Institute in Dallas, Texas, conducted research to evaluate the attitude toward obese individuals among students majoring in exercise science. To no one's surprise, the students displayed a strong bias toward obese individuals.

Gwyneth Paltrow while preparing for her role in *Shallow Hal,* tried on her "Fat Suit" and paraded around the hotel lobby. She described her foray into the plus size world as humiliating, as a slender and attractive actress, she was not used to the obvious fat bias.

Two American psychologists, Leslie Martel and Henry Biller, whose book *Stature and Stigma,* provides some insight into height bias. They asked several hundred university students to rate the qualities of men of different height. The consensus of men and women, regardless of their height was that they viewed men less than 5' 5" as being less mature, less positive, less secure, less masculine, less successful, and less capable among other attributes.

According to the National Organization of Short Statured Adults (NOSSA), Tall men (6 feet 2 inches and above) received a starting salary 12.4% higher than graduates of the same school who were less than 6 feet, even when the shorter applicant was a man of higher intelligence.

In 2003, researchers at the University of Florida and the University of North Carolina found that each extra inch of a man's height commanded an additional $789 dollars annually. Over the years, that difference can result in thousands of dollars more for the tall person compared to his shorter counterpart. Even in dating, there was an established bias according to NOSSA. One hundred women were asked to evaluate photographs of men whom they believed to be tall, average or short. All of the participants, found the tall and average men significantly more attractive than the shorter men.

Sam Walton the founder of Wal-Mart who was worth billions with a "B," drove a four-year-old 1988 Ford pickup truck while wearing clothes off the shelves of his own stores. In the book *Sam Walton Made in America My Story*, Sam Walton relates the story of Bob Clark one of the truck drivers for Wal-Mart. Clark had begun working with Wal-Mart in 1972, and by 1992, had accumulated in excess of $700,000 in profit sharing. Now imagine either Walton or Clark walking into an upscale men's store or restaurant. What kind of service would they receive if their financial status were unknown.

Remember the classic line from Julia Roberts in *Pretty Women*. Roberts, who was playing the part of a prostitute, enters an upscale clothing store in Beverly Hills. She is ignored and treated rudely by the sales staff. It is only when she returns dressed in a chic outfit and carrying an armful of shopping bags, that she confronts the previous sales staff. She inquires if the sales person works on commission. The sales clerk sheepishly says yes and Roberts holds up the bags saying, "Huge mistake." It would be nice if that was just in Hollywood, but it happens every day by people not treating others with respect and dignity.

Perception is reality. I had several experiences in which I was not in a suit, but dressed in neat casual attire. On occasion, folks would comment, "You don't look like a Secret Service agent." I knew they wanted to see the sunglasses with the squiggly earpiece.

Finally, do not forget the bias of your memory. So often, your memory recall might be tainted for numerous reasons. You may have recalled a situation from years ago in a fractured state, in which you are not recalling the entire situation. Perhaps you have heard a piece of stale gossip concerning someone. These encumbered memory recollections could also result in an unwarranted bias.

Look at your perfect self in the mirror. Is there something that someone else could find a bias with you? Your weight, your age, your tattoo or your skin color? Perhaps years earlier, you were prone to workplace errors. You are now experienced, but would you want your status gauged on your conduct from years earlier? We all make those instant judgments. We must give pause and give that person the opportunity to succeed. Stand in their flip-flops.

Chapter 21
The Brain

When I was in an active chase after a bad guy, my anticipation of good produced an increase of dopamine production in the midbrain. People love to feel good. Why not make their day better than when you first meet them. Leave them with a smile. We all know people that as they approach, we have a warm smile cross our face and a pleasurable feeling. That same jazzed up feeling we experienced when we first started dating our spouse.

The tollbooth operators stand in that lonely booth inhaling car fumes in all kinds of weather and collecting fees from blank faces of hurried motorists. I slow down, call out their name, and give them a genuine heartfelt greeting. If one is missing for a while, I ask them where they have been and thank them for collecting the money to help pay for the road and expedite my journey. I bet most people never thought of them as humans.

Their face lights up when they see me. Not one of them know my name, but they all know me and I would like to believe I made their day just a tad better. The limbic brain region will cause a physiological change to the body when the face displays various emotions.

Dopamine is a neurotransmitter in the brain and is closely associated with rewarding behavior. This is normally associated with pleasure received from addictions, consumption, sex and praise. Research suggests that the firing of dopamine neurons is a motivational substance because of reward-anticipation.

This hypothesis is based on the evidence that, when a reward is greater than expected, the firing of certain dopamine neurons increases, which consequently increases desire or motivation towards the reward. Dopamine production increases in anticipation of pleasure. For me it is Girl Scout Thin Mint Cookies, mint chocolate chip ice cream, or a good New York style pizza. For others it might be cocaine, sex, or skydiving.

Dopamine levels impact your attention and anticipation of rewards. Those that suffer from attention deficit disorder have lower levels of dopamine. We all strive for feeling good. We want to spend time in a positive environment that will stimulate our dopamine levels.

We are all motivated by different factors. For some it is money or fame as in an extrinsic manner. Many more are intrinsically motivated. That is from some inner drive. It all comes down to maximizing pleasure and reward. As you get to know someone, you can learn what their motivations are. Great leaders identify those needs and capitalize on them to motivate towards success.

Dr. Steven Reiss, Emeritus Professor of Psychology of Ohio State University proposed that there are sixteen basic human desires. Think of Maslow's hierarchy of needs on steroids. The desires were determined after a study of six thousand people. These desires represent intrinsic motivational values for people in business and social settings.

The desires are:

Acceptance, curiosity, eating, family, honor, idealism, independence, individuality, order, physical activity, power, romance, saving, social contact, status, tranquility and vengeance.

If you can incorporate some aspect of as many of these desires as possible with your conversational partner, you will strike accord with their intrinsic motivations. This is not rocket science. If you look closely at the list, you can probably identify your inner desires on the list.

Chapter 22
Brain Process

I am not going to force you to become an anatomy student, but I will give you a brief overview of how the brain helps us in communication. If you do not care, skip ahead one chapter. The hypothalamus is the copasetic part of the brain. It keeps everything chilled and online. The limbic system is the part of the brain that controls emotion and behavior. The limbic system of the autonomic nervous system is the set of brain structures that will save your life.

Life is good. You have just rolled out of your heavenly bed after a great night of sleep. You have turned the coffee pot on and are walking outside to retrieve the newspaper. Not a care in the world. Then you hear the whooshing whistling sound and look up towards the blue sky to see where the noise is coming from. At that point, you witness a piece of the space shuttle hurtling towards you.

The different parts of the brain are working simultaneous to keep all systems go. Each part is interconnected through various lines of communications known as neurotransmitters. The thalamus distributes incoming sensory information such as sight, sound, touch and taste.

The eyes and ears have observed the danger. The sensory cortex interprets the data and passes it along that this incoming stimuli requires additional examination. The hippocampus is the area that stores conscience memories. Let's see, have I seen this falling from the sky before and is this normal? It compares the incoming stimuli to determine the contextual basis and passes it off to the amygdala, which determines a threat and stores memories of fear.

The amygdala has decided that a piece of the space shuttle travelling faster than a bullet train towards you, is not safe. It regulates the anxiety in our body. The amygdala is screaming at the body that it should be in a high state of anxiety with the approaching obstacle.

The hypothalamus that has been keeping everything tranquil, now sounds the alarm bell and tells the body to stand where you are, fight like a young warrior, or run Forrest run! Regardless of the action taken, the alarm has triggered a number of processes. The pituitary gland is now stimulated to release hormones that cause the heart rate to increase, pupils dilate to enlarge the incoming light, the blood is redistributed towards the major organs, and the muscles become more rigid to withstand the assault.

In the instant that your ears and eyes perceived the space debris about to ruin your wonderful morning, all the systems have been fully employed. This is how the Limbic System of the brain operates. It is instinctive without much thought or reason. It is our most basic survival tool.

When reason enters into the equation, the prefrontal cortex is the part that takes over. This part of the brain located in the forebrain is the center for reasoning and decides if there is truly concern to act or not.

When people are engaged in conversation, the prefrontal cortex is reasoning what words to use or not to use. It is controlling when to use a handshake. The prefrontal cortex will tell the body how to sit or stand. It will also tell you what to wear.

The limbic system acts without thought, and therefore is the most honest relay of emotional thought. It is normally beyond our control and as such, is spontaneous. As we are dealing with people, it is often difficult to conceal the limbic response. There will usually be some leakage of emotions. This is where many times you can gauge their true intentions. The reverse is also true. They can gauge your response as well.

Chapter 23
Personality Types

Many of you have been previously exposed to the Big Five personality types commonly known as OCEAN, or Openness Conscientiousness, Extraversion, Agreeableness, or Neuroticism. I wrote earlier about Sam Gosling's, *Snoop: What Your Stuff Says About You,* and his research into snooping. His research is quite interesting in his ability to examine a person's environment, such as a dorm room and determine personality traits and trends.

I think a great deal can be gleamed from a person's personal space. You can make assumptions of what type of personality they have, but I am more concerned with identifying common points of interest with the stuff in their personal space.

Identifying the individual personality types is good and I believe there is some good to have that knowledge, especially in longer-term relationships. What I am more focused on in this book, is more geared towards how to initiate the beginning of the conversation. The Big Five Ocean theory will come into play, as the relationship is developed, deepened and strengthened. It will become a factor after the façade is chipped away and the security blanket is yanked off the bed, and away from the grips of the friend.

Sometimes the various personality types can be like reading your horoscope. On any day, a certain part will pertain to you.

As I read over the different personality types, I have a hard time putting myself into one of those squares. As I start to read it, I sit there and say oh that is my type until I read the next description.

I do not like labeling people just as I do not always believe in computer and statistical analysis. When you get into a checklist mentality, you fail to look outside the box. It limits your thought process. Sometimes that is necessary and other times it is not.

As an example, on January 11, 2002, retired General Joseph Foss was detained forty-five minutes in the Phoenix Airport, when his Congressional Medal of Honor set off the TSA screening alarm. He was on his way to West Point to give a speech. Prior to allowing this dangerous 86-year-old war hero to move along, he was compelled to remove his belt, boots, etc. The airport screener was following the guidelines put in place. The checklist mentality removed rational thinking.

I prefer not to worry with personality types during the initial meeting. I have never heard a politician ask an aide if the person they were meeting were open, conscientious, extraverts, agreeable, or neurotic. It might come in handy to have that knowledge prior to engaging in a business negotiation or battling an opposing attorney in court.

Chapter 24
Preparation

The microbiologist Louis Pasteur said, "Fortune favors the prepared mind." You have to be in the game not just physically, but emotionally.

Preparation is not just dealing with researching your subject, but also preparing your body and in particular your mind. If you are unprepared, you can be exposed and suffer the consequences. Almost as important, is to have your emotions stabile and in good order before dropping into the conversation pool.

I have listened to countless politicians as they are arriving at events and fundraisers and they are briefed by their staff. They are told whom they are meeting, bullet points about the person or organization, and the names of family members. When they bounce out of the limo, they are now prepared to engage in a positive dialogue with their host and show a genuine interest.

There was a group of us travelling in a thirty seat chartered bus. We were to be driven from our hotel to the event site. This was a well-known site to almost all the local inhabitants. The driver took a wrong turn and was turned around by security. He had to make a number of additional turns to return to the correct entrance. Later that evening, he once again made a wrong turn. He was able to get us back on track without too much inconvenience. It was obvious he had not driven the few routes the day before. Perhaps he was a late inning replacement due to illness and had not had time to research the routes. His errors should have been an embarrassment to his professional status. He was not prepared.

One of the best ways to prepare is to be informed. You should be reading a metropolitan newspaper every day. Not just horoscopes and cartoons. You should read the news and sports section. If you are in a hurry, just read the first couple of paragraphs of the key articles and glance over the other articles. If you are cheap or refuse to get up early, read the online version.

Yeah it requires getting up a little early, but you should be starting your day with a healthy breakfast. Even your mother told you it is the most important meal of the day. Now you feed your mouth and brain.

The television news will also cover the major stories. Be warned that watching the news can put you in a bad mood, especially watching the late night news. I interviewed one person who claimed he watched too much news and was suffering from anxiety. He was a news junkie and was all stoked up over some of the current events. This resulted in him saying some disparaging remarks that caused his arrest and my intervention.

Reading the news allows you to converse or at least be aware of the subject matter in a group discussion. It reduces your ignorance factor. Do not try to be a Cliff Claven from *Cheers* and know everything. More importantly, do not share your uninvited opinion on everything. Sometimes, it is better to keep your mouth shut and look stupid, then to open your mouth and prove it.

Dennis Waitley in the *Psychology of Winning* said, "If you believe you can, you probably can. If you believe you won't, you most assuredly won't." Do not overestimate your intelligence and do not underestimate others. Wars are started by leaders believing they are stronger than their adversary.

Dr. Paul Ekman the facial recognition expert advised that people who have practiced were better at decoding the face. Ekman said that for some people, they dramatically improved their performance in as little as thirty minutes.

Every time, I am en route to conduct an interview, I visualize what I expect and how the meeting will transpire. Quite often, it does not go the way I planned, but it will set my mood. I visualize the other person's position. I imagine as to how they might respond and the reason behind their conduct. I stand in their flip-flops and look at life through their perspective.

Whenever I was called to testify in court, I never entered court unprepared. I would look up the opposing attorney. I would review all the reports and anticipate the questions they might ask. I would attempt to predict what angle, or what defense they would pursue. I conducted my own mock court, as if I was being examined and cross-examined on the witness stand. I did that in the privacy of my home, or in the car sitting in a park.

While watching the Olympics, I watched Lindsey Von, the gold medalist downhill skier, prepare for the run. She had her eyes closed and her hands out in front of her making a point. Her hands and body weaved through the layout of the course visualizing in her mind every turn.

I research the person and write down the questions I have for them. I usually do not start out with the list, but it is there for reference. By writing and reviewing the questions, I usually have them cemented in my brain. During interviews, I always start on a positive tone. If the conversation heads south, I can adjust, but it is difficult to start in the cellar and climb up the stairs.

On one occasion, I was meeting in an undercover role with three folks that were engaging in a fraudulent scheme. I was playing the part of the owner of a marketing consulting firm. I knew my back-story and tried to play the part well.

One key aspect of my role was to string the suspects along and buy some time. I told them that I was leaving the next day for an Alaskan cruise and would not be back for a couple of weeks. One of them started asking a lot of questions concerning Alaska.

It turned out he had lived there and knew a lot about the cruise industry. Fortunately, the evening before, I had researched all about the itinerary and other information concerning the cruise, and I was able to have an informed discussion on this topic.

The surprising part of the back-story, was I had shared that I had started in real estate. Two of the three at the table had also been in the real estate business. Neither one of them asked me a question about that side of the business. This could explain why they had left real estate and were pursuing a life of crime.

I have a confession. I am a reformed procrastinator. The more tasks I delayed, the more work piled up. The problem was like a bank loan. The longer it took to payoff, the more interest compounded on the principal. I have a quote on my wall to remind me, "Don't wait one more minute! Develop a *Do It Now!* Attitude as a tool to achieve success." I ripped that off a Think and Grow Rich Calendar from 1997. I believe in not letting time control you. You control your time.

In preparation, you must explore and identify the why. Why is it in their best interest to cooperate? Why is it in their best interest to purchase from you? You have to identify the obstacle. Then you can deal with the barrier and respond. What is the pink elephant in the room? Get it out in the open. If there is a problem that will inhibit success or restrict movement, then discuss it up front.

We all have some garbage in our life. Preserving your mental health and attitude is important in your relationship with others. De-stress your life. Exercise, watch your diet, and obtain your identity through your family, not your job. Avoid over consumption of anything but a good time and a good laugh.

I prepared what I call the "Happy List." On a sheet of paper, I wrote three categories. I titled them work, home and the city I live in. Under each category, I would write all the positives for those three categories. On bad days and we all have them, I would examine the list and reframe my bad day. My list would put a smile on my face and remind me of all the good things in my life.

If I have a big event that I am travelling to, I usually crank up the iPod to my upbeat playlist or listen to positive pump me up message from an inspirational speaker, such as Zig Ziglar or Gary Vaynerchuk. I want to leave the negative baggage behind.

We all get sucked into an occasional negative emotional vortex. I cannot tell you how many times, I was pumped up only to walk into a firestorm at work. I could feel the energy being sucked out of me like a hemorrhaging artery. In John Hoover's book *How to Work for an Idiot: Survive & Thrive, Without Killing Your Boss*, he explores the frustration of the relationships between the boss and the subordinates and how best to deal with the boss.

I tried not to step into the glue of office politics. If it did not directly affect me, I tried to ignore the conflict. I am a very principled person and have a strong belief in what is right and wrong. It always bothered me when people were treated unfairly. As Hoover pointed out, "If I'm working for somebody less talented and intelligent than I am, and I allow that person to make my life miserable, who's the idiot?"

I had a coworker on the police department that came in every morning as the second hand graced 9:00AM. He would take his gun off, and place it in his desk, and then pull the pen out of his pocket, and scratch another day off the calendar. He would follow that with, "I hate this place." I liked him and we were lunch buddies, but I felt bad for his lack of enthusiasm. I often thought if I ever got to the point of being that miserable, I would quit.

The interesting observation was that even after he was eligible to retire and despite being financially comfortable, he stayed on the job. Perhaps he was not as miserable as he thought, or he was comfortable in his own misery.

My advice to my children when they were about to enter college was to, "find a passion." It is the only way to make it through the valleys of despair that we will all endure. No job is perfect. I may not have always enjoyed the hardships and the bureaucracy, but I enjoyed my work. I know some people that are miserable in their jobs. It is difficult to mask that from the outside world.

Have fun! Life is short and we don't have any do over's. Have a little levity. The perception of a Secret Service agent is the stone face gargoyles wearing sunglasses and earpieces. There is a fair amount of humor and practical jokes behind the scenes. I have heard of doctors telling jokes during open-heart surgery. Cops have been known to gossip about office politics or affairs between two cops, while ignoring the body at a homicide crime scene.

Chapter 25
Practice and Advance Preparation

I was not one of these parents that forced my kids to practice hours and hours and expected perfection on the playing field. My children became interested in studying Irish dance. On their very first performance, it was obvious they had difficulty recalling the steps for their routine. It was also obvious they did not enjoy themselves and were embarrassed despite being novices.

I encouraged them to practice so that the steps were natural. It would require practicing outside the class time. I told them that the day dancing is no longer fun, it is time to quit. The only way it becomes enjoyable, is through proper preparation and in that instance, it came from practice. Due to the cold winter, I knew the garage in the winter was not a viable option. We built a dance floor in the basement. Their comfort level increased and was commensurate with their enjoyment and success.

Preparation includes knowing everything you can about your product. When I was a young police officer, I would go home at night, look over the street map to see all the places I had been, and learn the streets in my district. I knew every street as well as the hundred blocks. I drove those streets and looked for shortcuts, and how traffic altered certain roads at certain times. I was a student of the road system. My life, that of my fellow officers, and those that I was serving, depended on my knowledge of those streets.

Bill Gates was not born a computer wizard and business entrepreneur. As chronicled in his book *Outliers* by Malcolm Gladwell, he explores what it takes to be successful. Ten thousand hours of practice seemed to be a constant theme among highly successful athletes, artists, and entrepreneurs. Gates had access to unlimited internet computer time while still in high school. It did not matter if they were musicians, writers, or hockey players, they all required a devotion to practice to achieve their level of success. That included Bill Gates.

When you wake up in the morning and you are standing under the spray of the hot shower, it is a good idea to start mapping out your day and visualizing the goals of the day. My wife would find it humorous, when I would call my voicemail or send emails to myself pertaining to items that needed addressing the next day. Outlook has a task list and appointments. I love checking items off the list.

There are those days that things do not go as planned. You catch a splinter in your toe, or rip your pants. Just remember there will be a tomorrow. There are not too many people being thrown on the gurney of the ambulance, screaming about their uncompleted inbox. You can only try your best to accomplish your tasks.

Advance Preparation

In my world, we called this Intel. Sun Tzu the ancient Chinese military strategist and author of *The Art of War,* was quoted as saying, "If ignorant both of your enemy and yourself, you are certain to be in peril." It is always nice to know who your adversary is in war, or in this case your new conversational partner. I am not going stalker here, but I am saying a few Google searches or gathering information through applications. Trust me. Your competition and the people you are meeting with are conducting the same inquiry on you.

Early in the Presidential campaign, Senator Obama was coming to town. I arrived at the office earlier than I usually do, just to allow for any unanticipated events. I drove the Suburban to the private residence hosting a fundraising event. I wanted to make sure that I would be able to navigate down the narrow street and into the driveway.

On my way to the airport, I found new road construction that had begun the day before. This resulted in the road closure of a street that we identified as a primary route. I quickly consulted with my police counterpart and we came up with a quick alternative. Imagine if I had not double-checked and turned down that road with the motorcade? Chaos.

I was about to enter a meeting with a high-level supervisor. He was not known to be a very sociable individual. He was quiet and not very conversational. I had known him for several years and had never established a long lasting dialogue. I knew his son was attending college and playing football. I conducted a few minutes of research to look at their record, the son's position and statistics, as well as the news that they were invited to a bowl game.

I entered the meeting and I asked him how his son was doing. His sense of pride was evident in his facial expressions and body language. I asked him if he had plans to travel to the bowl game. I cracked through the veneers and he relaxed, which had the same effect on me. Some people might consider this sucking up. I considered nudging the doors of opportunity and developing a relationship. My goal was to make that meeting more relaxed, not to obtain a promotion or gain favor.

Avoid over preparedness. When the President is travelling, we are required to prepare briefing papers, so that everyone is aware of the chronology of events and the list of contacts with telephone numbers. One person, in preparing for the arrival of the President, decided to type up a separate piece of paper with all the contact names and numbers. Then they laminated the sheet.

At first, I thought it looked professional, but then I wondered how much time and resources were spent on essentially a duplication of effort. Sometimes you get so focused on the preparation, you reach critical mass, in which you have spent so much time organizing and preparing. Then when the light turns green, you are still trying to start the car because you ran out of time and did not put gas in the tank.

If I am speaking at a venue, I like to walk in and get a feel for the site before game day. That is not always possible. I will check Google images or videos to see if there are any previous photos. If my hotel is in a different location, I will walk the route to the site, so that I visualize the location and gauge the time and distance.

For dignitaries, I would walk the route they were traveling so I knew it like the back of my hand. I would walk it backwards and forwards and look behind every door. If they were traveling in a motorcade, we would explore every route so that you would know where every pothole and bump in the asphalt. The pen and paper were always handy. As ideas or questions came into my mind, I would scroll them down. A recorder or memo function of your cell phone will do the same.

There were times that an interview would not go well. I always self reflected to see what I could have done wrong. If a suspect lawyered up, there was nothing I could do about them invoking their rights. I am a life-long learner and look at failures as learning experiences. I always self evaluate my performance.

We all have rejection from time to time. On a personal note, I completed three novels. I sent out upwards of a hundred query letters to agents seeking representation. Two of those novels are coated in dust waiting to be used as a two-pound doorstop. I never gave up and the completion of this book is proof to not give into the self-doubt and the proverbial dream stealers. You know the type that mocks you at trying to be successful.

If your output will provide material benefits, it is always a good idea to visualize the rewards of your success. In National Lampoon's Christmas Vacation, Chevy Chase was striving for a new swimming pool for his family. He looked out his kitchen window and could visualize everyone playing in the pool. It may sound goofy, but it does not hurt to post pictures of your goals as a screen saver, on the mirror in the bathroom, on the refrigerator, or on the visor in the car. Do not let the pictures become yellowed with age or clouded with dust. Change them every couple of weeks to refresh the perspective.

Stay current and be informed. Learning is a continual process. My wife presented me with an iPod the first year they came out on the market. I enjoy an eclectic mix of music. I also enjoyed audio books. I had an early mix of personal development stuff mixed with "how to" for business and sales. The iPod supplied me with a never-ending supply to my insatiable appetite for learning. My car was a rolling classroom. I would jot notes on occasion. Sometimes, I would pull over to write notes that are more extensive. I re-listen too many of those books. We all fall into bad habits and it is a good idea to go through re-tread school. Despite having fired a gun for over thirty years, I was still required to re-qualify every three months.

The other advantage to listening to audio books and presentations was that when I was trapped in gridlock, my stress never increased. I was able to sit back and use the delay as an enhancement to my learning. I listen to at least two to three books a month. That is in addition to my reading of the same amount of books, three magazine subscriptions and the daily newspaper. Need some reading ideas, check the bestseller list or my reference section.

Many people often wrongly quote the study of Yale graduates in a goal setting study. However, in 2007 at Dominican University of California, they completed a goal setting study. With 149 participants, who were professionals from around the world and different genders, they monitored the effectiveness of writing goals. The conclusions of the positive effect of writing your goals on paper, were supported.

Those who wrote their goals accomplished significantly more than those who did not write their goals. It just goes back to organizing your thoughts and focusing on the elements of success. Regardless if you are writing out goals for personal wealth, the traits of a potential mate, goals to achieve from an interview or job seeking strategy, it helps to put the pen to the paper.

Since 1986, University of Kentucky scientist David Snowdon has been studying 678 nuns from the Sisters of Notre Dame in Mankato, Minnesota. He has been researching their personal and medical histories as well as testing them for cognitive brain function.

A surprising result of the study is the discovery that the way we express ourselves in written language, can be a predictor of our susceptibility to Alzheimer's disease. Snowdon analyzed the autobiographies of almost two hundred nuns, written when they first enrolled in the convent. He discovered that the sisters who had expressed the most positive emotions and more dense complex writing styles as girls, ended up living the longest, and that those displaying symptoms of Alzheimer's had expressed fewer positive emotions. We are what we think.

Chapter 26
Observing

Sharon Kay Thorton from Amite County, Mississippi, had lost her vision nine years earlier due to a rare disorder called Stevens Johnson Syndrome. She became a candidate for a rare ground-breaking surgery at the Bascom Palmer Eye Institute in Miami. The surgery performed frequently overseas was achieved for the first time in the U.S. The team of doctors extracted an eyetooth from her mouth. After drilling a hole through the tooth, they fit the hole with a small camera. The tooth was implanted in her left eye and has restored her sight.

In the post surgery interview, Kay asked people to close their eyes for one week and then open them. You will see more clearly. She said her image of Duane Chapman of *Dog the Bounty Hunter*, was not at all the clean cut Marine type she had envisioned, "His hair is so long! For all these years, I had it in my mind how people looked and when I see everybody now, I just go, you're joking!"

Think about this. If your doctor informed you today that you would lose your sight tomorrow and today would be your last day to see, would you spend your last day sitting in front of the flat panel TV, or trying feverously to reach the end of the internet? In all probability, you would run outside and see as much of the world and as many of your close friends as you could. You would hang on every crease in someone's face, the beauty of the monarch butterfly floating between the radiant flowers. These are items you see every day, but have chosen to ignore.

If you walk down any busy sidewalk in a bustling metropolitan city, watch all the people with ear buds planted in the ears or a cell phone cemented to their head. They are oblivious to anything other than the walk and don't walk sign as they meander through the crowd towards their destination.

As I was digging through the rubble at the World Trade Center, I prayed everyday that I would find something to bring closure to the loved ones who had not been able to say goodbye. One day, I found a females cardigan sweater. I pictured a twenty something year old wearing the sweater to fight the morning chill on a beautiful clear blue-sky day.

She had probably awakened in the morning to her favorite radio station. Brushed her teeth, contemplated her day at work, and gathering with friends after work at a local watering hole, or perhaps a date. She grabbed a cup of coffee, not savoring the aroma or the warmth of the cup. She dashed out the door, not realizing that she would never see the apartment again. She rode in the subway with hundreds of other anonymous commuters, not understanding that within hours she would be dead.

Perhaps, it is the fragility of life that I have witnessed over the years, or perhaps it is focusing on the small things that have kept me and others alive, that causes me to focus on small often overlooked elements in our daily existence. It is also that ability, which has always assisted me in striking up a conversation with a near stranger

I am always pleased to witness a sunset with a multitude of colors, as if God himself had stroked the canvas with his paintbrush. Living in an area abundant with wildlife, I love watching the interactions of all forms of life.

Observing and processing those views through our brain in this hectic world can be difficult. It is difficult to slowdown and really pay attention. It can be challenging to slow down your anxiety at meeting someone new, and trying to enlarge your focal plane to pay attention to them, and their surroundings.

At times, we do not see what we see. Our eyes capture it in the focal plane, but our brain fails to cognitively process the image. We all have had occasions where we are looking for the car keys. We look and look. We scan every surface and still cannot find it. That is until your spouse walks in and picks them up and jingles them like a dinner bell and says, "Is this what you are looking for?" There they sat in an obvious spot on the kitchen table.

At the Frick Collection in New York, they have been offering a class on observation. The Art of Observation was based on a class offered by Yale to medical students. The Frick Collection initially offered the class to the Weill Cornell Medical School. It has since expanded to include other medical schools in New York. After focusing on select works of art by the masters, the students then examine x-rays or photographs of patients to look for subtle often overlooked differences. Similar classes have built upon the success and are offered across the country. The Frick Collection expanded the offering to officers of the NYPD and the FBI, who then viewed photographs of street scenes and individuals.

In research published in 2008, in the *Journal of Internal Medicine*, the paper titled, Formal Art Observation Training Improves Medical Students Visual Diagnostic Skills, examined the effectiveness of observational training. Medical students at Harvard were selected to attend a nine-session class, *Training the Eye: Improving the Art of Physical Diagnosis*. The twenty-four students that participated in the class increased their skills in observation by thirty eight percent over the control students. Improving the diagnostic observation skills by medical students have been replicated in a number of other studies.

We do not always see what we see. The brain will often overlook details in the visual plane that should have been obvious. This can be attributed to what is called inattention blindness. The term was coined by Arien Mack and Irvin Rock in 1992. Our brain can only process so many stimuli from our sensory input, before it becomes overloaded. As a result, our attention acts as a filter to focus solely on the conspicuous. The remaining chafe is discarded into the recycle bin. Nevertheless, what is conspicuous?

There are a number of factors that would affect our attention. The conspicuousness of the item, the mental workload, expectation, and capacity. Mental workload is the amount of activity that the brain is processing. If the brain is inactive, such as the security guard whose only stimulation comes from relying on visitors and employees hitting a buzzer on the door requesting entry. The guard becomes conditioned to the buzzer for stimulation, while the rest of the time he is bored to death. Expectation is where people do not expect anything new and become complacent of their surroundings and activities. Capacity can be affected by impairment through a few cocktails or sleep deprivation.

Daniel Simons of the University of Illinois at Urbana-Champaign and Christopher Chabris of Union College have conducted extensive study in this area. In their fascinating book *Invisible Gorillas and Other Ways our Intuition Fail Us,* they describe how quickly we can become blind to stimuli occurring around us.

The book's title is based on an experiment in which he videoed six students. Three are dressed in white and three dressed in black. They are passing a basketball between like dressed members. The idea is to count the number of passes between the members. Most people become so focused on keeping up with the ball and counting the passes that they fail to recognize the student in the gorilla suit, who walks through the middle and thump their chest. I have shared this YouTube video with a number of people and only about half noticed the gorilla. I also fell victim to this.

I was in a chase after a vehicle in which the driver had engaged in several felonies. It turned out the car was also stolen. I had attempted to block the car and he drove around my car. There were five police cars trying to catch this fellow. The chase began inside the city in the early hours of the morning. For thirty-five miles, we chased this car at speeds in excess of 100 mph down a dark and curvy highway. At those speeds, I focused only on the suspect's car and I suffered from inattention blindness pertaining to all other surroundings. You may experience the same condition while talking on the cell phone while driving. The suspects eventually abandoned the stolen car and were caught.

I have often been asked why Secret Service agents wear sunglasses. The reason typically defers to being outside on a sunny day. Most people believe it is to prevent people from watching our eyes. It is true that our eyes are constantly scanning the myriad of people in the crowd. It is a daunting task, as you walk along the rope line in front of a political candidate looking for the unordinary.

As we scan, we are looking for the "something" out of the ordinary. Perhaps it is the face, or what they are wearing, their demeanor, or the placement of their hands. Any danger will start with their hands wrapped around a gun, a knife, a grenade or a detonating device. The hope is that you will observe something to trigger the alarm before you have to focus on the hands. At that point of recognition, your reaction time is reduced to milliseconds.

While teaching a class on security assessments at St. Leo University, I realized that I became more aware of security enhancements around buildings. The students acknowledged the same behavior, or recognizing strengths and deficiencies in the security apparatus of apartments, corporate complexes, retail space, and hotels. We all tended to pay more attention to our environment.

We get used to the mundane. Remember the term paper that you read over several times looking for errors. Confident of your work, you turned the paper in and received the corrected copy with several glaring errors you missed. When I write and get to the point of serious editing, I will change the font and spacing and sometimes, I will read aloud to provide a new perspective. I still miss errors. I am sure you picked up a few of my mistakes.

On one occasion, I was meeting my daughter to hand off her laptop that she had left at home. We agreed to meet at a halfway point. I pulled up to a stop sign and looked for cars. The coast was clear and I hit the gas. I barely averted disaster, when at the last moment I slammed on the brakes to avoid striking the flaming red golf cart. The golf cart driver's look of contempt was obvious. How did I miss the bright red golf cart? Just like those folks counting the ball passes and did not see the gorilla, I too missed the gorilla. I was not looking for a golf cart, but cars. Inattention blindness had caused my failure to observe.

It happens more often than you think. I watched a video of a shopper texting on her phone. She was so engrossed in her texting while walking through the shopping mall, she failed to observe the huge fountain in front of her. As she continued the tapping of her keys, she fell right into the glistening water of the fountain.

Observing is a platform for exploration and developing relationships. The observations will be your introduction into identifying common points of interest, as well as weaknesses. Once you have established your mutual commonality and weaknesses, you can then begin the interview process.

To become good at observing, you must be open to all senses. Your body is always open to the sights and sounds, but how about the feel of a new couch, the smell of a new car, or the taste of a great meal, in which you decipher a particular spice.

You must avoid the trap of tunnel vision. When you enter stressful situations, the brain tends to become more one dimensional, and your peripheral vision is narrowed. There are ways to reduce stress, but sometimes it is easier said than done.

Most times if you have done your homework, you will find that you have a common point of interest with this adversary. Your goal is to turn them into an ally. Expertise in this endeavor will come from experience and practice. Like the medical students, perhaps a few hours in an art museum will strengthen your observation skills.

Exercises:

While you are sitting there reading, just relax. Practice some relaxation techniques. Set the mood. A little new age or spa type music will start the calming effect. I like the music of Ryan Farish or Yanni for this purpose. Close your eyes and shutdown the outside world. Start from the top of your head and relax. Work your way down to your forehead, eyes, cheeks, nose, mouth and jaw. Think how your jaw is tight. Now go to the shoulders. It is all right to slump. Relax your spine and abdomen. Place your hands on your legs and relax the arms. Move down to the hips, your thighs, calves and feet to the toes. Go down this checklist and conscientiously relax each part. It is amazing how tight certain parts of your body can become. Your breathing should be relaxed and eyes closed.

I know some people will sit there and call this a bunch of wind chime music and incense burning foo foo. I suffered from migraines and went through biofeedback sessions. It did not help with the headaches, but it did teach me how to relax. I wished that I had used it more often.

Listening

Set a timer for two minutes. Close your eyes and listen. Do it inside your office, your car, your home and outside. Listen to all the noises you tune out and do not hear. I love sitting outside in the morning at sunrise. I hear the wildlife welcoming the day. I can sometimes hear water trickling from the spillover in the pond, the birds, frogs and the nearby air conditioner units. When it is real quiet, I can hear the ticking of the outdoor clock. When the pool pump starts up, I hear the pump and the water bubbling. I can hear cars driving. On some days, I can hear wave runners on a nearby lake or an occasional airplane overhead. The sound of children playing brings a smile to my face. How often do we hear these sounds, but really do not hear them?

Inside the house, turn off the television. What do you hear? I hear the overbearing sound of lawn equipment outside. The humming of the refrigerator. The quiet crunching of the laptop, and the tapping of the key board. The ticking of a clock. The sound of my wife's pencil writing in the Sudoku book. The turning of the pages.

Write down the thoughts and describe what you hear at these locations. Try this once a day until you feel you have mastered this technique. Maxwell Maltz in *Psycho-Cybernetics*, advocated that habits are formed after twenty-one days of repetition.

This exercise will take a little more effort. Go into the pantry and the refrigerator. Open five items and inhale the aroma of each. Most items have a distinct odor and we often do not take notice of their scent. Coffee, orange juice, fruit, jams, snacks, potato chips, whole potatoes, and candles. Take a whiff of your spouse's cologne or perfume, and the soap. These are all subtle scents that we are exposed to everyday and ignore. When you come home from vacation and you walk into your home, discover the unique essence of your home.

Disclaimer. Do not stare at any one person or building too long, or you risk the chance of being accosted by the local gendarmes for being a stalker.

Stereotype alert. The majority of your observations will be based upon prior life experience, in which you form opinions and make judgments. The input for that knowledge comes from personal experience, the media, or friends, and family. People will argue that you should not stereotype. It can be dangerous territory.

Example: You could look at someone driving a pickup truck with bumper stickers for the NRA and Greazy Spoon Café. The assumption would be the driver is an outdoorsman with conservative ideals. However, if I told you that the driver was an economics professor from Harvard, and had merely borrowed his in-laws car on vacation, you would form a different opinion.

Observations only provide an insight, but not an omniscient view. We can prejudge, but avoid being judgmental until you have seen the rest of the story, as Paul Harvey would say.

Chapter 27
Observing Cars

Herbie the Love Bug was a fun film along with its two predecessors. Herbie is a Volkswagen Bug that has a personality. He takes on the testosterone laden NASCAR stock cars and defies logic to best them in a head-to-head race. According to a study by Florida State University Professor Dennis Slice and a team of researchers at the University of Vienna, they would describe Herbie as cute and non-aggressive, due to the structure of the front of the vehicle.

In the *Journal of Human Nature,* Professor Slice was quoted as saying, "The most unique aspect of the study was that we were able to quantitatively link the perception of cars to aspects of their physical structure in a way that allows us to generate a car that would project say, aggression, anger, or masculinity, or the opposite traits."

A third of the participants were able to attribute human or animal attributes to the physical elements of the cars. Such as the eyes were the headlights. They were also asked to rate each car on personality traits. Almost every rater agreed on the dominance or submissiveness of the rated car

I know that at times, I have reacted differently to various vehicles on the road, without ever laying eyes on the vehicles driver. Say for example the perceived aggression of a sports car versus the family oriented minivan, the affluence of a European sedan, or an older car that is all tricked out. How quick are you to allow each one of those vehicles to merge into traffic in front of you?

This study could suggest that perhaps, there is a hidden road warrior in all of us. Just as we make split judgments of people, we do the same concerning inanimate objects like cars.

When you are approaching a potential client, you might have an opportunity to assess their car. How? If it is in their driveway or in their assigned parking space, or when they meet you at the restaurant. The color of the car, the condition of the vehicle and the type, often speak of the person's personality. A red corvette may scream, "Look at me," and a Black Mercedes may say, "I enjoy the finer things in life." A Silver Volvo may say, "I enjoy being conservative and safe." On the other hand, it may mean, "I inherited this car, or had too good of a deal to pass on."

I was conducting business at a hotel. While walking from the parking lot, I noticed a fluorescent green Camaro. I thought I had observed the vehicle in the past, but was not sure having visited so many hotels. Another vehicle caught my eye. A white Range Rover with a Tampa Buccaneer specialized license plate.

As I was talking with the sales manager, I asked her if that was her green Camaro? She said yes and asked how I knew. I told her it matched her personality of being spunky and outgoing. Impressed, the general manager asked what kind of car she drove. I told her a white Range Rover because she enjoyed luxury and stability. They were astounded at the perception. Luck or skill? A little of both.

The license plate themselves might provide an insight into their core beliefs. In Florida, we have over 110 different license plates supporting various environmental causes, charitable endeavors, the military, and all the colleges. Take the PBA license plate. The fee raised by the selling of the plate, contributes towards the Police Benevolent Association Heart Fund. The fund disperses death benefits to families of police officers killed in the line of duty. If you saw one of those plates, you could assume they have some tie to law enforcement, or are big supporters of combating crime.

Another reason could be to show a potential ticket writing police officer that they are an ally. I'll bet a paycheck that cops are less likely to write a ticket to someone driving the same type of car, driven by the same person, and committing the same violation, then one that does not display the PBA license plate. You are displaying an allegiance and the relationship has been established.

The license plate frame and front license plate will many times broadcast their favorite college, professional sports teams or other interests including type of dog or the high school they support.

Most cars will have some indication of where they were purchased. Sometimes it is the license plate frame and other times it is a decal or metal tag affixed to the rear of the car. You can ask questions concerning the dealership, or if it is from a different town, it could indicate where the driver hails from. Yes, cars get resold. It is a way to stimulate conversation.

One of the greatest lessons my dad taught me when driving, was to scan vehicles for body damage. He said, that quite often the damage is indicative of a weakness in their driving. Sure enough, I have observed countless times that when I see a car with rear end damage that it might be prone to stop short, or the car with a caved in fender that turned into me without signaling. I have commented to myself, "Now I know why they have that damage."

Bumper stickers are always interesting. I laugh at some cars that are rolling billboards. "My Kid is an Honor Student at Einstein High." Meaning: they have kids and they are proud of them. The lettered oval travel stickers are displaying their favorite place to vacation or a status symbol for where they vacation. OBX for Outer Banks of North Carolina. When I lived in Virginia, they were abundant. NYC is obvious, but they should mail out a decoder book for many of the others. Marathons runners proudly display the 26.2 sticker.

Religious and political stickers are easy. Whatever they have so prominently posted on the rear end of the car is a clear statement of interest. Radio stations provide insight into their music or political interests.

Parking decals can indicate school affiliation or place of employment. The condition of the car can also give an insight into the person's organization. If it is covered with road salt from the last two winters, and it looks like they are living in their car, one could assume they are somewhat disorganized. If in that clutter you see eight discarded Starbucks containers, it is a good bet that if you showed up with an extra latte from Starbucks, you might ingratiate yourself.

Check the rearview mirror. Some folks like to dangle some trivial item of importance. It used to be baby shoes, and then graduation tassels. I observed one girl who dangled a Barbie doll from a noose attached to the mirror. Her way of fighting the perfect body image in today's society, or just being a little rebellious.

Chapter 28
Home Sweet Home

When I was on house hunting trips, there were times we would pull up in front of a house, pause and then proceed on without ever stepping a foot on the asphalt. The exterior condition was not up to par. I had learned over the years that people may keep the outside of the house nice and the inside looked like the house of horrors, but not once did I find the opposite true. A poorly maintained exterior telegraphed that the inside would be mirrored. Could there be an anomaly, sure.

As you walk by a home, you examine the yard. Is it well maintained? Does the house need painting or a new roof? Are there security cameras on the outside? Does that mean they are paranoid, concerned for safety, hiding, or were left over from the previous owners. I have seen several times, when questioning suspects, they have used external cameras to detect and warn of the presence of police. I have also interviewed mentally unstable individuals that every square inch of their house was under video surveillance due to their paranoia.

Do they have flags or banners displayed? Swing set in the backyard or a basketball hoop out front. An abandoned bicycle in the yard could give an indication of children and their approximate age and gender. A black bicycle with training wheels would indicate a possible boy under ten years old.

With the enforcement of homeowner's covenants, many homes adherence to the rules are strictly enforced, thus preserving the vanillaness of many neighborhoods. Despite this harmonious approach, many people still try to achieve some individualism.

The façade effect is that many people will maintain an exterior image. I have observed many times that the exterior façade is immaculate and that image is shattered once you venture past the threshold of the front door. Rooms without furniture, or furniture that is not congruent with the exterior. I have seen people still living out of boxes long after the U-Haul left the driveway. Some people have piles of mail, old magazines and clothes scattered all around. One house I entered, had enough hurricane supplies for the next ten years and could have opened a surplus store. There is a reality television show called, *The Hoarders*, that documents the compulsive collecting of some.

Is this an indication that they are disorganized and sloppy people? Perhaps. My initial assessment could be correct. It would obviously mean this is not a priority and I would want to make copies of anything I gave them, so that it did not fall into the black hole and never see the light of day again.

Once you cross the threshold of the front door, you have now entered their personal space. Most everything on display is for public consumption, and is an extension of the public persona the person is looking to present. Take a whiff of the area. Scented candles, a stew in the Crockpot, a litter box, or athletic locker room scent.

I heard of one office story, in which there was a horrible odor emanating from inside the office. The employees were convinced that there was a dead rodent in the ceiling. They lifted the ceiling tiles and searched with flashlights. After additional investigation, they found the culprit was not in the ceiling, but the locker room gym bag of one of the employees.

Pictures in the entryway or viewable to the public are there to impress. Family photos or those "look at me" photos. Examine those photos. Who is in the picture and what is the background? The deeper you get into the house the more personal it becomes. Home sweet home is your sanctuary. Obviously if you make it to the master suite, you will find the inner most signs of their existence. It is private and not meant to be shared. You will rarely get a glance unless the host is providing a tour. At best, you might get a glance from a distance. Curio cabinets and china cabinets also hold sentimental items.

Look for what is missing as well. As you look at the photos and they are of celebrity shots and none of the family, it shows what is important. They want you to focus on their celebrity friends. The families fall further down the pecking order.

In the book and the movie the *Blind Side*, Alabama football coach Nick Saben is recruiting Michael Oher, a prized five star recruit in the home of his foster family, the Touheys'. At the time, he was the coach of LSU coming off winning a national championship.

He knew the value of relationships and that those relationships included everyone that would have input into the decision-making process. He made a comment about how much he liked Mrs. Touhey's window treatments. He could have just left it with, "You have a lovely home." Sounds like Eddie Haskell in *Leave it to Beaver*. Saben was more specific and said the window treatments not curtains. Use specificity.

The office is similar to the house. Items on the desk or the wall opposite of their desk are those most personal. It is what they want to view and be reminded of on a daily basis. Items facing the door are for the benefit of visitors.

They could be plaques and certificates of achievements, trophies, photos or art. Look at each item. Is it an "I Love Me Wall?" or family and vacation photos?

One time, I was in our pediatrician's office and noticed a picture of the Maroon Belles Mountains outside of Aspen Colorado. I asked him and he confirmed the site. Although I did not ski, we talked about Aspen and Colorado for a few moments. Several years later, while on vacation, I snapped a photo of my children at the same spot. I gave him that photo, as a small thanks for the years of service he provided to our family.

Buildings

What does the office building say about the occupants. The lobby is adorned with marble and a glass atrium, or is the hallways narrow and dark with a musty odor. The building does not always project much about the occupants. An older building could mean they are resistant to change and enjoy the status quo, or perhaps they are frugal. The sleek modern building may say they like to impress and spend money. Most employees have little input into where their office is located.

I met with a doctor who specialized in infectious disease and travelers with rare disorders. Her office was the nicest doctor's office I have ever walked into, with hard wood floors and fountains. It became a topic of conversation when I spoke with her. She said that many of her patients suffered stress from traveling, and she wanted to present a calming experience.

Do not over evaluate the buildings. There was a time I was in a doctor's office with my wife and the waiting room was very upscale. I whispered to her that I now knew where all our money was going. I did give him props for making his patients as comfortable as possible. As opposed to the office for a bone doctor, who has a cramped and uncomfortable waiting room. I felt sorry for the patients with various orthopedic impairments who were constantly shifting in the uncomfortable seats.

Chapter 29
Clothing and People

What does clothing say about us? For some it is important to wear the latest trends and styles. At one time, labels were worn on the inside of clothes and now they are prominently displayed on the outside. I was at the counter for the Limited and asked the sales clerk if the there was a discount for the shirt I was purchasing that displayed its name. I figured I could get an advertising discount for promoting their name. She looked at me as if I was nuts.

As we have become more brand conscience, people like to promote their brand allegiance. Even sunglasses now promote a brand. Keep in mind that knockoffs are everywhere. Shirts and hats, quite often are adorned with logos for sports teams, high schools, colleges, restaurants, vacation destinations, and Harley Davidson.

Do their clothes fit them or are they ill fitting? I have known some people that could make a tuxedo look bad. Is it their shape, their cut of clothes, or they genuinely are not into appearance? Perhaps due to a sudden weight loss, their clothes are baggy.

People Watching

Studying people can be fun. You are spying on them and making up fictional stories based upon their appearance and interaction with others. Are they business associates or are they more intimate? How close are they sitting together? Where are their feet pointing? What is the level of eye contact?

One time while having lunch with my family, an acquaintance sat down at a table in front of us. His lunch partner was not his wife. It became obvious that there was more than business being discussed. To save all of us the embarrassment, I leaned forward and said hello. It was as if I threw a cold bucket of water on the two diners. They became distant and awkward towards each other. They left at the first opportunity.

Exercise

Go to the food court or sit on a bench at the shopping mall. Just observe and people watch. The airport is another great place. If you have a municipal park with crowds, pick a spot to observe. While driving and while sitting at a traffic light, watch the pedestrian traffic.

Watching

Our eyes are constantly scanning. In 2001, a study conducted by scholars at the University of Illinois and the Air Force, detected that expert pilots scanned with their eyes significantly more than novice pilots between cockpit instruments and the visual approach. Here is evidence that the more you practice, the more accomplished you become.

As you drive down the road, consider your eye movements. Your eyes are rarely fixed for more than a few seconds in one area. As you maneuver a 2,000-pound sled of steel down the interstate at 70 mph, think of your eye movement. You look at the rear view mirror to check traffic approaching, you scan the side view mirrors and windows, the instruments, the traffic, the car broke down on the side of the road, the GPS, the traffic signs, and the location of the vanilla latte in the cup holder.

The exception to this focus is the driver applying makeup, or reading the newspaper as they drive. As stupid as these people are, their eyes are still scanning perhaps not as often. They are not focused on the task, despite their assurances to the contrary. Their eyes still scan for some input. Even talking on the cell phone has been measured as having as much of an impairment as alcohol.

Are you a big focus or a narrow focus person? The difference is being able to see the larger picture of the optical plane versus the smaller narrower plane. The next time you are about to pull out into traffic, how do you decide when to pull out? Do you look at the first crease in the flow and jump out, regardless if you are going to cause that person to have to hit their brakes. Do you take in the big picture and realize there is no one behind that one car and you can pull out in a leisurely pace and avoid a road rage incident. If you are a narrow focus person, you need to work on that.

Observing is a trained and learned skill. Depending on the situation, your visual acuity becomes more aware. For instance, if you are walking into a parking garage at two in the morning, your eyes will be scanning for danger. If you enter the same garage with a group of six mixed gender friends, your observing abilities will decrease due to the comfort factor of friends as well as the verbal interaction.

Some of the best observers are fiction writers. As you read some of the bestselling authors, take note of the depth of their screen description. The metaphors can be thought provoking and obviously took a prolonged analysis of the scene. The amazing concept is that many times these scenes were not viewed personally by the writer, but were visualized through the authors imagination and taking their mind to that scene. This is especially true of historical fiction's literary interpretations of scenes.

Journalists are also excellent observers. They invoke all of their senses to cover a story. They take copious notes and transcribe those notes as the foundation for an in-depth article. The most copious note takers I have ever seen are attorneys.

There is a cartoon called *Hocus Focus,* distributed by King Features. The cartoon has two images and you are tasked with locating the six differences in the two panels. Some may be obvious and some are very subtle. It is a good test of your observational acuity and demonstrates how easy it is to overlook so many things.

Increasing your observational ability is not difficult. It takes time, practice and perseverance. Reading inanimate objects is much easier because there is limited movement in the field of focus. For example: parked cars, houses, offices, and clothes.

People are much more difficult to read and it requires more skill. As people are processing thoughts, their body language is constantly changing. You cannot gauge a person's body language, without establishing their baseline. This would be their normal conduct reflected in a more relaxed environment.

Three fundamentals to success are observing, interviewing and ethics. You can have all the goals, time management skills, and motivation in the world. None of that matters if you cannot make simple observations, interact with people and base your conduct on ethical principles. As Zig Ziglar would say, "Money will buy you a bed, but not a good night's sleep, a house but not a home, a companion but not a friend." Only through careful observation, can you see true success and make a genuine connection crucial for rapport building.

Chapter 30
The Hunt

We were on the hunt for a serial rapist. He had attacked several women and had failed in several additional attempts, but still managed to steal their purse. We had established the commonality that all of these victims had travelled on the same two roads and had stopped at a few different retail establishments. The assumption was that the suspect had observed them walking to their car, and he followed them home where he would confront them. We had a suspect description, a vehicle description and a partial license plate.

One late night while surveilling a grocery store that was a common stopping point for some of the victims, I noticed a car slow down on a dark side street. The car stopped and paused for a few minutes between a break in the bushes. When the car left, I could see that the color of the car matched, but was a different make. A Buick instead of a Chevy. To the untrained eye, they appeared the same. The license plate was also different from the suspect description.

I followed the car for several miles. He drove to the edge of the city limits, made a U-turn, and headed back to where we started. He passed the same store where he had started and I decided it was enough to stop him.

He was very cooperative and was well mannered. He told me he had taken the entrance exam for the police department. He gave us permission to search his car. We found a treasure trove of small articles from purses such as: bobby pins, earrings, nail files, combs, and hairbrushes.

I asked him his destination. His explanation of his destination did not match with his journey that I had observed. He had no idea that I had been following and observing him for the last thirty minutes. We had him! As we continued to hit him with his inconstancies, the facade began to crumble. He confessed to being a sexual predator and was sent to prison for a very long time.

Talk about being a great salesperson, we convinced him it was best for him to purge his conscience so that he could go to jail for most of his adult life. His efforts to become a cop were dashed, and the public was much safer as a result. Could you imagine if he had become a cop and had a license to pull unsuspecting females over at his whim?

Chapter 31
CPOI - Common Points of Interest

Establishing Common Points of Interest is one of the most important aspects of establishing rapport. I would rate appearance, smile and handshake ahead, but CPOI is definitely next. You are like an archeologist on a dig, slowly brushing the dirt away to find the skeleton that you are searching.

It starts before you leave the house or the office. Check the digital footprint on Google. The longer we are on earth, the more likely we have created a digital footprint. Try it. Run your competitors name. Google images might reward you with a photo. Be aware that it might not be the same person. Google Earth will show you the person's residence.

Check the business in the news and on the company homepage. You can determine new products in development or being deployed. You can explore the history of the company. Stock assessing websites will provide analysis of the company and their major competitors. If it is a small local company, check the local newspapers archives online.

As online social media is changing by the day, there are additional sources of information. Does the person tweet on twitter or maintain a blog. A blog will really provide an insight into their viewpoints and interests. If they maintain a public or fan page on Facebook, that is worth a look.

If their name or their immediate family has been in the news, there is a strong likelihood that they will be found. Run their address. You are on a treasure hunt. Sometimes, they will be listed as members or officers in different organizations. Look up the organizations. The spouse and children may be listed with a soccer team or the PTA. There are some search companies that you can obtain more information for a fee. Personally, I believe that is going too far into their privacy, and you are now crossing into the creeper stage.

One day, I was preparing to meet two executives with a successful company. I started my research online, when one of my colleagues entered the office and watched what I was doing. He uncovered my secret. He confessed that he was always curious as to how I could find an "in" with people that I was meeting. Now he knew.

I know people are calling me a stalker. Do you think the person you are meeting is probably doing the same thing? I will almost guarantee it. Before the internet became popular and you were meeting with someone, did you not try to find out the persons likes and dislikes? You want to be able to find something in common so that you and they can become comfortable.

Take Gary Vaynerchuk, the Wine Library TV guy. He has taken social media to an atmospheric level and exploded his personal brand and the revenue for the family liquor store. In his book "Crush It," he describes the various methods of using social media to leverage his business and personal brand model.

From reading his book, listening to his book, and following him in the social media arena, I could walk up to him on the street and start a wonderful conversation. First, I would probably pick up the pace of my speech, because he is a fast talker. I know he has a huge interest in wine, business development, social media, the New York Jets, and his family. He is also an immigrant and lives in

New York. With that varied of an interest, you can find a common point of interest to engage him in conversation. Gary is probably one of those folks that you could walk up to and say, "Hello." He would do the rest.

Chapter 32
Digital Jungle

We touched the surface a little bit already. Unless someone has been in a cryogenic state, they have deposited some digital droppings. Everyone is growing a digital tail. Have you checked out your name in the digital jungle?

You have seen those little boxes on blogs and WebPages. RSS(really, simple, syndicated) feeds. When websites or blogs update content, they push the information out through the RSS feeder. In turn, the feeder dumps the updates to a RSS reader that you have subscribed such as My Yahoo, Google Reader, or Feedly. It sounds complicated, but it is not. Say for example that you are a scrap booker. You subscribe to one of the many RSS readers and they will cull the blogs and websites for updated content and deliver that aggregated information directly to your inbox. Kind of like a daily newspaper. You subscribe to those feeds that are of interest.

Therefore, if you have a new client on the horizon, you can import information on their company as well as their competition's to the RSS reader. Every day, you will receive updates of newsworthy items that will educate you on your future client.

Set up Google Alerts on your client and their business. Everything pertaining to whatever alerts you set up will come your way. If a bomb thrower has left a poor review, you will be alerted in your email, as opposed to using a machete to fight through the digital jungle.

Technorati is a way to monitor all things blogs. Type in a key word and it will pull up all postings in blogs. If your future client or their business is mentioned in a blog of any sort, bingo you can find them. Type your own name and see what happens.

You can search Facebook and come up with the login page. It will show some of their favorites such as favorite products, movies, celebrities or politicians. It will also list some of their friends. If you want to go further, you will have to friend request them and break your covert status.

Another social networking site is LinkedIn, which is a business-networking site. You can see their employer and their job title, past employer, as well as where they received their education. If you join LinkedIn, you can also see their full profile.

As more people use Twitter as a social enhancement to their business model, you can search their posts. The one hundred and forty character snippets of concise language can provide nifty little morsels. You can do a Google search of Twitter for a name. Then you go to their Twitter and read their posts as well as everyone else. Twitter also has an advance search feature that you can use to dig up artifacts.

Chapter 33
Personal

Check for the wedding band. Go back to your single days and see if the person of interest is attached. No ring, no ask. Leave it unless they bring something up. If you catch the glistening of a ring, you can ask if their spouse works outside of the home. You never know who is staying at home with kids. That is a full time job in itself.

Most people are very proud and protective of their children. Many times, you can get someone to open up by discussing his or her children. You do not want to walk up to a stranger while you are wearing a trench coat, your hands slipped into the pockets, and start asking about their children. Creeper alert!

If you have made it past the introduction of the person, ask if they have children. If they have kids, you can ask what ages, sex and what schools they attend. Ask what their interests are outside of school. Most kids today are booked up solid between karate, soccer, dance, etc. If they are adult children, ask what college they are attending, their major, and where they live, or what careers they have chosen. If they live out of town, ask and explore their new hometown just as I describe below.

Are you from here originally? Their answer might indicate someplace you may have visited. If you have never been there, then be honest, and ask how they like the hometown compared to where they live now. Another angle is to say, "I've never been there, but I have heard good things or heard the art museum is nice, etc." Alternatively, you can ask what they liked most about living there. This can stimulate conversation and identify other interests.

If you must bring up the weather, put on a positive spin. When we have a dreary rain filled day, I usually say, it is days like this that remind me why I moved from up north, where we had this all the time. In 2004, Central Florida was hit with four hurricanes in a short period. I was fortunate to be spared any damage. It was easy for me to say this is the price for living in paradise. Others were not as fortunate. During that time frame, hurricanes were on everyone's mind.

Weather is an icebreaker and can be used to judge the level of conversation someone is interested in maintaining. If they grunt in agreement, move on. If they acknowledge the weather, accept it and move on. How long can you stimulate conversation talking about the clouds and sun, or lack of sunshine?

While staying in a hotel or passing through the maze of an airport, everyone has the commonality of travelling to or from somewhere. Ask them where are they from or where are they going. Is it business related, personal, or vacation? From there you can go off in many different directions. On the airplane, I am not a big talker. I like to slip into my own world. I might start talking on final approach or just as we land. If you start on takeoff, you might be stuck next to Gabby Gabe for the next four hours.

When I am flying, I am looking to accomplish some productivity. Many others are like that as well. Use meal or snack time to chat, but be conscience of your traveler's interests and goals. Other than the ones nodding off to sleep and watching the movies, many others break out a book, an eReader, or a laptop/iPad. These instruments are all common points of interest. How is that book? What genre do you enjoy? How do you like that brand of laptop/tablet?

People like to display mementos of vacations. The mementos could include photographs, knick-knacks, screen savers and calendars in their personal space. They might be wearing t-shirts, and hats. Ask about their vacation experience.

Be careful of picking up knick-knacks. Kind of like the china shop, you break it, you own it. People set up mini museums but do not want people to touch. A recruit at the University of Florida dropped the crystal national championship trophy shattering it on the floor. He had permission, but you do not want to be the one remembered for dropping some rare artifact. You can look over it and study it, but do not touch. If they pick it up and hand it to you, carry it like an egg.

Speaking of t-shirts, you can always ask about the content of the shirt. Most of the time the people are wearing personal billboards that scream, "Pick me! Pick me!"

I was at an event, and I was standing next to a fellow who was wearing a shirt with "839 K-9" on the left chest. I asked him if he was a K-9 officer. He said no, but went on to explain the fascinating story behind the group on the t-shirt. The group, of which he was a member, fosters bloodhounds and donates them to law enforcement. After raising the pups, they turn them over at a year old. The group was started by the parents of Lake County Florida Deputy Cody Snodgrass, who was a bloodhound handler killed in a motorcycle accident. The number 839 was his badge number. The man explained one training event, where one of the dogs picked up a scent that was five days old. I thoroughly enjoyed the conversation and learned something new.

On a reversal, I was car shopping and was wearing a shirt from "The Stand in the Gap," a Christian event for men in Washington, D.C. The sales manager recognized the shirt as he also attended and came over to me. We struck up a nice conversation. I was just tire kicking on that day. Six or seven months later, I called him on the telephone. He remembered me and we negotiated the deal right over the telephone.

It was on the weekend and the bank was closed. He gave me the keys to the car and had trust that my check was good. I did have an advantage because it was after Christmas and before New Years, and the dealership was dead. It was the easiest car buying experience I have ever had. We had established a mutual beneficial relationship started by my t-shirt.

It never ceases to amaze me the different activities people engage in their spare time. I have talked to a number of people who are writing the next fiction novel selected to Oprah's book list. Me too. Another friend paints and is quite accomplished. Another person I was talking to was a Civil War re-enactor. Some have more physical activities, such as tennis or golf.

People love their sports teams. They usually display their allegiance on their cars or in clothing. Tread lightly. Some are all or nothing. Friend or foe. You can usually figure out quickly whom they root for. You would be surprised how many females and business executives are NASCAR fans and love certain drivers while hating others.

If people are at work, you know their occupation. If not, you can always ask, "What line of work are you in?" Think like a journalist and ask questions to learn about their occupation. Maybe it is because I am curious, but I love to have people educate me on their occupation.

The furniture delivery fellows told us how they had sixteen deliveries to make on that particular day. They told us what time they left their homes to retrieve the truck, and how long they worked for the company.

The holidays are always a source of conversation. Any three-day weekend opens the door to ask if they have plans or are doing anything special. Christmas and Hanukah are good for asking if they have completed their shopping or decorating.

Look at the person you are talking to and observe their accessories. For men, it might be the tie, or the jacket, or scarf. Almost every tie that a man wears can be commented on. Some ties make a bold statement, while others are conservative.

For females, it could be their watch, purse or shoes. Many females take great pleasure in their collection of matching shoes and bags. In this day and time of concerns for sexual harassment, I avoid conflict by saying either my daughters would love those shoes, or my wife would love that bag. I can impress someone when I recognize the brand and compliment her Coach or Channel bag. That is the advantage to being the sole male under the roof. I became quite educated on the fashion trends.

Jewelry is another easy conversation piece. Comment on the watch for men or women and necklaces or earrings for females. If they are wearing a low cut blouse, you might want to pass on the comment about the necklace. You do not want to be labeled a creep. At one time, it was quite popular for some men to wear more gold then an Inca warrior. The trend for bling has subsided along with the hairy chest.

If you see a bookshelf and you do any reading, scan the shelves. People will generally read books of interest to themselves. Books can be the window of the soul. I can assure you if you examined my personal library, you would definitely find the core subjects of my interest.

If all the books are on scrapbooking, and you know nothing about the hobby, ask some probing questions. How long have you been doing it? You must get a lot of enjoyment out of it? Do you do albums for just yourself or for others as well? I know very little about scrapbooking, but with those questions, you can stimulate dialogue.

If they are driving an old beater of a car, it is a good indication that they are not big into cars. If they drive up in a fancy sports car and it is a brand new one, compliment the car. "Is that new? What kind of gas mileage does it get? Where did you buy it?" Many people enjoy telling the tales of beating down the salesperson.

What neighborhood do they live in? You might ask who was the developer or builder. Who was their real estate agent and would they use them again. Ask what are their favorite restaurants in the area, or you can share and ask if they have been to one that you have visited.

Most people in the professional world attended college. Many are proud of their institutions. With over four thousand schools in the country, most of the schools you have never heard of, unless it is a school nearby. Take a shot and ask, you might know someone else that attended the same school and ask what was their major field of study.

I entered a meeting with a professional and observed their water glass with the University of Virginia Cavaliers logo. I immediately engaged in a conversation about the University, Northern Virginia where we both had lived and Charlottesville the home of UVA. My family and I had visited the school and town several times. We were very familiar with the town and the restaurants. I told her one of my neighbors graduated from the school. She told me to pass along information concerning a local UVA club that might be of interest.

On her walls were numerous photos of her newborn daughter. I took an interest and asked some questions concerning her daughter. She proudly displays photos of her child and discusses the latest adventures. It is just that easy.

Chapter 34
Play the Elevator Game

Pick a tall building in your city. Stand in the lobby and look at the directory. Find a business near the top that might ring a bell and can give you some reason to be there. Perhaps you need to Google the company to find out about them. How about a medical office building. There are doctors and labs on every floor. Wait in the lobby until you see someone or a group walking towards the elevator. Follow them, not like a stalker, but so you are not alone. Hotels are another great place to play this game.

Look at this total stranger and find something unique. Then point it out. Their neck tie, purse, or ask them how they like their Droid cell phone or iPhone. The safety net is the weather. Sure is cold out today. If I find silence, at times I might ask, "So how is your day today?" They are forced to respond.

One time I was riding the elevator of my daughter's dorm with two male students. I was not aware of the school elevator norm that no one talks. Whoever was standing next to the floor selector would always ask politely what floor you were headed. Then it was silence.

That is until I entered. I happened to be glancing over the school newspaper. I noticed a sidebar article that some government was forbidding the nude hiking through the Swiss Alps. I mentioned this out loud to the horror of my daughter. The students chuckled and probably thought I was a loon.

The next elevator ride, I noticed a student wearing a NY Mets hat. I started to affirm his allegiance and if he was from New York, but I decided my daughter might never speak to me again.

You have nothing to lose. You probably will never see the person again. You are merely being nice and exchanging a compliment that will stimulate a conversation. You might just make the recipients day with a flattering remark.

A friend and I attended a charity race that was being conducted at Raymond James Stadium, home of the Buccaneers and the pirate ship. Due to the large crowd, we had decided this would be a wonderful opportunity to hang flyers for our charity race on the windshields of cars parked in the nearby lot. There were several other race directors and staff utilizing the same advertising routine.

After we had finished, we walked towards the stadium. I could see a security guard on a golf cart, pulling the flyers off the windows and tossing our hard work into the nearest trash can. Not wanting our efforts to be in vain, I hustled over to the guard and told him the offenders had received permission. This was true. I never admitted my involvement. His response made it very clear that this was a violation of a county ordinance, and he was there to enforce the statute.

I knew we were in trouble and there would be no point in reasoning with this overly officious man. We were exempt from the statute, due to the fact were advertising a charity event at a charitable affair.

I decided the best course of action was to delay and deflect. I told him that I knew this particular guard company was one of the most professional outfits and were normally staffed with former military or law enforcement. I complimented him on his appearance. I noticed he stood a little taller, hiked up his gun belt and puffed out his chest.

I started to draw his story out. He had been in law enforcement and the military. He was from St. Louis. A town that I was very familiar with and I explored his hometown with him. I could see many of the runners making their way out to their cars. My plan was working.

After talking with him for about fifteen minutes, he received a call on his radio. He apologized, but duty called and he expressed what a nice chat we had and to have a nice day. Our flyers remained where we had posted them. My friend was amazed at how quickly I was able to seize the conversation and redirect it to suck this fellow into the discussion. I was not disingenuous. I meant every word I had said.

Social Justice

When it comes time to socializing, keep in mind the party dynamics. Most times, birds of a feather will flock together. There will usually be a polarization effect.

A dear friend of mine has amazed me with his and his wife's ability to weave an eclectic group of partygoers into a cohesive group. The attendees have the host in common and some other traits that the host uses in his introductions. He used the fact that we had lived in Louisiana, as a common trait of introduction with a couple we had never met. Now we had two items in common, the host and a past in Louisiana.

Another time he introduced me to an attendee that was a private attorney, but had been with the government. We knew many of the same players and discovered we had both worked and lived in Miami. We met on the battlefield several months later, as he cross-examined me on the witness stand. He shredded me apart, but I felt better that it was him. I believe he left the debris of my carcass intact because we had established a friendship. After my time on the stand and during a recess, he came over and shook my hand as a conciliatory gesture. I told him he was just doing his job, but the next beer was on him.

I have watched the host make introductions repeatedly as he sprinkles little tidbits of informative nuggets into his introduction. There is still some polarization, but he exemplifies the meaning of a host of a party. As a result, I look forward to his gatherings and the opportunity to meet new and exciting people.

A law enforcement officer was preparing to retire, and he was approached concerning his interest in a position as a regional supervisor with a Fortune 500 company. He went through several interviews over time. He was invited to one last interview, the final interview. All of the finalists for the job were invited and the night before the scheduled interview, they had a meet and greet social mixer.

After the party, he was notified he had received the job. It turned out, the social mixer was the final interview. They wanted to determine how accomplished the last candidates were in interpersonal and social communication skills.

When you are at a social gathering, you will normally have pockets of different conversations occurring. I play I-Spy and eavesdrop. I flitter around like a covert spy listening to each conversation. I move from group to group, until I find something I am interested in and can ease into the group. No one wants to be like the geek at the school dance, left to sit alone miserable in his or her own existence.

Chapter 35
Developing Observation Skills

Observation skills are easy. You can become a student of observing. Sit in a parking lot of a bookstore and watch the cars park. You may even be sitting in the parking lot with one of my books. Look at the shoppers walk across the parking lot. Pick out conversational items as if you were standing next to them and having a discussion. Sitting in the inside of your car will prevent you from feeling foolish. The more you practice, the easier it will come to you. As you see how easy this is, try it for real on a stranger. You have nothing to lose. Go with the same sex. This avoids someone from getting the wrong idea. If you fail, you have lost nothing, but gained some experience.

On a house-hunting trip, we parked in the lot for a builder of new homes. I noticed the lone car had a license plate frame for the Wantagh Volunteer Fire Department. After we met the sales associate, she asked me where I was from. This is a classic line for someone that is house shopping. She added that she picked up a hint of an accent. I told her I was from Long Island, to which she inquired where. I told her Wantagh and she nearly jumped off her feet in excitement. I eventually put an end to the charade. Now she wanted to know how I knew she was from there. We had fun with this trick and we developed a good relationship into the post sale.

One of the most dangerous pitfalls that cops and the military can fall into is tunnel vision. As I discussed earlier, inattention blindness can be brought on during high stress situations and your field of vision narrows. I experienced this in car chases and it is for that reason many departments restrict car chases.

When you enter the office of the HR director looking for a job that has a lot at stake, you become nervous and tense. Your focal plane narrows and you only see the person behind the desk because you are locked on like two lasers. Big huge mistake.

The more you can relax and observe, the better off you are. You will increase your chances of identifying a common point of interest or an item of passion. This will immediately increase the girth of conversational topics that will assist you in crushing the interview and knocking it out of the ballpark. Swing for the fence. Strive for friendship, not a job. Strive for friendship, not a sale. If you make the interviewer a friend, you will increase your chance of being hired or completing a sale. I will repeat the last sentence again.

If you make the interviewer a friend, you will increase your chance of being hired or completing a sale.

Remember that people normally have mementos or achievements that they want to exhibit. They are dying for you to ask the story behind the item. Go ahead make their day and in the process yours as well.

I never put anything on my walls at home or in the office that I was embarrassed for others to see. Whatever I put on display, was meant for public consumption and thus public discussion.

In one of my offices, I had the array of trophies and certificates that reflected the milestones of my career. My young daughters had created some personalized gifts in school for their dad. One of them was a yellow paper tie with #1 Dad written in blue sparkly. It had a blue ribbon to hold it around the neck. I took down those meaningless symbols of achievement and replaced it with my daughters tie. That had more significance to me and I would gladly speak of my children. My other daughter's penholder adorned my desk until I retired.

Most people are not very observant. Think of when a person that shaves some facial hair off or change their appearance without notice. People notice something has happened, but cannot figure it out.

On one dark morning, I was going on shift on the police department. Somebody yelled out to me to be careful because there was a snake in the bushes to my right, just outside the door. I looked and saw the bullet hole in the deceased snakes head, relaxed, and laughed at the ploy of a mischievous coworker.

I joined him and we watched several people stride past without noticing the snakes presence. I walked over, moved the snake out of the bushes and coiled the dead reptile into a striking position. I wish we had YouTube back then. It was hilarious to watch the reactions. They went nuts. Several times, I thought there was going to be gunfire. Still, several highly trained and veteran officers were oblivious to the snake until we yelled to them. The Invisible Gorilla?

Write your observations. Like an artist painting on a canvas, the picture is better visualized. Write down your observations to help to cement the process in your brain. If you are taking notes from an actual interaction, it will assist you in recalling trivia from the previous encounter. You can also incorporate the notes into their profile that you maintain on your contacts.

Rent or buy the movie *Sherlock Holmes*. He is the existential observer of life. He employs all the senses to investigate and solve the crimes and dilemmas that he faces.

In the medical profession they have a saying that when you hear hoof beats, look for the zebra stripes. Most people thinking of hoof beats would associate that sound with horses, not zebras, but zebras have the same sound. In the medical community, just because someone is fatigued does not necessarily mean they are suffering chronic fatigue syndrome, but perhaps from Lyme's Disease or thyroid issues or some other malady.

Listening is the most underrated observational skill. You can listen to what people are disclosing about themselves, their viewpoints, passions and interests. Hearsay may not be admissible in criminal court, but it is admissible to your court. You must gauge the veracity of the information and determine if the source of the gossip has an agenda. Many times, hearsay is not one hundred percent accurate. Not due to intentional distortions, but memory recall might have been impaired for various reasons.

Remember the telephone game we played in school. One person would whisper a statement to another. By the time it reached the last person, it rarely sounded like anything that was originally said.

In the *Invisible Gorilla*, Daniel Simons and Christopher Chabris discuss the illusion of memory. Everyone remembers where he or she were on 9/11. As the two researchers discovered, despite assertions as to where people were and what they were doing on that horrible day, their statements often conflicted with each other. I too remember where I was on 9/11. I was at the school in Sarasota with the President. Despite being a participant in history, I cannot recall who was standing next to me. That is why eyewitness identification is so often flawed. Memories are not as concrete as we often believe.

Sometimes too much information is overwhelming. Columbia University professor Sheena Iyenger conducted a test on jam sampling and buying. In a grocery store, they set up a tasting booth of six jams. Thirty percent of the shopping tasters made a purchase. When they repeated the experiment with twenty-four jams, they had more shoppers stop to taste, but only three percent bought. They could not make up their minds with so many choices. The brain became overloaded and paralyzed with indecision.

I had a similar experience with a slab of marble. A contractor gave us a choice of five colors. We made the choice quickly. We were then told to go to the marble company and select the specific slab. Once there, we were told our selection was open to any color in the yard. We spent an hour and could not decide. We finally went back to our original selection.

As you drive down the road, you might observe a sign promoting a service. You are focused on driving and catch the main writing, but with too much information and your travelling speed, you cannot read it that fast and it is too small. Your mind cannot process it that fast. Sometimes in life, we have to slow down.

Chapter 36
Verbal Truths

We listen to people and speak all day long. How many are speaking the truth? We take most people on face value that they are sincere in their dialogue.

Politicians are priceless when it comes to speaking and are masters of deception. One of the primary clues is the response latency. That is the time it takes to respond to the question. Remember the Balloon Boy who was supposedly whisked away by a huge Mylar balloon, while the entire nation tuned in for the updates? Balloon Boy's father displayed a classic delayed latency during a subsequent interview. The question was asked of his son why he went into the attic by the journalist. The boy responded with the shocking statement that he was hiding in the attic for the television show. Dear old dad was in a basic state of shock. The cortex must now respond and is in a position to formulate an answer. Quite often, these gaps are populated with stalling words such as ahhh or ummm.

Another manner of delayed response is deflection. Like a mirror, they are beaming the rays back to you. They may ask you to repeat the question for clarification. They might ask you to rephrase the question.

I was testifying in Montreal, Canada. The court proceedings are conducted in French, and therefore there was an interpreter to translate to English for my benefit. On certain questions, I would ask for a clarification on a question. The interpreter asked in French, received the response and translated to me. By this time, I had already come up with a thorough answer. I was not lying, but merely buying time to come up with the best answer. Just because someone delays their response, does not mean they are untruthful, but it does send up caution signs.

On the other side of the coin, a too quick response sends a message that you have rehearsed an answer to an anticipated question. This happens in debate prep, where a candidate is asked every conceivable question. As the question is asked, they anticipate the question and jump the gun just a little.

We all take a moment to formulate a response to an inquiry. Just be mindful the longer it takes, the more disingenuous you sound. A normal response is about one second. In a study in 2002, by Professor Robin Lickley, of Queen Margaret University in Scotland, determined the longer the lapse between the question and the answer, the greater chance of being perceived as untruthful. It merely raises a flag to your intended recipient that they may view you as less than forthcoming.

Bella DePaulo, psychology professor at the University of Virginia, and Deborah Kashy, an assistant professor of psychology at Texas A & M University in a 1996 study, discovered that people lie every day. According to their study of students who maintained journals, they lied about thirty percent of the time in different interactions.

Many of these distortions were of the white lie variety. "Does this dress make me look fat?" "I can't go out tonight, I have to study."

There are also lies of omission in which certain elements are left out of the story. It might be they forgot, or perhaps it was embarrassing. The person might feel the missing data is irrelevant and not necessary.

Substantiated lies are those that the person feels is substantiated, necessary, and often closely associated with the white lie or fib. Think of the affirmation of the Tooth Fairy, or avoiding to hurt a friends feelings, or to avoid their own humiliation.

The other is a lie of entitlement. Fudging on an expense report or pumping up the charity donations on the IRS. You substantiate your actions through a sense of entitlement. The company did not give me that raise or promotion last year. They owe me this.

The most serious lie is the intended lie. That is to cover or conceal the truth. Did you misappropriate the funds from that account? No. You want to avoid exposure and or the punishment. In an effort to avoid the covers being ripped off of you, the truth is intentionally distorted.

Politicians are notorious for responding with long-winded verbose answers, but fail to answer the question asked. By the time the answer is finished, the politician is hoping the interviewer has forgotten the initial question. President Obama is noted for providing long professorial answers consuming large chunks of time. He may not be deceptive, but he is monopolizing the time, and thus reducing the time you can ask follow-up questions.

If they salt in qualifying statements that are not necessary, beware. "To be perfectly honest…" "I want to tell you the truth." "The truth of the matter is…" There is no reason to add these if you are in fact telling the truth. Your response should stand on its own. People use "honest" all the time. Honest is honest. Is "perfectly honest" more honest than plain honest? You be the judge.

Pronoun usage can also indicate truthfulness. When using "I," you are taking responsibility or ownership. When you are looking to place some distance between you and the answer, you talk in the "we, they, and you," vernacular. I would really see this in statements from criminals when they were talking of victims or accusers. Instead of using the person's name, they use, "that girl" or "that car." It shows a dissociation of the person or item. The clearest and best-known example of this method is when President Clinton described Monica Lewinsky as, "That Girl."

How are you at delivering your thoughts to others? Anyone that has sat in a lecture hall at college has been victimized by the professor with such great intellect, but they could not reduce their knowledge to layman's terms. Are you talking in such jargon that the recipient of the message has eyes glazed over. On the other hand, are you assuming the person in front of you has a lower intellect, so you talk down to them? People can detect this condescending manner and it is very demeaning.

Aldert Vrij, professor of Applied Psychology at the University of Portsmouth, UK, has focused his research in the area of deception. He is one of the foremost authorities on lying. There is a great deal of junk science out there. Vrij's extensive research has determined one single trait that is of a higher consistency with deception. That is most people not being truthful, are less expressive with their hands and arms. That's it. Period.

Good verbal skills are essential to communicating your thoughts. Communication that can be easily distorted to the favor of the communicator.

Chapter 37
Para-Linguistics

The tone of your voice can be altered for effect. We can emphasize certain words or put a hint of sarcasm on top. No one likes a condescending tone or a contemptuous tone. Be careful on the tone. You may place emphasis on a word, but many tones are not received with appreciation.

Pitch can be altered by stress. When I was on the police department, one of our officers keyed up the microphone and yelled some inaudible information. No one could understand a word he said, other than his call sign. He sounded like a pack of barking beagles and you knew something bad was happening. It turned out he had encountered a tornado on the ground coming towards him, and he had jumped into a ditch to survive the destruction.

On another occasion, an officer had driven into a crossfire between two groups of individuals. Despite the stress, he calmly radioed the situation and the request for backup. The dispatcher later remarked, at how calm the transmission was in such a tense situation. The dispatcher said she could hardly believe the officer was involved in a shootout.

Control your voice. If you are entering a stressful interview, be wary of your octave rising to the point that it becomes noticeable. Take a deep breath and exhale slowly. Breathe!

It is easier to breath while standing, and thus easier to increase your volume. If you are addressing a large group, stand up if possible. If you are in a more intimate setting then speak loud enough for those in attendance to hear.

If people have to strain to hear you, they will tune out. It is too much effort. Likewise, if you are blasting out at a decibel level of a rock concert, folks will hear the voice, but not necessarily the message.

Speed of delivery is important. Keep in mind what is the baseline. I had a coworker that was from Mississippi and was probably one of the slowest speakers I have known. If someone is speaking at a normal pace and when asked a question, or are telling a story, and their speed slows down, beware that they are searching the brain to complete the idea that has not been fully formulated. It does not mean they are being deceptive.

I have encountered many people who due to a traumatic event, were wound tighter than a rubber band and were spewing conversation faster than a racecar at Daytona. They understand the urgency of their situation and wanted the story out.

In the writing profession, we are taught to make every word count. Less is more. Some people are just chatty. Most of them know who they are, but just enjoy talking. Anxiety can amp of the level of conversation. When I was preparing to board a flight to Afghanistan, I noticed a political aide who was talkative. As we reached the critical apex of whether we could fly and land prior to darkness, her level of conversation accelerated to nonstop. Her pitch also increased with her level of anxiety.

People who speak fast are viewed as not being as trustworthy. People assume you are like the small print on a contract, speaking so fast that you cannot comprehend the message. To some, it appears the fast talkers are hiding something. Check your wallet and make sure it has not been lifted. Take a breath and slow down on your delivery.

Avoid the monotone speech. Vary the pitch, speed and volume to maintain the interest. Just avoid the extremes. If you want to draw someone's attention, speak louder and slower.

In a 1999 study by Timothy DeGroot, of Catholic University and Stephen Motowidlo, of the University of Florida, they determined a correlation between vocal cues such as pitch, variability, speech rate, pauses, and amplitude variability with supervisor performance ratings at utility companies and publishing companies. Those that varied their vocal delivery attained higher credibility and evaluations.

In a 2002 study, Nalini Ambady, Wendy Levinson and others researched the tone of speech in sixty-five surgeons. Those that were viewed as projecting dominance and less empathy in their voices were identified as being associated with a higher incidence of malpractice claims. In less than ten second audio clips, the doctors with higher liability were identified. In the discussion section of the report, the researchers concluded that "how" a message is conveyed might be as important as "what" is said.

Pay attention to your speech delivery. Record yourself and listen. Look for critical input from others. Paralinguistic's is a crucial element in the tripod of communication. It is a lot to remember.

Chapter 38
Nonverbal behavior

"What you do speaks so loud I cannot hear what you say."

—Ralph Waldo Emerson

The words tumble off our tongue like a waterfall of communication. Many times, we become focused on the arrangement and content of words, as we search for a meaning. Words can bear a significant meaning, but they can also be rehearsed like an actor preparing for a scene in a play. Our days are constantly filled with role-playing. We try to appear sociable with a neighbor, who hosted a loud late night party, we are cordial to a former lover that betrayed us, or we cover our resentment towards a boss that has treated us unfairly.

When it comes to communication, the words we speak are only a small part of our communication. You have heard actions speak louder than words. As we encounter various individuals and situations, our body will display various nonverbal behaviors due to stress, tension, or repressed emotion.

As a verbal deliverer of communication, many times we are not aware of our display of nonverbal cues that can offset the intent of our verbal dialogue. As the recipient of the verbal communication, our brains are processing all the sensory stimuli. We intently listen to the words searching for a meaning and preparing our response. Many times, we are also processing the nonverbal behavior to determine the veracity of the statements. Are the words congruent with our nonverbal behavior?

We have all heard of the study, "That we only use ten percent of our brains." It has taken on the persona of the urban legend. It is inexplicably not true. If that were truly the case, our brain would atrophy to the size of an alligator's brain. A person that is healthy without significant brain impairment is using the entire brain to process and move.

Along the same avenue is the statistic often quoted, "That 93% of our communication is nonverbal." This information is based on a study conducted at UCLA by Dr. Albert Mehrabian. His research was based on the utterance of a single word in which the human lab rats would deliver the word with different intents. Even Dr. Mehrabian has criticized the ninety-three percent model. He claims the intent of the study was to monitor feelings and attitudes, not channels of communication.

Christopher Witt PhD., has written a great book on communications, *Real Leaders Don't Do PowerPoint. How to Sell Yourself and Your Ideas.* Witt said about the 93% model, "Nonsense! That idiotic claim comes from a misreading of a small group of studies done by a psychology professor more than forty years ago…that had very limited scope."

I would agree that our nonverbal behavior could make up a large proportion of the total communication pie, but it does not approach ninety-three percent. Have you watched television without the sound? Do you know what is the message being delivered? Absolutely not.

If you are one of the few people without an iPod and forced to listen to the radio, you are missing nonverbal behavior. The broadcaster is communicating though verbal delivery only. True, the tone, pitch and speed that the words flow through the microphone provide a tremendous amount to the base of communication, but the words and choice of words have a lot to do with the message.

Polygraphers always ask mundane questions of the examinee.

"Is your name Joey Bagofdonuts?"

"Are you right handed?"

"Are you a certain age?"

These questions are used to establish a baseline so that when they ask, "Did you steal the Holy Grail?" you should have a measured response. How measurable depends on your body's response to the comfort factor of the question.

Your responses should increase over the baseline, but if it is a question that makes you uncomfortable, the body's stress will increase disproportionately. Many times, there is an underlying reason for this response. For example, if a person grew up in a family whose parents were addicts, lived in poverty, and running from the police, that person could respond with a higher emotional response when asked a pre-employment question concerning drug usage. The examiner should be able to deal with the response during the subsequent post-test interview and reframing the question to measure a more appropriate response.

We have all seen the so-called experts in interpreting body language featured on television. How does one become an expert? There are no credentialing committees and no academic thresholds to gauge someone's expertise in this relatively new field. Critics have cast those assessing body language, as being no better than psychics. Sometimes I have to concur.

I strongly agree that many times body language can be over read. I have heard some of these self-avowed experts propose some preposterous assessments. Never ever, rely strictly on body language to play gotcha! It is one tool to use out of your toolbox. It is very difficult to read someone on the first occasion of meeting them. You might be able to see some obvious signs of discomfort in which you need to assess your approach. Never assume as many of these talking heads propose as to what the person is thinking. Pure speculation.

I will discuss body language in a larger context in developing relationships. I am knowledgeable in monitoring body language, but I do not profess to be an expert, whatever that maybe. My friend, Joe Navarro who retired from the FBI, is a body language expert. Joe has an advanced degree in psychology, has written books on the subject, studied body language for decades and taught seminars on the subject for years. Despite that impressive resume, Joe claims he is still learning. I believe for a more detailed examination of body language, read his book titled, *What Everybody is Saying*.

Dr. Paul Ekman is one of the leading researchers of body language and more specifically the face. He has studied facial expressions for most of his life and is unquestionably, the foremost expert, on recognizing and interpreting facial expressions. His work is the inspiration behind the television series, *Lie To Me*.

Juries have become enamored with the "CSI effect." That is, they are expecting fictional state of the art science not developed, to be used in the courtroom. One time, we had a caller insist that we have a stamp tested for DNA because she watched *CSI*. She was informed that the DNA database was in its infancy and we needed a suspect to match the collection from the stamp to a suspect. She understood that she had overestimated the ability of DNA matching.

With *Lie To Me,* everyone has become consumed with microexpressions. These fleeting tells can be observed by anyone that has had some level of training. Even Dr. Ekman has warned against relying on a single behavior to determine deception. A suspect I was interviewing in a fraud case, had a face exploding with facial expressions and twitches. It was obvious that he had a physiological impairment. That was supported by his attorney, who confirmed the problem.

I am not a behavioral scientist and I do not have a PhD in psychology. I do possess well-developed clinical skills to interview people and interpret their responses. My ability to assess people and to observe their behavior was the key to surviving thirty three years in law enforcement, keeping my partners alive, and those that I was responsible for keeping safe up to and including the President. I can say with complete certainty that I had people lie to me and on more than one occasion, they fooled me.

I love to people watch and watch their interactions. I was at a charity event and observed a couple that was experiencing a rift. I could not hear a word, but I watched their body language like a voyeur peeking through the blinds. Few other attendees paid any attention. It reached a point where he leaned in towards her. One foot stepped closer as he belittled her with his finger jabs. She defiantly looked up at him, while attempting to control her anger. She widened her stance and took on an akimbo stance with her hands on her hips. One foot faced ninety degrees in the direction she wanted to exit and flee. The couple's anxiety dissipated and they walked off. A time later, I caught a glimpse of the couple and everything appeared normal. I was no longer in a position to monitor, but they appeared to be at peace with one another.

We all have personal traits or ticks. My wife refers to my idiosyncrasies as "MR Traits." Many of these would be pacifying behaviors. These occur, as we are bored, nervous, or stressed. I have a friend that constantly tugs on his shirt around his waistband. This is a preening gesture and is his normal baseline. It could be that he is concerned about his appearance and trying to ensure he has room in his shirt. He does it in all environments.

I cannot stress enough how important it is to use a holistic approach to interviewing. Do not get all wrapped around the axle of reading body language. This is not some parlor trick. You have to spend time and develop their individual baseline. This occurs as you are in the getting to know someone phrase, and bringing him or her into a position of comfort.

Most doctors are so busy rushing from one patient to another; they rarely have time to determine the baseline of their patients. I notice my speed of speech increases with a doctor, because I can sense their urgency and know I have to get to the point as they are juggling china plates in the air. My baseline would be altered for that environment. The more comfortable I become with that doctor and their office, the more regulated my behaviors would become.

You do not want to play gotcha! I saw the foot point away towards the door. You are bored and want to leave. Oh, I did not realize you have tendinitis in your ankle and need to move your foot to alleviate the stiffness. Never ever, focus in on one behavior to label a person. You would not want people doing that to you. Many of these experts will label someone as showing signs of deceit, when all they are displaying are signs of discomfort.

If you observe multiple displays or sudden changes in someone's behavior, this can lead you to exploring the causes of that exhibited behavior. Never ever, jump to conclusions. Take the display of behaviors on their face value. Do not read too far into them.

The other point to make here, is to monitor what you are projecting. I am not talking about assuming an exterior shield and present only positive nonverbal behaviors. First, it is difficult to keep your own leakage from occurring. Like a thermostat that monitors the temperature, monitor your own activity. See if you notice that your feet are pointing towards the exit instead of the person of interest. Then look at the direction of your torso. I catch myself at times pointing away from the person I am talking with and I will readjust so that my torso is pointed directly towards the subject. Watch yourself first!

Chapter 39
Aspects of Body Language

Telephone Verbals

If someone in your circle receives a telephone call, watch their behavior. You have no idea what is being said on the other end of the phone, but you will be able to see all kinds of nonverbal behavior exhibited. What is humorous is that the other person on the other end of the phone can't watch, but the person in front will roll their eyes, illustrate with their hands or will do a drum roll of impatience with their hands.

Whether you realize it or not, many times some of this behavior is messaged through our voice pitch and speed without you knowing it. The same with impatience. Think of how you handle a telephone solicitor while you are right in the middle of an action scene of a movie on TV. Zig Ziglar encourages sales associates to smile and stand when they are talking on the phone. That positive energy will be conveyed through the telephone.

Reliving History

When my youngest daughter would hurt herself, she would come to us crying. We would ask what happened. She would re-enact the event, minus the impact. If you watch people who are telling a story, you can see many times, as they are reliving the story, they will display some of the same behaviors they probably displayed during the event. This goes for facial movements and body movements.

Pacifying

Children will often seek comfort from the softness of a blanket, sock, or a stuffed animal. They often insert a thumb or a pacifier to soothe themselves. As we grow older, it becomes more difficult to drag a blanket or a pacifier around.

We still seek to calm our nerves and relieve anxiety. Smoking is one form. One day standing outside the New York Stock Exchange prior to a meeting, I couldn't help but notice the very high percentage of floor traders arriving for work that were sucking that last drag of a cigarette. This is in a day when smoking is becoming more taboo in the professional environment. Watching the frenetic pace of the traders on the floor, it is no wonder they look for forms of relaxation and pacifying.

Back in the day when I had a mustache that adorned my face, I would stroke the hairs. Often it occurred without thought. It was usually when I was bored, contemplating, or anxious. After I shaved the facial hair, I continued that behavior and over a decade later I still occasionally stroke the naked space above my lip.

Pacifying behaviors are looking to soothe and comfort. You can see people rubbing or stroking parts of their body or clothing. Other forms of pacifying are the biting of lips, wetting lips, licking the inside of the mouth, stretching, cracking wrists, knuckles or playing with jewelry. I have watched some people with necklaces, pull the gold into their mouth and begin sucking or biting the accessory.

In the movie "*The Blind Side,*" the inspiration behind the book of the same name is Michael Oher. He is a homeless youth from the projects in Memphis and is fortunate enough that an affluent family takes him into their home. He eventually becomes a first

Mike Roche

round draft pick of the Baltimore Ravens as an offensive tackle. When he was placed in high stress situations such as the classroom or an interview exploring possible violations with the NCAA, he rubbed his thighs with his hands. That was his pacifying routine. From that action, you could tell when Mr. Oher was anxious or suffering some stress. Some people will use this technique to dry their sweating hands, which can be another stress indicator.

Activity around the mouth is often associated with the early association of breastfeeding or sucking on the bottle of formula. This was one of the first reinforced positive experiences, in which we obtained needed nourishment. We all have these traits.

I have read many times that these behaviors are associated with anxiety. This is not an all-encompassing view. I would agree stress could exacerbate these habits, but there are other explanations. Watch a child as they are watching their favorite show like the *Wiggles*. The thumb goes in the mouth. Are they under stress enjoying their favorite show? It is strengthening the enjoyment, by engaging in a soothing conduct. It has nothing to do with anxiety. If someone is twisting their wedding band while watching an enjoyable movie, it is unlikely they are experiencing stress.

Women will cover their necks when they feel threatened and may gently stroke the front of the neck region. It is a vulnerable area and thus a part of the body they want to protect. Every woman has watched the proverbial shower scene that is in every scary movie. The neck is usually exposed and is the main connector from the brain to the rest of the body. If the female's hand finds its way to the neck, there is normally something going on. You need to find why they are uncomfortable. It could be the financial decision they are about to make, or reliving the argument with an ex-lover that morning.

One afternoon while at a car dealership, I watched a woman with her spouse and a salesperson. I noticed her hand moved to her neck region and gently stroked. I could tell she was bothered. Was

183

it from the impending financial decision or had her mind drifted to some previous bad news.

Blowing air through their lips is a pacifying routine. Tiger Woods, while providing his scripted mea culpa after his exile from cheating on his wife, exhaled deeply. This was a pacifying routine to help calm himself down and control his emotions. You hear test takers and those about to engage in a sporting event or artistic event that requires concentration and control, exhale deeply. Asthmatics and COPD patients are often heard controlling their breathing with exhales.

Preening, is often seen in primates and you will see humans engage in the conduct as well. You can watch some people picking lint off their garments. Some of the behaviors would be adjusting their necktie, pulling up their socks, or pulling on another part of the clothing.

When I was in junior high school, I was wearing some ankle boots. The movement of my feet would draw the top of my socks from the calf to the ankle. I was always tugging on my socks even when it was not necessary. I was self-conscience of my appearance and avoiding embarrassment.

Michael Moore, the movie producer, will wring his hands as he starts a speech. He is a publicly displaying an anxiety that most people experience prior to speaking in public. It does not mean he will be making inaccurate statements, it means like most people, he is uneasy when making speeches in a public forum.

I watched one associate while talking in a friendly group setting. He always appeared confident, but he was slowly rubbing his hands, as if he was in a hand washing routine. This was his normal behavior. Do not make more of a normal behavior than you have to.

Chapter 40
The Head of the Matter

Let us start with the "top down" look at nonverbal behavior. Why not the hair? We spend billions a year on hair care products and services, as well as hours of our lifetime in front of the mirror, seeking the all too evasive "look."

In the terms of nonverbal behavior, the hair is used as a pacifier. One of my former coworker's in a state of frustration, would exhale deeply and run his hands through his hair like a comb. His hair was left in disarray looking like Einstein. This was his trademark.

Most people enjoy the stroking of the hair or the scalp. I know the hair does not have feeling, but the movement of the hair will stimulate the nerve endings of the root.

Girls more commonly than men, will play with their hair primarily due to the length. I have also watched men with longer hair play with their locks. They will commonly scratch the scalp. Do not look at this as anything more than pacifying. For girls at a club, it can be a sign of flirting.

Due to the time and money spent on our hair, we care about our appearance. Some people are very concerned about their look and therefore are self-conscience of the appearance of their hair.

A gentle touch to ensure proper placement is nothing more than that. It can be a distraction, so avoid overdoing it.

The head will nod up and down in agreement and shake side to side in disagreement. There are times that someone is advocating a position they do not feel passionate about, or may actually disagree with. They may say they agree, but their head is shaking side to side as to say no. Is what they are saying congruent with the action of the head?

Eyebrows – Forehead

Personally speaking, I have trouble monitoring the forehead. It is easily overlooked. Some people look like a Shar Pei dog with all kinds of wrinkles. Others have foreheads that hardly move due to all the plastic surgery and Botox injections. Hats and hair can also obscure the forehead like a curtain over a window.

On the other hand, the eyebrows are connected to the forehead and as a result will move in concert with the skin of the forehead.

Frowning occurs when the eyebrows tilt down towards the nose. It reflects a multitude of emotions including concentration, displeasure, fear or sadness.

When they arch upwards this is indicative of surprise, being receptive, or happiness. Representative Nancy Pelosi is expressive with her brows. Due to intervention techniques, her eyebrows might be the only part of her face that is free to move. A simple eyebrow flash when making an initial greeting is a bonding agent. This helps in rapport building along with a quick wink of the eye. Expressive eyebrows are those people that use the brow for accentuation and to draw attention to the message. Be cautious of the skeptical eyebrow flash. They are not buying what you are selling.

Eyes

If you remove the "e" in eyes, you are left with yes. Sure, it may sound a bit hokie, but the focus of your eyes will more likely lead to a yes. Combine the eYES with a smile, and a good handshake, and you are well on the way to a yes.

Blinking is a natural effort to keep our eyes lubricated. A normal blink rate is from a low of around four when reading to around forty. This can vary widely due to physiological and environmental conditions. If a person has a sudden increase from their norm, this could be an indication of anxiety, or it could mean an eyelash fell into the eyeball. During allergy season, some people will blink more often to lubricate their irritated eyes. Keep it all in context. Look for changes in the normal rate, up or down.

When President Clinton was asked about his relationship with Monica Lewinsky, his blink rate jumped off the charts. People with faster blink rates are not viewed with as much trust. Professor Aldert Vrij of the University of Portsmouth, UK, who is one of the leading researchers in the field of deception, has found the blink rate of limited association with those being deceptive. I have seen a number of folks blink rate increase dramatically when faced with a question that makes them uncomfortable. Are they being deceptive? Not necessarily.

When my children were young and they were pleading with me to purchase ice cream or to stay up later, they would usually resort to "pretty eyes." Girls will employ the technique of fluttering the eyes in a flirtatious manner. Some will use it as a technique in teambuilding for support.

Eye blocking is physiological response to discomfort. The eyelids will partially cover the eyes, or hover in a partially closed manner. The eyelids will shield the eyes from an intrusion or a question that is viewed as unpleasant.

The eyes are said to be the link to the soul. Perhaps. Certainly, dilation or constriction will indicate level of excitement. If their eyes are the size of beach balls, it means they are either excited, on drugs, in a dark room, or dead. Constricted pupils would indicate being exposed to bright light, or not excited. I believe females are more apt to pick up on this trait then men, unless the eyes are a brilliant color out of the norm. When I was a street cop, we would look for the pupil size as an indicator to sobriety, along with slurred speech and falling down.

Get in the habit of judging the color of the eyes. Start with the actors and models in TV and magazines. Then make it a point to ascertain the color of the eyes of everyone you engage. Do not stare. Just a quick glance. That glance will help in the bonding.

There is a lot of discussion concerning eye gaze. Many folks believe that liars will not look you in the eye. From my experience, I can tell you that it is absolutely not true. This is also supported by the research of Aldert Vrij. Many people that are being deceptive will look you straight in the eye, almost daring you in a defiant manner. The liars stare is very common. Alan and Barbara Pease assert that liars will maintain strong eye contact seventy percent of the time. Others may look away, this does not mean they are not being truthful.

Eye gaze can be directly attributed to cultural norms. The Asian culture in particular, due to the hierarchical status and cultural politeness, tend not to look you in the eye. People with lower self-esteem may not hold your gaze. In the Middle Eastern culture, it is rude to make eye contact with a female.

In a bar situation, a person that holds the gaze for a few moments could be expressing interest. Especially, if followed with a coy smile. When you are in direct conversation, it is best to hold on to their gaze probably two thirds to three quarters of the time. No one enjoys a stalkers stare. Move your eyes around the room to break up the monotony.

Think of when you are driving. The majority of your time is looking through the windshield at traffic and hopefully not trying to read the text message from your BFF. As you are driving, your eyes are glancing out the mirrors, at the speedometer, and at the cars around you.

Monitor eye aversion. When people suddenly avert their eyes, it could indicate they are looking to disrupt the conversation. If you have the floor and your conversation partner averts the eyes suddenly, pause at the first opportunity to provide them the chance to provide input. Eye aversion could also mean an embarrassment reaction to the topic being discussed. This could also be the result of a cultural norm or a personal experience flashback.

I have talked to a number of people, who will tend to drift off and look past you. Is it perhaps my conversation has gone long, or they remembered they forgot to take the trash out. When that occurs, ask a question to draw them back in, or shut down the story and allow them to leave. I call it the blah blah yeah yeah eyes or the zombie eye look, because most of the time they are tuned out. We have all had those coworkers that could never have a short conversation. Ask to borrow a pen and they will tell you the history of ink and writing.

There have been discussions concerning people looking up to the left or the right when asked a question. First, many people do not track that way. There has not been any substantive scientific evidence to support this concept. I have seen some people that do track that way, but I have never relied upon it as a strong indicator. The proponents advocate that when asked a question concerning the retrieval of information from the brain, their eyes will look up towards the left. If they are making a story up from the imagination side, they will look up and to the right. Scientific evidence does not support this theory.

Ahhh, the squinting of eyes. Caution alert. It means careful deliberation of the incoming information, usually leaning towards the negative. It can also indicate anger. Think of two spouses in discord. An alternative is that merely the light is bright. My baby blues are sensitive to bright light and therefore, I squint in the sunlight. Perhaps, the squinters just left the eye doctor and their eyes were dilated.

Chapter 41
Nose and Below

If you see someone flaring their nose like a bull getting ready to charge the matador, you might want to find an excuse to leave the room. It is never a good sign.

Much has been suggested about the Pinocchio effect on the nose. There have been some suggestions that as someone is deceitful, the blood pressure is elevated causing swelling in the nasal cavity, which results in people rubbing their nose.

It has been pointed out that President Clinton when being deceptive about an affair, increased his rubbing of the nose. I will not dispute that this occurred, but remind you that everything should be taken into context. If someone suffers from allergies, this could induce itching of the nose. Aldert Vrij, Professor at Portsmouth University, who has focused his study on the detection of deception, failed to substantiate the so-called "Pinocchio Nose Effect." The nose does not enlarge in size in response to deception. There has not been any substantive scientific data to support nose touching linked with deception. Let's stop with the fiction and move on.

The bewitched effect. If someone crinkles their nose, they might be trying to make themselves or you disappear. I am guilty of this fleeting gesture if something does not meet with my approval. It is a fleeting gesture and again should be viewed in context. Remember what your nose does when you smell something putrid? The nose crinkles with displeasure. If you have allergies, be mindful not to crinkle the nose, or you jeopardize sending the wrong message.

Mouth

Have you ever listened to a bad joke and gave a halfhearted smile? You wanted to be polite and avoid conveying your true emotions. False smiles of obligation are easy to detect. Politicians like to give polite smiles, as they are introduced. When there are true emotions displayed in the smile, look at the outside corners of the eyes. The skin will form crow's feet and are easily recognized. False smiles will fail to deliver crow's feet. The skin will remain smooth. Go to the mirror and try this yourself. Practice your smile.

Are the lips disappearing or are they swallowing their lips? My lips are sealed. I am not saying anything and not letting anything in. The mouth is the gatekeeper. The tighter, the more negative to the point the corners will create a sad line. I watched this in one episode of *The Pitchman*, in which the contestant was asked a difficult question concerning the marketing audience of their product. The lips almost disappeared. They had not anticipated this question and obviously had difficulty with a response. They were obviously in bad trouble and were declined funding for their project.

A tight smile or smirk is often accompanied with a gentle nod of the head. If you are using a smirk, you could be conveying a negative smugness or sarcasm. With an upturn of one corner of the mouth and you have turned the smirk into a mischievous smile. Folks will wonder what you are up to.

Pursing lips is an indicator of angst, turmoil or disagreement. The lips pucker up ever so slightly. One time I was going to meet the body language expert, Joe Navarro for lunch. He suggested a Thai restaurant. My email response said, "Joe, I am pursing my lips. How about …" I provided two alternative restaurants for his choice. I was using a little humor for one of the foremost experts in reading and teaching nonverbal behavior.

I worked for a supervisor that was a chronic lip purser. When I saw that response, I knew he was not in agreement with me. He often would add a head nod as if to say I agree with you, but I always knew he was about to deliver an alternative suggestion. With most people, you can recognize this warning and ask for input to resolve the conflict. With some people including that supervisor, their input was not always welcomed. They tended to offer poor alternatives. You will have to be the judge if you want their input.

If the mouth slips to the slide, this can show disagreement or consternation. The nose may track with the mouth, but not always. If you see this, you might consider that the recipient is not in full agreement.

A sneering mouth and combined with the rolling of eyes is contempt. Contempt is bad. People who show contempt are not and probably never will have a friendship with you. Psychologist John Gottman, in his study of marriage counselor patients, was able to predict with ninety percent accuracy the longevity of the marriage. Contempt was the strongest clue displayed by the couples headed for trouble.

If the tongue sticks out and retracts quickly like a lizard, this is a clue that the person is being sneaky or concealing. It can be used when you make a coy joke. Remember when as kids, you would stick out your tongue in a taunting manner? In adults, it is difficult to get away with such immature behavior. So, as adults we are more discreet and therefore more concealing of the technique. It could also be that they are touching their lips with moisture. As you can see, with most displays of body language, there is often more than one explanation.

Licking lips is providing moisture to the lips. Is this a result of anxiety or physiological response to medication or hydration? I know quite often, if I cannot carry my security blanket of a water bottle, I will pop a mint or a piece of gum in my mouth to provide moisture. Just because someone is licking their lips does not mean they are anxious. If it occurs in response to certain line of questions, along with hesitancy, this could be a signal of anxiety or reluctance to answer. Monitor the activity of your curious tongue.

The hands over the mouth are an indication of low confidence. The conduct is often associated with reluctance for the words to come out and we are shielding our mouth from view. It is a negative gesture and not well received. This is similar to placing the hands under the table or the magician's sleight of hand.

I had a coworker who was one of the toughest people I knew. He was a veteran, who had seen combat and was the real deal, but he constantly covered his mouth. He was a shy person and lacked confidence when engaging in public dialogue. Rest assured everything he said was the truth. Just keep in mind if your hand is in front of your mouth, it will raise a flag of concern.

Fingers in the mouth are pacifying and an indication of uncertainty. It is also a dirty habit considering where the fingers may have been. If you watch the fingers slip inside the oral orifice, it is a good assumption that something is bothering them. Make sure you keep your fingers out of the oral cavity. You will lose any positive standing.

The Face

Dr. Paul Ekman has spent his life devoted to uncovering the language of the face. His research and findings are extraordinary. He and his colleagues at the University of San Francisco have identified forty-three individual muscles in the face that can be combined into 10,000 different expressions.

While conducting his extraordinary research, he identified limbic leakage that occurred in fleeting moments across the face. These micro expressions appear in a fraction of a second. They are difficult to pickup, but with study and practice, you can become proficient at distinguishing these expressions.

He classified the seven universal emotions that regardless of the culture, they all appear the same. Those are: anger, fear, disgust, contempt, sadness, surprise, or happiness.

Here is a little practice for you. Stand in front of the mirror and relive the moments that would have elicited those emotions. The face you make is going to be similar to the ones you will see from people you are meeting. I hope that you will not see a client flash contempt or anger, but now you will know what to look for. Of more importance, you will know what you want to project. Self-monitor your own expressions. It may be harder than you think. Can you conceal a true surprise or anger?

According to Ekman, he has identified eighteen different smiles. The smile is the most easily recognizable facial expression. We have all faked joy or contentment. Opening up the pretty box on Christmas only to find out it is a fruitcake from Aunt Edith. A genuine smile not only lifts the corners of the lips upward, but it will create the crow's feet on the side of the eyes.

Think of when you were furious at the betrayal of an ex-friend, lover or spouse. You probably experienced the tightening of the lips, narrowing of the eyes and furrowing of the brows. The tighter the lips, the angrier you were. Go to the mirror if you are unsure.

Sadness can be associated with stoicism or being poker faced. There is no mistake when the corners of the lips turn down. An interesting point came from Paul Ekman's research. When they spent the day forming sad faces, their overall health declined on the day in question. It was an unintended consequence. They replicated the emotional state on subsequent days. Turn that frown upside down, and you will feel better as well as projecting warmth.

Surprise can be real or a feigned expression. The surprise birthday party that was not such a surprise, but you acted elated to conceal your devious knowledge. The flashbulb eyes and the wide-open mouth. We all have seen it and it is a positive emotional state.

Contempt is the worst of the facial expressions. When you see this, you may as well roll up the circus tent and go home. I discussed earlier the findings of Psychologist Dr. John Gottman, who analyzed married couples engaged in conflict resolution dialogue. When he detected contempt from one partner to the other, there was definite trouble in Camelot. He and Professor Bob Levinson could predict with an astonishing ninety percent accuracy as to the viability of the marriage beyond three years by studying the behavior and their perception of the past.

Blush equals embarrassment. It happens to everyone and everyone has felt the flushing effect. This is evidence of autonomic nervous systems instant reaction to embarrassment.

Chin-up

Lifting the chin and looking down the nose is considered a superior position. The interview of Sarah Palin by Charlie Gibson was a classic demonstration of this conduct. Charlie had his glasses perched at the edge of his nose. He may have been looking over his glasses at times and through them to read the paper. I find myself striking the same pose with my reading glasses. Despite the reason, it comes off as a condescending position and was held up as proving his dislike for the interviewee. I make it a habit to remove my reading glasses when I engage in conversation. It indicates interest and eliminates a false sign.

Neck

The neck is loaded with nerves and muscles. Many times when someone really crosses me, I can feel the nerves in the back of my neck short-circuiting. You can see people rub the back of the neck because of stress, but also because they have been working at the computer all day, or they slept wrong. Keep it in context.

In the movies, it is always the neck that is attacked. It is strangled, sliced, punched, and choked. It sits there between the shoulders and the head fully exposed. The neck is the bridge transporting the messages from the brain to the rest of the body. As such, we tend to be protective of the part of the body that is vulnerable. Females in particular, when they feel threatened or uncomfortable will cover the neck with their hand.

If a female tilts their head as they are speaking or listening, it is showing comfort as they are exposing that side of the neck. The tilt can also be used during a period of contemplation similar to what a dog will do. They are projecting an open channel of listening. It will unwittingly send a message of comfort. In the bar scene of a Hollywood movie, the starlet, will use this as a flirtatious gesture. You can witness it yourself at most hookup joints on a Friday night.

Chapter 42
Under the Head

Shoulders

Shoulder shrugs are associated with pensiveness or indecision. You know when you, "I don't know." If a person gives a synchronized double shrug, the person is more committed to that thought. A half or partial shrug, say with one shoulder or the other, displays less commitment. This may also occur in conjunction with some facial movements particular with an upward eyebrow flash. Sometimes you might see a smile or a smirk accompanying the shrug.

Think of how you are conveying your uncertainty with shoulder shrugs. Half shrug, full shrug, or no shrug. If you are asking a subordinate if they can work this weekend and you get a half shrug, it leads one to believe they are not fully committed to the answer.

Chest

Puffing of the chest is a territorial display that is very negative. I was in a discount store in Miami and watched two elderly men become engaged in a confrontation. The wife of one of the elderly men had interrupted the sales person while talking with the customer. The customer in a very strong manner, rebuked the women for her conduct.

Her husband attempting to fight for her honor, challenged the customer. They engaged in a spirited debate over the proper decorum of the women. They both shuffled toward each other and puffed up their chest to make themselves appear larger and a stronger adversary. When it reached the point that the next step would be punches, they disengaged and huffed at each other as they retreated. These two men were no younger than seventy years old. Who says only kids fight.

Posture

Chair slinking is a sign of comfort or disrespect. I cannot tell you how many times I walked into an interview room with a suspect that was facing serious charges, and they wanted to show a disconnection. I would always instruct them to sit up. They might not like it, but they would comply.

This goes into body splays. People who are slumped over or spreading the legs and arms are taking up all kinds of real estate. They own the entire sofa. It is based either on extreme comfort or on disrespect of the other occupants of the room. Many times these couchsteaders, will straighten up when a stranger enters the room or someone of a higher status appears.

In 1982, Psychologists G.E. Weisfeld and J.M. Beresfeld in a study, determined that people who adopt a tall standing posture tend to be seen as more dominant than those who adopt a slouched posture, and that those who are trained to stand tall feel more confident and optimistic. I guess my mother was right when she told me to stand straight or sit up.

People will fidget due to how uncomfortable they are. If a question is being asked, and they suddenly start to act like a wiggle worm, that is a warning of anxiety. Keep in mind that people suffering from back or leg conditions will fidget.

When I am giving a speech, I will notice people are starting to shift in their seats, as we get closer to a break. Those banquet chairs or folding metal chairs can be brutal. Keep it in context. If you are in an important meeting, pay attention to your shifting body. It can send the wrong signals. Once again, shifting in the chair is not indicative to deception.

Synchrony

We like alignment in appearance, which means straight lines. If someone is standing or sitting, the head through their feet should generally be synchronized in a straight line. If the head and body are straight and the legs and feet are heading out the door, there is some discomfort going on. Likewise, if the torso is leaning in one direction opposite of the head and legs, ding ding ding. Something is going on.

Chapter 43
Upper Extremities

Arms

Crossing arms across the body is often associated with a closed body language. I know many people including myself, who will cross their arms to relax. If you notice that crossing becomes tighter and appears to be giving them a hug, this is not a good sign. The person is either cold or very uncomfortable. When dealing with a business encounter it is best to limit the arm cross. I can tell you that quite often in stressful discussions, both participants will cross their arms.

While conducting criminal interviews, I would observe this behavior occur frequently. The arms were crossed and shielding the body. There were quite a few times, they would complain of the temperature being too cold. This is a physiological reaction to stress, but not necessarily deceit. If you were sitting in a police interview room, how would you sit? If you were waiting for the HR director or the procurement supervisor to enter a room, how would you sit? Monitor your own body language.

Joe Navarro brings up a good point. You seldom see people at home crossing their arms while watching television. Many people will start out in a sales environment with their arms crossed. As they become more comfortable, they will ease the grip and perhaps drop the shield. Quite often, my colleagues and I would stand around an airport tarmac waiting for the late arrival of a dignitary. We were all among a group of people that we were acclimated to and comfortable with. However, I would look around and see many people, including myself, crossing their arms for comfort and out of the anxiety of boredom.

Females quite often will cross their chest. Sometimes, this is due to them being self-conscience of their breast size, or again where they feel the most vulnerable. Expectant mothers will often drop the arms to unconsciously cover the womb. She could also be experiencing Braxton Hicks contractions. This is another situation that a particular display of body language could mean several different clues.

In their book, *The Definitive Book of Body Language*, Alan and Barbara Pease put forth the belief that those that cross their arms across their body, limit their openness to inflowing information. Their research indicated that those displaying the arm cross, learned and retained thirty-eight percent less than those with an open posture.

People will often throw up a shield over the torso. Females in particular will use a purse, books, a menu, a sweater or other items to place an obstacle between the other people. I have found myself doing this as well while carrying a portfolio. It is always best to keep such obstacles to the side to present a sign of neutrality.

I was interviewing someone concerning an allegation of wrongdoing. I was facing them in a seated position. She was holding a glass of water in front of her. I asked her to place the glass of water on the table, so that I could obtain a better read. She had no idea what I was doing. It allowed me to become comfortable that she was telling me the truth. How was she telling me the truth? There was no recoiling of the body. I did not observe any negative facial clues. She leaned towards me, maintained eye contact and said an emphatic no. Then as she had more time to contemplate the situation, she was able to recall aspects and inconsistencies of the scenario that would exonerate her. If she had held that glass, it could have impaired the freedom of movements.

Arms at side are the most neutral you can get. If they are behind you and concealing your hands, you take on a regal stance of higher dominance. Not good for mutual cooperation. I have seen cops, lawyers, professors, and royalty stand in this manner. It is a position to demonstrate whom they think is of a higher authority.

One day while stopped at a traffic light near the courthouse, I watched a man in his sixties, well dressed, and standing in this manner. His partner, who was younger and not as well dressed, stood a considerable distance from him. She was outside the intimate zone. One of her feet was at a right angle pointing away. Her hands were in a low closed steeple position. It was obvious that she was talking to someone of higher status and did not want to be there. Again, I have assumed this stance and watched as coworkers assumed this stance, as we waited at the airport for a tardy dignitary.

Arms akimbo is a very dominant stance. This is the position in which hands are on the hips. As a uniformed cop, I assumed that stance frequently. Parents will use the akimbo stance with their children when they are less than pleased with the crayons decorating the white wall. While watching a college football game, I watched as an offensive lineman was called to the sideline after being flagged for unsportsmanlike conduct. His coach was in the akimbo stance. The lineman also struck the same pose indicating his displeasure at the situation. You could say they agreed to disagree.

Half akimbo is a display of power, but more muted. It works well in the boardroom for females without the jesting stance of a full akimbo. If you drop the hands from the waist to the hips, it softens the dominance.

I entered a home to interview an older gentleman, who had some apparent mental health issues. He was being investigated for verbal threats. After the initial contact, I stepped into another room to interview a family member. The officer that had accompanied me was very professional, but perhaps too professional.

The officer was talking with a very dominant voice and stood akimbo. I heard voices raising and then scuffling. Sure enough, the situation had deteriorated into a physical altercation. We were able to quickly subdue the fellow without injury to anyone. I can tell you that was the first time in ten years of focusing on mentally ill individuals that the situation escalated to violence. I believe the dominant stance and tone struck by the officer exacerbated the situation.

When we put our hands behind our heads and interlock the fingers like a prisoner of war, we are showing a sign of comfort and a degree of dominance. Many times in a business meeting, the leader of the group may assume that position, but rarely will subordinates in the presence of a superior, mirror the pose. I find myself engaging in this position at the kitchen table with my family. I found an old picture of myself home. I had returned from college and I was striking the pose next to my mother with a very contented smile. At work, I catch myself rocking back in my chair talking to a coworker, while slipping my hands behind my head. I try to avoid this behavior. I will drop my hands when I catch myself striking this pose. I like to maintain good rapport.

Chapter 44
Let Me See Your Hands!

Hands can be used as many different instruments. They can be used as detractions, illustrators, weapons, pacifiers, comforters, explorers and tools. Magicians and card players use their hands as distractions.

In the law enforcement community and specifically the Secret Service, we looked to the hands as purveyors of weapons. We generally did not worry about a head butt. We all saw when a shoe was removed from a foot and launched by the hand at President Bush during a press conference in Iraq. As we work along a rope line, we are looking at the display of hands as folks are jostling for position.

Hands are used to provide a comforting touch to a loved one or a friend. You will see older people that will pat the knee of grandchildren in a comforting gesture. It can be used as a bonding gesture. We reach out and gently touch someone on the leg or the arm. President Obama uses this technique quite frequently during face-to-face dialogue.

Keep your hands where I can see them. Poker players do not respond well to players slipping their hands under the table. Neither do most people. If you are at a table, try to keep the hands level or above the height of the table. At times when we are listening, we will have our hands in our lap. When talking, bring them up to portray confidence.

Hands are like the paintbrushes on a canvass. They are the illustrators of our verbal diatribe. They emphasize or add a little salt and pepper to what we are serving with our mouths.

Palms-up can be used as a sign of openness and seeking an ally. I have nothing to hide, look, my hands are empty. We are presenting an open gesture to input and that we have nothing to conceal. David B. Givens, Ph.D. the Director of the Center for Nonverbal Studies in Spokane, believes the palm up gesture is one of the most important gestures you can utilize. Givens advocates that displaying the palms-up, makes an emotional appeal for listener support, cooperation, and understanding.

When the palms are facing down, it shows more confidence in the message. It is also viewed as more dominant. I used this as a cop in a gesture to calm people down. It also delivered a message that I really was not too interested in what they had to say. I conveyed what I had to say was more important. You will see President Obama display this gesture during a spirited debate.

When the hand goes up in a stopping motion like a traffic cop, it has only one meaning. Cease or stop. If both hands go up, it serves more as a calming gesture, that I need your attention. President Obama displayed this tactic often during his interview with Brett Baer from Fox News. As the interviewer's questions were becoming irritating to the President, he deployed the stop sign hands.

Sweeping gestures are pointing direction of attention. Such as sweeping towards their chest or opening towards the recipient. Females in particular will often bring their hand over their heart at a sentimental or kind thought.

When the person does the tomahawk chop with one hand chopping into the palm of the other, they are not rooting for the Florida State University Seminoles. They are making a point. An emphatic point. If you use this display, use it sparingly as it is an aggressive gesture and not always well received.

The fingers are for directing attention. I know I have been guilty of the finger point. It is very dominating and aggressive. It is screaming, "Let me tell you something. You have to listen to what I am saying." The two-finger jab is as soft as a double barrel shotgun firing a load of buckshot. TV personality Bill O'Reilly is a huge finger pointer. When he becomes really heated, he breaks out the double jab. Donald Trump jabs that finger across the table as he says, "You're fired!" As mom would say, don't point.

Politicians have learned that jab can be a negative aspect. They use a two-finger circle point. By closing the thumb and pointer finger in an oblong circle and bringing the fingers into their hand, they still emphasize the point, but with a softer approach. Steve Jobs was a master at using this technique in his product launches. If you raise the remaining fingers and place them in an oval, it becomes the ok sigh. All is good.

Shaking hands or trembling can be indicative of nervousness. It can also be caused by many other conditions. Patients with Parkinson's, Lyme's, MS, and ALS also may exhibit trembling hands. Cold can also cause tremors. I have witnessed many people complain of the cold in an interview room, due primarily to nerves as opposed to the environmental conditions.

Steepling is the act of touching fingertips together to form the appearance of a church steeple. It is a sign of authority, confidence, or emphasis. Ladies have a tendency to drop their hands lower across their bodies. The higher the hands the more authority you convey. Secret Service agents will steeple their hands when working near a crowd. This is to portray authority, as well as to deploy the hands quicker towards an aggressive act.

If there is a particular point you want to make during a presentation, throw up the steeple. Use it like the Fastpass at Disney. Use it once per hour. The steeple will place an emphasis on the main point you want to convey. If you use it like the saltshaker on fries, you lose the impact and come across as being bossy.

Remember again your mother said, "Don't point." You never want to point with steepled hands. Especially, if you press the hands together and have the palms pressed against each other. You have presented a double barrel shotgun steeple and you are looking down the gun sights of your thumbs lining up your target.

A wide stance steeple is where you separate the hands about shoulder distance and chest high. You can use this while making presentations or speeches to deliver some emphasis. Pretend you are holding an invisible beach ball.

If people have collapsed the steeple into a clasped like prayerful hands, it can be a sign of concern or worry. It is not associated with high confidence. This can also be a display of comfort. If you are making that first impression, stay away from the prayerful hands for the first few minutes. Do not over read this position of the hands. Many times, we employ this as a passive gesture of absorbing the input and listening.

Raising the finger up is seeking attention, as in I need your attention. It is also used for emphasis and generally is not a negative gesture unless overused.

Every now and then people will flash the middle finger. This usually occurs when the hands are seen resting against the face. Do they really intend to flip you the bird or is it completely unintentional. Who knows, but beware it will make people think and worry about what is behind the middle finger.

The thumbs up are a sign of confidence and everything is good. Athletes, to politicians, to astronauts use it to convey a confident message that all is good. Looking over my wedding photos, I was snapped giving the thumbs up to my buddies, as I escorted my bride out of the church. That confidence has lasted over three decades. Be mindful that this is not a universally accepted gesture. In some foreign countries, this gesture is considered offensive.

When the hands are exposed, the higher the thumbs, the more confidence the person has in their position of resolution. If a person is speaking with hands steepled and their thumbs are up like a gun sight, it is a good bet that they feel confident. If the thumbs disappear or drop, that would lead to a sudden loss of self-esteem. Either due to a subservient position within the room, as in the boss just walked in, or their positions was challenged and they have lost their confidence.

Disappearing thumbs occurs when there is a lack of confidence, or an increase in anxiety. That is where the thumbs get tucked back into the hands. I was in an interview of a mother of a suspect involved in a fraud. Obviously, she was concerned about her child's involvement. When she was asked to convey information that she knew was damaging to her offspring's situation, her thumbs were swallowed by her hands. She was not being deceptive, but she did not want her kid doing a long stretch of prison time.

People with their hands in their pocket can be a sign of uneasiness or lack of confidence. It is sometimes used in a laid back casual setting. We have all stuck our hands in the pockets for warmth. It is best to keep them out in the open. I was in a group setting with friends. We are all comfortable with each other. I lost count of how many had a hand in their pocket.

What changes this pose dramatically is when the thumbs are exposed. I worked for a supervisor that was very confident. His trademark was his hands were always in his pockets if they were not holding something. His thumbs were always exposed and sticking out of his pockets.

I was watching a ceremony at the White House involving several doctors wearing their white coats for effect. One of the male physicians had his hands in his lab coat pocket, but his thumbs were exposed. This is common in the medical community. The other male doctor was in a regal stance with his hands behind him and the two females were in a fig leaf pose that I will discuss shortly.

Genital framing is seen many times by cops who will hook their thumbs in the gun belt. It evokes a sign of dominance. In the bar scene you will see men doing this. It screams out. "Come on ladies check me out. I am a stud puppy." Females generally do not display framing and can be turned off when faced by this gesture.

Females will commonly collapse their hands into the pelvic region. It is generally considered that the person is subconsciously protecting their vulnerabilities. It is many times the default position for females not in a comfortable setting. Yes, I have seen many a man assume the same position as well.

The two female doctors at the White House ceremony, who are no doubt very confident with their level of success, felt somewhat uncomfortable standing next to the President and in front of the press corp. Their hands shielded the genital region. Many men will strike this pose as well. Had the one doctor not had pockets in his lab coat, he may very well have had his hands in the fig leaf position. It just means we are feeling slightly vulnerable. Think about this pose. Do you strike this pose in the comfort of your home? Perhaps if your parents or in-laws were present and there was tension.

The regal stance with the hands behind your back while standing (like being handcuffed), is a more formal position. I have also witnessed people assume this position out of boredom. Remember the comfort versus discomfort factor. Are they comfortable or is there some stress. Boredom can create an inner stress. How you are standing and what are you doing with those awkward hands of yours?

The hands will tend to illustrate less when we do not have confidence in what we are saying. This was the one clue that Dr. Aldert Vrij noticed in deceptive people. They tended to illustrate less. Take it in context. If we have confidence in what we are saying, we tend to speak with more passion portrayed through the hands illustrating for effect and emphasis. Someone that is not being truthful and not feeling the love will illustrate less. Baseline is very important. Some people are more animated with their hands. Growing up in New York, many of my Italian friends were very expressive with their hands. As I travelled through the Middle East, hands become almost an extension to the verbal language.

Many times during an interview, the interviewee will clasp his hands and sit them in their lap. It is a relaxed position for most. They are open to input and evaluating. It is a neutral position. If you find yourself at a table assuming this position, it is best to move them to resting on the table. Make sure your hands are not clenched to the point that your knuckles are white.

Try to avoid resting your head or chin in your hands. The more support you provide, the more disinterest you are projecting. We commonly use a finger resting against the side of the face to display interest and active listening. It is hard sometimes to maintain interest for extended periods.

Anyone that has watched a horror movie will see nail biters in the audience. Walk across campus before a test, or in line for a rollercoaster and you will see people in high stress biting their fingernails. This is a big no-no when you are trying to impress others. The same would apply for picking at your fingernails. You would think people would know better, but think again. I witnessed a chewer during a job interview. I will bet he never realized what he was doing. Stress can cause all kinds or reactions.

Chapter 45
Other Stuff

Haptics

We all crave to be touched. Often hospitals provide volunteers to rock infants that are not being provided the necessary endearments of love from parents that are unable to visit. Studies have continually shown the need for the attribution of love through the sensory of touch. As we spend more and more time in our cubicle and in front of the computer monitor, the stimulation of the physical touch is craved. I have no scientific study to base those beliefs, only the observation of the paradigm shift of the electronic age.

In his 1969 study, British psychologist John Bowlby, whose groundbreaking study of the attachment theory of psychology, developed the belief that the central ingredient for peoples' lives was through their intimate attachment to other humans. He intimately studied the relationship between infants and caregivers. Most people enjoy the gentle touch of reassurance.

The hand can also be used to make a physical connection with another person. This is called haptics. President Obama when trying to capture the attention of the interviewer will reach out with his hands and touch the interviewer with his fingertips. It is a gesture, we used as children to get the attention of our mothers. It can also be used to show, that what I have to say is more important. If the other person is agitated, it can be used in an effort to soothe them.

When we are touched appropriately, we develop a positive reaction. In strained relationships, touching is minimized or done so for social graces. Quite often, strained relationships will achieve touching with fingertips, as opposed to the full hand touch. President Obama touches politely with his fingertips. If he placed the entire hand on the knee, that could be viewed as inappropriate.

Females will generally touch more than males. Just watch the average social gatherings of a girls' night out. There is a lot of touching among friends. Males tend to be reluctant to touch females, fearing the wrong impression and being shackled in a jail cell.

On a date, a male placing his hand at the lower back of the female, provides a touch of reassurance. It is demonstrating, "Let me show you the way." The touch should be subtle and not feel like a jumpmaster pushing the parachutist out of the plane. The same touch can be used in other environments as well, but be careful as not to come across as too much of a parental guide.

A supervisor may provide a haptic touch of encouragement or reassurance to a subordinate. It might be a pat on the upper back or the shoulder for a job well done. I cannot stress enough caution in this area. In this age of sexual harassment lawsuits, a touch witnessed by others, could be construed as a platform for litigious intentions. When in doubt, don't.

While conducting interviews of suspects, on occasion when the situation was warranted, I might touch the knee region or the upper arm to the shoulder with a reassuring touch. This developed an unconscious bond. I was letting them know, it was all right to relieve their anxiety in the form of a confession.

Do not be a lingerer. Lingerers can be viewed as creepy. Subordinates should never touch a boss unless a moment of levity occurs and the boss is cracking a joke. You reach up and touch their arm for emphasis of the humor.

The gentle touch on the arm develops a bond. I was eating at Stonewood Grill, one of my favorite restaurants. The server, who was doing an excellent job as always, gently touched my bicep in response to a lighter moment. Did that earn her a higher tip? It didn't hurt. Most people would not even notice that gentle fleeting touch, but your brain felt the touch. Studies support this "Midas Touch" theory of non-sexual touching to increase the tipping to servers, who provide a gentle unassuming touch on the hand or shoulder of their customer.

On another occasion at the same restaurant, I watched an elderly man sitting by himself eating. I felt sorry for him eating without company. Then I watched the server sit down across from him and engage in some conversation for a couple of minutes. I thought what a nice gesture this was. As he stood up, he patted the customer on the shoulder. I pointed this out to my family and later spoke with the manager about this genuine display of empathy.

People like to touch or stroke others and inanimate objects. People receive solace from petting their dogs. Many retirement homes will have designated days, in which pets are brought in, so the residents will receive the satisfaction of the sense of touching the pets. We all enjoy the gentle touch of a parent or loved one.

Microgestures

They can occur as spontaneous reflexive movements in response to unwarranted stimuli. As an example, when a member of congress heckled President Obama, his left elbow raised up like a running back would deflect a tackler. I have seen people unintentionally presenting the middle finger, or a sudden leg jut as if to say get away. These will be momentary flashes and often will not be repeated. It is often difficult to determine the cause behind the motion.

If my wife and I are watching a movie with torture, I can usually see my wife kick her foot upward. That scene is bringing discomfort to her and as a result, her brain is trying to kick the disturbing images away. Look for the suddenness of movements in response to a stimuli.

Chapter 46
Proxemics

Proxemics is the name given for establishing body distance. We all have certain zones of comfort. These spatial zones are changing in response to our social climate. For example if you are in a crowded nightclub with heart thumping music, your zone of comfort will be much closer, say six to twelve inches. If you were at a company picnic and stood that close to your boss's spouse, you could probably cross yourself off the holiday bonus program.

A police officer that I knew had a history of invoking combative behavior in suspects. He had developed good defensive skills as a result. He never worked on his spatial zone awareness. He liked to crowd people so close that you could smell his tobacco stained breath. His conduct accelerated the tension and instigated combative situations that could have been avoided.

There was clip that was shown repeatedly on the news of Harry Reid and Nancy Pelosi. They walked out together as equals. She spoke at the podium first. He reached up and put his arm around her outside shoulder like a spouse or girlfriend and certainly not a colleague. She repulsed at that moment, her body instantly pulled away, first with the hips, and then the rest of her body followed.

Determine the persons natural comfort zone. After the initial grip and grin, most people will retreat to their normal space. The social zone is between two and four feet. The intimate zone would be less than two feet. If you encroach, they will typically ease back to the normal range in a polarization effect. As they become more comfortable with you, they might inch closer into a more intimate zone.

Obviously, most family members will have comfort zones that are close and more intimate. The distance between a male and female meeting for the first time, will normally be a few inches further apart. Do not get hung up the measured distances of the various zones. That is not as important as monitoring the self-imposed zones of your partner. Throw away the tape measure and respect their bubble.

It is humorous to watch people who are in one position and then as they like or dislike what is being said, will increase or decrease their distance from the purveyor of words. This can be seen in reality television shows. Watch *The Apprentice* or *The Pitchman*. People that are listening to dialogue will lean towards the listener or at least maintain neutrality. If they do not like what is being said, they will try to put space between the language they do not like and their body.

The pulling back of the body screams, "Let me out of here!" The show *The First 48* follows a team of homicide detectives attempting to solve the murder within the first 48 hours. In the interview room, sometimes it is difficult to see the movements of the suspect, due to the poor camera resolution. One thing that stands out, is once the investigator launches the accusation, many times the suspect will recoil and lean away from the accuser. This does not mean they are guilty, but like anyone, they are uncomfortable with the accusation.

If you want to appear interested in the conversation, just lean in with your upper body just a tad. If you are at a dinner table, lean towards the conversation. Do not lift your backside up and get close enough to smell the cologne. No one can hold a position forever and will occasionally stretch by sitting back. Do not be offended. I know several people with bad backs that cannot lean forward for an extended duration, nor can they sit for extended periods with their back against the cushion.

Your torso should be directed at the conversationalist to provide interest. If the person is sitting to your side, you should angle towards them. If a person is turning their chest away from you, that is a good indication of disinterest or impatience.

Most football coaches will direct their tacklers to focus on their opponent's belly button. The ball carrier may give a head bob or throw a leg in one direction, but the true intent of the player is the direction of the belly button. Point the belly button towards your interest. I catch myself on occasion with my torso not pointed directly towards my target. I have to self-regulate and adjust.

One time, I was attempting to have dialogue with an individual that I was confronting. After the initial introduction, he turned his back and engaged in busy work while talking to me. Not only was it disrespectful to me, it demonstrated his attempt to avoid the confrontation. Typically, you do not want to expose your back, because it makes you vulnerable, as you cannot see what the person is doing behind you. They could be preparing to bury a meat clever in your spine.

Chapter 47
Feet and Legs

The lower extremities are often overlooked and can be huge indicators of behavior. Many times, it is difficult to monitor the feet and legs because of tables and desks. In interviews rooms, it was always difficult because of the interview table. The Tampa Police Department is one police department that has no tables in their interview room, only chairs. I love that. It provides an open view of the person across from you.

While watching an episode of *The Pitchman*, I was watching one hopeful entrepreneur. I noticed the back of his chair was moving vigorously. As the camera panned out, you could see his legs were feverishly jacking up and down. His demeanor above the table appeared calm. He had a lot on the line and was as nervous as a long tailed cat in a room full of rocking chairs.

The next time you are in a protracted conversation when you have another destination to travel to, look down at the position of your feet. Quite often at least one foot is pointing in the direction of where you would like to go. Watch in any meeting and if the speaker is at the tail end of reading some data dump, observe the attendees and see where their legs or feet are pointing.

I was interviewing a former NFL athlete that was twice my size. We were in a mental health facility, and let us just say I was not on his guest list. His body language and statements made it clear, he did not like my presence. I noticed his feet pointing towards the door. As I displayed empathy towards him and used calming body language, I noticed his feet shifted towards me. When we stood to say goodbye, he shook my hand and asked again, what my name was. I had earned a new friend.

At a restaurant one day, I observed a diner with his feet crossed and his knees were about twelve inches apart. This was a relaxed position. When the attractive server who was somewhat provocatively dressed approached his table, he uncrossed his feet and his knees came together. If I had spoken with the man, he probably would have had no idea his legs moved. Why did he do this? He was uncomfortable with her presence. This is quite typical of people splaying their legs in comfort. When a stranger or someone higher in the hierarchical chain approaches, the legs will close up.

While on a break from teaching, I was munching on a sandwich at a restaurant. I was seated at a small booth facing a pub height table and chairs. I watched one couple take a seat. I noticed the male had his foot propped on the bottom rung of the stool of his partner. He was comfortable enough to step into her territory. Both of their belly buttons were facing each other until their meal arrived. I watched similar behavior between two couples at a resort swimming pool restaurant. One was a senior citizen couple and the other two high school sweethearts. Despite the age difference, they both expressed comfort and intimacy with each other.

People can demonstrate their impatience when they begin rubbing their thighs. It is a pacifying act, but is also a strong signal that someone is ready to jump on the horse and giddy-up. This quite often is accompanied by accelerated head bobs and yessing or oking to hurry things along.

While interviewing an individual for a financial crime, I noticed she varied her leg behavior. When we began asking questions, the girl's leg was leaning in, or directing away depending on the anxiety of the question.

If people are in the flamingo stand with one leg on the ground and the other crossed or holding the wall up, this signifies comfort. As a street cop, I would observe individuals standing like flamingos. Once the patrol car pulled up in front of them, they normally would plant both feet. This would allow the felony fliers to be in an escape position. The flamingo provides little balance and thus an appearance of comfort. With both feet on the ground, you can brace the body or escape.

When people cross their legs, it often indicates comfort. They are not looking to escape. Now when the leg is crossed in concert with leaning back in the chair and hugging themselves, there is some serious blocking going on. You would need a hammer and chisel to chip the shield away.

I interviewed a female on one occasion that was desperately trying to stay out of trouble. She was a lot more flexible than I am. She pulled her legs up and with her arms pulled her feet into the chair so she was almost peeking over her knees. She erected a human fence posted with, "Do Not Enter!" She was also rubbing the toes on one foot so vigorously that I thought she would ruin her pedicure. Her entire body was repulsed with discomfort. She finally admitted her guilt and the admission had a cathartic effect as her body relaxed. She had nothing further to hide.

During the section on first impressions, we discussed walking. Stride can be attributed to caution or confidence. If I do not want to be on stage, I might unintentionally slow my gate. On the flip side, I might take a deep breath, marshal up the courage and stride an empty skeleton of confidence. Parkinson's patient will tend to shuffle their feet. Do not over read on the gait. Keep in mind what first impression are you projecting in accordance with your gait.

Posture is vitally important to first impressions. As my mother would say, "Stand up straight and keep your shoulders back." Her voice still resonates with me. Taller people are viewed with more confidence. The taller you stand, the better you will be received.

People with rounded shoulders or stooping are viewed with less confidence.

Feet jiggling or kicking can be a distraction to your conversational partner. My wife, when there is a sudden onset of stress, will kick as if she is punting the football away. I will ask her what is wrong. When someone's feet are bouncing up and down, there is some underlying anxiety.

Interlocking feet is something I do all the time and is quite common. If I were to pull my feet under the chair that I was sitting, that could indicate non-comfort. I was interviewing an applicant. He was an excellent candidate, but when I inquired about his previous marriage, his feet hiked up under the chair. It was still a subject of discomfort. Did it mean he was hiding something? No. The subject made him uncomfortable.

On another occasion, two of us were interviewing a suspect in a fraud case. I had already researched her background. When she sat down her feet were withdrawn under her chair. As I explored common points of interest and established rapport with her, her feet came out from hiding. As the interview began refocusing on the crime, her feet once again withdrew and disappeared under the chair.

The next behavior, you usually will not see except in the boss's office. It is what we call the rollercoaster seat. These people are the ones that are so terrified, they look like they have reached the apex of the coaster and are about to plummet down the summit. The only thing they are missing is the rush of air blowing their hair. Their arms are griping the chair rails, perhaps some white knuckles. Their back is pressed against the seat back and their feet are cemented to the ground or tucked up under the chair. If you look at their face, it might even look like they are pulling a few G's. Obviously, you will have to identify their fear. This would most commonly be seen in a human resources environment.

In summary, let me say again, due not jump on a single gesture as evidence of comfort, discomfort, or especially lying. With over thirty years of experience in observing people in various situations, I never ever focused on one event. **You must process all forms of communication for congruency. Is what they are saying and how they are saying it consistent with what their body is saying?**

I was conducting an interview of an individual. He was stoic and consistent in his body language. His body was reading a constant 98.6. The temperature began to increase as I explored his time spent in combat. We were in a deep discussion concerning the action and firefights. As he recalled that time, I noticed his feet that were firmly planted on the ground were now kicking out under the table, and his hips were shifting in the chair like he had a rash and his eyes averted for a moment. Those behaviors disappeared once we left the combat experience and explored other areas. He properly reacted with some degree of emotion.

This is a very good example of not over reading. Some might think that this onset of movements could indicate deception. All this meant was that he experienced anxiety and discomfort when his mind drifted back to a high stress environment. Stand in his flip-flops, or in this case his combat boots, as he was throwing lead down range and having bullets returned to him, as he tried to survive the experience. It is not a pleasurable experience to have someone trying to kill you.

In initial meetings that are brief, you may not have time to determine a baseline. You can pick out certain traits that exhibit discomfort. Such as the feet pointing away or the arms clenched across the chest. Use this information as a general guideline. As you have read, there are sometimes opposite meanings behind certain nonverbal behaviors.

The last point I want to make, is that as you read over these gestures, did you think of **how you present yourself. Conduct constant self-evaluation and assessment.** These points can assist you in presenting a more attentive pose with guests, clients, customers, or patients. We all have certain gestures that could project the wrong image. Focus on yourself and then monitor the behavior of your conversational partner.

Chapter 48
Narcissist the Crux of I

One key aspect of my job has depended on developing relationships based upon mutual respect and trust. The depth of my rolodex is a testament to the relationships that I have developed. Not just in law enforcement, but in many different areas of business. I live by the old belief that others matter more than I do. At my retirement party, I was moved by the eclectic mix of attendees. There were people high in hierarchy, but also attending were administrative employees at various companies and agencies that valued our mutual respect. I treated them all the same as colleagues and as friends.

My mother had a term known as the "Great I Am's." Perhaps, I failed to head the valuable lesson from my mother. Here I have written a book that I am expecting people want to read what I have to say, and that I have something to say that people need to hear or should hear.

Tiger Wood, in his mea culpa scripted conference expressed all the symptoms of being a narcissist. He professed a sense of entitlement because of all his hard work, and that due to his success, the rules did not apply to him. Ooops.

By 2006, 1 in 4 college students agreed with the majority of the questions concerning the Narcissistic Personality Disorder (NPD).

Twenty-five percent! Perhaps that is to be expected as college students are more focused on self, as they are selecting majors, careers, and relationships. That is a thirty percent increase over the baseline average two decades earlier. College students of today have high self-esteem that exceeds that of the students in the 1960's by a whopping 80 percent.

As we take a step back and view the American society as a whole, we realize that 1 in 16 members of the American culture have met the criteria to be diagnosed with NPD. This does not take into account those that are high on the narcissism scale and fail to fall under the diagnosis of NPD.

Drew Pinsky in his book *The Mirror Effect*, describes the process by which provocative, shocking, or otherwise troubling behavior, has become normalized, expected, and tolerated in our media culture, and is increasingly reflected by our own behavior.

What is Narcissism? It is defined in the DSM IV-TR criteria as:

A pervasive pattern of grandiosity (in fantasy or behavior), need for admiration, and lack of empathy, beginning by early adulthood and present in a variety of contexts, as indicated by five (or more) of the following:

1. Has a grandiose sense of self-importance
2. Is preoccupied with fantasies of unlimited success, power, brilliance, beauty or ideal love
3. Believes they are "special" and can only be understood by, or should associate with, people (or institutions) who are also "special" or of high status
4. Requires excessive admiration
5. Has a sense of entitlement
6. Is interpersonally exploitative
7. Lacks empathy

8. Is often envious of others or believes others are envious of him or her

9. Shows arrogant, haughty behaviors or attitudes

The traits that comprise narcissism are:

Authority – superiority, power and control. Most managers have to possess a certain or healthy amount of this trait. The worst one is the control freak or dictator.

Entitlement – Being owed. You believe that you have earned the right. Many internal thefts are attributed to a sense of entitlement.

Exhibitionism – Mostly seen with celebrities and athletes, but also with wannabees who are willing to act like idiots to garner attention.

Exploitivness – the renting of people or hijacking their qualities for their own good and self-promotion.

Self Sufficiency – the confidence of people in their own ability. We all need a certain amount for basic functioning. As in drinking, it is good in moderation.

Superiority – dominating belief that they are better than others and seek appropriate attention. An elitist viewpoint.

Vanity – Inflated view of self and appearance. Most of us want to look our best. It is when it becomes an obsession as in going into serious debt for plastic surgery, or clothing, and status trophies. Are you guilty of not being able to pass a reflection of yourself without slowing down and checking the image out?

Most people including this author all possess one or more of these traits. It comes down to the severity or the degree of each trait. A healthy dose of confidence is necessary for success. The problem comes into play with a lack of empathy. They can wear a mask of attractive social skills. They can be well liked by casual acquaintances or those necessary for self-serving success.

Empathy is the ability of a person to recognize and relate to another person's situation. You cannot treat others, as you would like to be treated, if you cannot relate or understand how the other person is feeling.

Senator John Edwards after being exposed as an slithering adulterer behind the back of his cancer stricken spouse said, "Becoming a national figure, all of which fed into self focus, an egotism, a narcissism that leads you to believe you can do whatever you want, you're invincible and there will be no consequences." That is until you get caught red handed. Then you deny, deny, deny, deflect, and demand proof, and finally make counter accusations.

Narcissists have a fundamental belief that they are superior over others. They are not always folks that have been cocky or arrogant. What we are talking about here are people that believe they are very special combined with an explosive mixture of possessing little to no empathy. They may feign empathy, but it is used as a manipulative tool for their own self-wealth and personal achievements.

They tend to be collectors. They become collectors of people, trophies, and status emblems. These collections are whatever they deem of value to themselves.

I interviewed an applicant for employment with our agency. His resume was quite impressive. In fact, I thought he was over-qualified. As I talked with him, I learned he was on a treasure hunt through life collecting "look at me" trophies.

While being an underclassman in college, this applicant had achieved the highest honor for an academic achievement. He failed to compete again. He was a sportsman and again recognized for his achievements. Once obtaining the top award, he stopped competing. In his professional life, he reached the pinnacle of his profession with a sought after certification. Yet, he wanted to give that up to start all over again. I wondered how long he would stay with us, before he chose to leave in pursuit of another trophy.

Beware of the closet narcissist. They do not exhibit the neon flashing signs. They may offer obligatory empathy, but they could not care less. They may ask how was your weekend or how do you feel. They rarely ask any follow-ups. If they do, it is to feign interest. They do not seek others out, unless the other person provides some benefit to their ego. The biggest problem with a closet narcissist is like the Wizard of Oz, they operate from behind the curtain. They can be manipulative and spiteful, but they will usually use emissaries to spread the misery.

Narcissism is not just used to describe Donald Trump and Fidel Castro. It is used to describe an ever-growing section of our society. In business you not only have to know how to recognize and placate those individuals, but perhaps more importantly to recognize your own narcissists traits to smother, so as not to alienate your clients or associates.

Chapter 49
Inoculating Against the I

If you have made the unfortunate error in entering a relationship with a narcissist, get out now! Narcissists make poor relationship partners, they make worse clients and even worse business people. They are selfish and lack empathy towards anyone.

The ME generation has been spectacular for the business world. Their sense of entitlement has become pervasive in their reluctance to delayed gratification. They want it now, not tomorrow or next month. With the current turmoil of the economy, this will damper the spending habits of narcissists.

In 2010, the release of the I-Phone 4 resulted in long lines at many of the retailers well before the scheduled release and the opening of the individual store. Jason Bateman, the child actor, from *Silver Spoons and Arrested Development* and mostly mired in a mediocre acting career as an adult, was one of those with an insatiable desire for the new phone.

Two thousand customers were patiently waiting for their opportunity to purchase the new cell phone at this Los Angeles location. Bateman was too important to wait in that line. He was escorted to the front of the line despite the booing and jeering crowd. Apple defended the passage due to the presence of paparazzi, and that he was a loyal customer. I guess the other 1,999 were not loyal enough customers.

If we were to give Bateman the benefit of the doubt, we could blame it on the Apple Store staff. A person with any empathy would be humiliated and embarrassed at the special treatment and decline any such offer. If it were the paparazzi, then sit inside the store signing autographs until it was your turn. Another alternative would have been that you could have gone home and ordered it on the internet and wait two days for the delivery. Yeah, so he would have missed out on the bragging rights. Who cares?

Many sunsets ago, I received a tip from an informant concerning the location of a career criminal. I was not the case agent, but I went out to locate the suspect. Enlisting the aid of another department, we located the suspect. As we approached him in the parking lot of a library, I knew he was going to run. I watched as his eyes started scanning his options. His face was happy, then flashed fear, and then concentration. His knees lowered just a tad as his torso turned and the race was on. After a lengthy foot chase, we caught the subject.

This man assumed the identity of dead children and was quite proud of his accomplishments, as well as his intellect. I played to his strengths in assessing that we were lucky to have caught the break and he was ingenious. I also praised him on his speed and if it were not for him worried that I was going to shoot him, I would not have caught him. He also had a considerable sum of cash stashed in his socks for an unexpected getaway.

He provided enough of a confession to keep him in jail, but I lacked all of the details to effectively conduct a comprehensive interview. The next day an overbearing supervisor used a confrontational style and the suspect closed up tighter than a hurricane shelter in Key West. Fortunately, a FBI agent was able to reestablish the rapport and she obtained a full confession. She used the approach of praising him for his brilliance.

He was an absolute narcissist and we were able to manipulate him and use his over inflated ego against him. He could not contain himself to brag of his exploits. He could not care less about the victims or the identities of the dead that he had dishonored.

You are probably wondering how this ties into interviewing and developing relationships. You must recognize that to be successful in developing relationships and interviewing, you must put your own ego to the side and recognize the other person's importance. Because they are. People love recognition. It stokes their ego and boosts their dopamine levels.

People do not like to be told they are wrong. Our society has become overwhelmed by the aspect of avoiding damage to the sensitivities of people. People are easily offended and we are so worried about their self-esteem, people are unwilling to point out errors.

I am aware of a law enforcement SWAT team that will remain anonymous. On occasion, they train against a red team of role players. The red team is instructed not to win or try too hard, but merely challenge the SWAT team. The agency is concerned about the fragility of the confidence of the team. I hope the real bad people are so sensitive. The fix is in. Everyone is a winner.

My parents the rest of the Greatest Generation, who endured the stress of the great depression and World War 2, maintained relative tranquility. School and workplace violence was unheard of in the past. What changed? My revelation came in reading Jean M. Twenge's book, *ME Generation*. She followed that up with The *Narcissism Epidemic* written with her coauthor Keith Campbell. Their works provide an in depth exploration into the world of Narcissism.

Bobby Bowden the famed coach of Florida State University was once asked how the players have changed over his forty years of coaching. His humorous reply was that the players of today like to play the "I Formation." "I" want this and "I" want that.

Chapter 50
How to Deal with the I-Bombs

Narcissists enjoy being the center of the universe. As long as you serve to benefit and enrich their lives, all is good. If at any time, you fail to recognize their importance or your services are no longer needed, you will be dropped without pause from the circle of trust. If you reach a point where you challenge their status level, not only will you be banned, but in all probability, a full-blown frontal assault will occur.

Long-term relationships with a narcissist can be toxic. Reverend Dennis Corrado of the Oratory Church of St. Boniface in Brooklyn, speaks of the concept that you do not need toxicity in your life. He was specifically speaking of some people in your life that are toxic. I fully embrace that position in social settings. When it comes to business, we are often placed in positions of working for and with people that are toxic. You must weigh the importance of that relationship and search your soul for guidance in accordance with your principles.

Narcissist can be manipulated and their weakness exploited. How do you identify a narcissist? They tend to be very charismatic and social. They have a large opinion of themselves. They will not always be verbose and publicly sharing of those comments. By monitoring their conduct, you will be provided insight. There will be signs that they look down upon others and hold grudges. They often have long memories. They tend to attract not the best and brightest, but the best at enhancing their image through adulation. They like "Yes Men." Deep down they are not nice people.

They are trophy, status and emblem collectors. If they have an office, look at the walls. They will commonly have an "I love me wall." In one such offender's office that I entered, there was not a square inch of wall that was not covered with photos of themselves in poses of action or standing alongside various celebrities. This was all to provide some significance to their lives.

They are quite often preeners. They love to groom themselves, because they are in love with their image. They cannot walk past a mirror or a window without checking themselves out. They will often have a strong sense of entitlement, but will not always share those beliefs with others.

The narcissistic employee will quickly embrace the attitude of "I am doing this because they owe me." There is no sense of ownership or loyalty. Employees are less likely to fall on the grenade and take one for the team. We have certainly observed this behavior in sports, where on some teams they have become a collection of individuals striving for individual success.

Dr. Wayne Hochwarter, the Jim Moran Professor of Management in the Florida State University College of Business, asked more than 1,200 employees to provide opinions regarding the narcissistic tendencies of their immediate supervisor. Their responses were not good. Dr. Hochwarter said, "Having a narcissistic boss creates a toxic environment for virtually everyone who must come in contact with this individual." He went on to say, "The team perspective ceases to exist, and the work environment becomes increasingly stressful. Productivity typically plummets as well." The employees reported lower levels of job satisfaction, increased stress and lower levels of productivity.

Critical feedback of employee's inadequate performance is a delicate trail fraught with peril. When I was in a position of providing feedback, I made sure that I sat down with the employee, went over the situation and praised the overall effort. Then I focused on the points of concern, and tried to enlarge their framework of existence to stand in the recipient's position. If you received this report, would you understand this paragraph? On the other hand, if this report is being reviewed by management, is this the product you want to be recognized for? Is this your best effort? You want management to take notice of your performance. Your hard work deserves to be noticed. Your overall effort was very good, but I believe with these corrections, you can become excellent. You have provided them a selfish reason to improve.

Show empathy. Most people expect empathy. If you are a narcissist and have never had any adversity in your life, have never been married, and never had children, you need to fake it in a believable manner. Watch some movies with those situations so perhaps you can see the effects on people. Think of *A Christmas Carol*.

I watched in disbelief once when a supervisor asked an employee about his personal crisis. The employee gave a quick overview dealing with the deteriorating health of his family. I could see the boss was quickly uninterested and dismissed the conversation with a request for an additional task from the employee. Through the employee's body language, it was easily recognized that they were in despair. It was just as easy to read the supervisor, who was uninterested and did a poor job faking his concern. The employee, who had returned early from sick leave out of conscience to duty, quickly recognized his dedication was being taken advantage of and not appreciated.

Contrast that with a supervisor I worked for that called me every day and volunteered to mobilize the resources of the office to help my family and me. If asked, I would go through a ring of fire for that supervisor.

Narcissists have the ability to ingratiate themselves with people that can enhance their career and serve a selfish purpose. They can pull the wool over the proverbial eyes of superiors. We all fall victim on the short-term basis to the manipulation of the narcissist. Think of Eddie Haskell of *Leave it to Beaver*. "That is a very nice sweater you are wearing Mrs. Cleaver." June Cleaver recognized the efforts, but many do not and fall victim. As they rise through the ranks, they undermine the moral of the organization and many times implode due to their own unrecognized ineptitude. Quite often, they are shuffled to some nondescript assignment of purgatory.

I have watched several noted politicians dictate heartfelt thank you cards to people who have made life a little easier or went out of their way to be a gracious host. There is nothing better than receiving a genuine thank you card from those that appreciated your efforts. It is better to receive than to give. Narcissists do not like to dish out praise, but love to receive accolades.

Everyone knows a suck-up or a tail kisser. Whether you are a narcissist or not, the apple polishers are always striving for the same thing. They are trying to ingratiate themselves in a manipulative, disingenuous and corrosive manner. Every organization has them. The boss that falls victim to this manipulator, allows a cancer to infect and spread throughout the organization.

Narcissists love suck-ups. These smoochers are telling the narcissist how great they are. The boss embraces this conduct at the detriment of the organization. It puts them on a higher pedestal and they love the adulation.

The other employees look at the favoritism and it undermines their initiative. They will normally disassociate themselves from the narcissist and their followers thus, allowing a divisive crevice to fracture the continuity of the team.

Be humble. If you are a narcissist and many people do not know that they are, try on a coat of humility. Even if you are not a narcissist, a coat of humility never goes out of style and will keep you warm, not to mention it is a coat that you can share with others to provide comfort. The book, *29 Gifts* by Cami Walker, provides simple inexpensive or free ways to enrich people's lives.

Research has indicated that narcissists are less likely to display aggression towards those that have established some commonality. Go back to common points of interest. Look to establish that commonality. I am not advocating inviting them over for a barbeque.

With narcissism on the rise, the herd is getting larger. Similar to a large herd of cows, they eat all the grass until it is all gone. No one is looking out for each other. As a result, all members of the herd are competing for adulation and attention.

If you display genuine attention and interest in a narcissist, you have just thinned down the herd. You can be cordial to all of them.

Many I-bombs do not know who they are. If you suspect you might fall into the trap, go online and look up the test for narcissism. If you score high, then you need to keep that in mind when dealing with others on the playground.

With a narcissist, you have to avoid direct criticism. They revolt at efforts to correct their conduct. Remember, they are never or rarely wrong. If you can reframe the information in such a way that it is positive for their interest, you are on the way to striking gold. You can hop in the backseat for the ride. It might be a bumpy ride without shock absorbers, so make sure you wear your seatbelt. Caution and survival is the rule of the day.

Chapter 51
Mimicry

"Everybody is like a magnet. You attract to yourself reflections of that which you are. If you're friendly then everybody else seems to be friendly too."

—Dr. David Hawkins

Isopraxisis is the fancy word for mirroring of another person.

With most people, we see some degree of mimicking. Whether it is by style of dress, actions, manner of dress, or speech, we all do it to some degree. This is not necessarily a bad thing.

Most people adapt and change to fit in. Everyone wants to assimilate to others. When I left New York for Arkansas, my accent stood out like a wart on a nose. It was obvious, most people recognized my speech, and at times, I was at the receiving end of ridicule. As time went on, my New York brogue began to dissipate. I began to acquire more of a southern accent. I would never be confused as being from Arkansas by the locals, but I no longer stood out.

After several years, I returned to New York on business and while shopping in a store, the clerk asked where I was from. To her astonishment, I told her I was born and raised less than an hour away. She had difficulty believing my explanation. I was now from nowhere. I was no longer totally native, but acceptable to both parties.

Marco Iacoboni, PhD wrote a detailed book on the effects of mirroring and mirror neurons in the brain. In his book, *Mirroring People: The Science of Empathy and How We Connect with Others* he said, "We have an instinct to imitate one another - to synchronize our bodies, our actions, even the way we speak to each other."

In research conducted at the University of Nijmegan in The Netherlands, they followed restaurant servers and monitored the tips provided my customers. Those that mimicked the customers' orders received tips that were twice the control group that only said, "Coming right up." Rick van Baaren who was one of the researchers told *Nature* in a 2003 article, "Mimicry creates bonds between people - it induces a sense of 'we-ness.'" We all strive for acceptance, right?

Professor Tanya Chartrand of Duke University and John Bargh, professor of psychology at New York University, call this the "Chameleon Effect." Their research led to the groundbreaking study on the natural tendencies of people to imitate speech and physical expressions.

In a study published in the *Journal of Personality and Social Psychology*, Chartrand and Bargh asked 72 college students to sit down individually with an experimenter and discuss a set of photographs. With half the human lab rats, the experimenters maintained a neutral, relaxed seated position. The other half mimicked the posture, movements, and mannerisms of the other students. Therefore, if someone rubbed his or her nose, the experimenter would copy the behavior. After the conclusion of the experiment, students whose behavior was imitated, rated their experimenters as more likable. They also reported having had smoother interactions with the copycats.

In 1999, Chartrand and Bargh studied participants who viewed photos. They discussed their observations with two different individuals. One who displayed a tendency to rub their face while the second would shake their foot. Bingo, the participants showed an increase in the same behavior and without being aware of their mirroring.

Less can sometimes be more. Remember how annoying children can get when they parrot your conversation. It starts amusing, but quickly wears thin. It is the same in real life. Although you are attempting to establish rapport, if the person you are emulating becomes aware of your mirroring, it will become obvious, self-defeating, and annoying just like the parroting kid.

In another study of the chameleon effect, Chartrand and Bargh discovered that students who rated high on empathy were more likely to imitate others. Narcissists would have difficulty in this department. People like to be around empathetic people. You know, "I feel your pain."

As you are talking with people, you can mirror some of the words used within their discussion. Just season the stew a little. If someone is talking about repetitive sales volume, as an important facet of their business, you could use the term repetitive sales volume in the discussion. That perks up their ears like an alert puppy dog, and lets them to know you are listening.

If they cross their leg, follow suit and cross yours. If they lean in towards you, then edge towards them. Do not do it action for action. Pause a few moments before mirroring or risk being exposed. Hold your hands like them and mirror their posture. Space your legs at the same distance and the same angle. If their arms are crossed over their chest, you follow suit. If they smile, flash one back. Now, you might want to avoid mimicking a finger in the mouth or nose.

I have heard some practitioners of mimicry, advocate mirroring the same blink rate and breathing. I have enough challenges monitoring and controlling my breathing without mirroring someone else. What happens is you focus so much on your mirroring that you lose focus on the context of the conversation. My father suffered from COPD. If I were to mirror his breathing, I would suffer lightheaded dizziness. If I mirrored the blink rate of my partner, my belief is that it becomes a distraction to your thought pattern.

Keep it real. I advocate subtle delayed mirroring of your partners mannerisms. Follow the body inclination, arm, hand and leg movements. Flash back a smile and a genuine laugh. Keep it simple and subtle (KISS!).

Mimicry is a top-secret technique to bonding that few people possess the knowledge to use as a leveraging tool. The evidence is clear on this aspect, and I felt it was important enough to devote a chapter just to this technique.

Chapter 52
Interviewing

"I never learn anything from talking. I only learn things when I ask questions."

—Lou Holtz

Everyone has watched the Hollywood version of a police interview. Good cop, bad cop routine. Alternatively, just bad cop screaming and yelling at the suspect and sprinkling a little violence in there to scare a confession.

I am guilty of using enhanced interrogation techniques repeatedly over the last thirty years. My technique improved more as time went on, as I experimented and found what worked. I made subtle changes.

The two most important enhanced tactics that I employed were patience and developing relationships. I had to show I was not in any hurry and that person was the most important element at that time. Now I did not bring an overnight bag to camp out. Every situation is different. Certainly if you are a pharmaceutical salesperson visiting a busy clinic, you are going to be pressed for time. It might take multiple visits to reach a comfort factor.

If someone is coming to your office, as in a HR environment, make those people comfortable. People do not like change or new areas. Help them to adapt to their new surroundings. When you help, others feel important, it places them more in a zone of harmony. The more I can put someone at ease, the more likely I will succeed.

I use an acronym EASY that ties everything together. E is entry. Remember you must make a positive first impression. A is Assimilate. You want to incorporate yourself with the subject. S is State your purpose. Y is You own the outcome by making them more important.

In Hollywood, you watch many of the cops screaming at some hardened criminal who has recently been out of jail. He breaks down and gives up the goods. In real life, most jailbirds live in a world of violence and therefore are not intimidated by shouting. A youthful offender may be prone to break under those conditions, but I have seen situations where they could actually be a harder nut to crack, because they are not as wise about the system. The mature offenders once presented with the overwhelming evidence would usually shop for a deal.

In very few instances, was I not able to obtain someone's cooperation. I would paint a full picture for them. I laid the cards on the table. There were times I used props or insinuated that I knew more or possessed more evidence than I had. Those that I worked with that enjoyed the same degree of success, used the same techniques. We relied very heavily on developing rapport with the suspect and having the patience to use those skills. It is not rocket science. Treat the other person with respect, the same respect you would want to be treated. Stand in their flip-flops.

Very little of my time interviewing was spent with suspects. Think about this. Most of the cops' job is collecting evidence and taking statements. Most of the people I interviewed were other law enforcement officers, business leaders, associates, victims, and information purveyors.

The best time to conduct a cooperative interview is in the morning after the cappuccino has kicked in. Right after lunch is not as productive, because the body is slowed from the heavy lunch. If cocktails are involved it helps to loosen inhibitions, but it can also impair judgment.

During most interviews, I will take some notes or at a minimum, when I get outside, I will jot down notes of the meeting. I will send a short email thanking them for their time and it was nice to meet them. Sometimes they respond and sometimes they do not. If they beat me to it, I will respond quickly.

Be cautious when you are taking notes in front of people. People become suspicious of what you are writing down. If you are jotting down a future appointment or a question for the client, that is fine. You might wait until you get out to the car, or when they leave to write down some retrievable notes. I can tell you that people are always wondering what you are scribbling.

The next time I meet them, I will inquire into something they had said in the past. If your memory is not deep enough, keep notes and organize them in alphabetical order in the computer. People are shocked when you ask how their kid's baseball team is doing.

I have a friend that had a photo of her grandfather with the 1919 Boston Police Department. Several years later, I read a book by Dennis Lehane, *The Given Day*, which described the 1919 Boston Police members who went out on strike. I called her and recommended the book to her. She could not believe that I remembered that conversation of perhaps two minutes in duration that occurred three years earlier.

On another occasion, I was meeting with an executive of a company. As we sat down and began our meeting, I started into where he was from and what college he attended. I also brought up a telephone conversation we had four years earlier and thought he had mentioned he had lived in Atlanta. Bingo! That demonstrated that I thought a great deal of our interactions and that they were memorable.

I have had a number of folks that demonstrated my importance to them. David Harris-Hack, a sales associate with Marriott has developed a long-term relationship with me. We were having a conversation and he recalled a discussion from several years earlier over a pond behind my home. He did listen to me!

Connie Paul, a sales manager with Wyndham Tampa, would always ask follow up questions concerning my family. When my wife was fighting breast cancer, Connie would always ask about her health. She was wonderful at deepening our rapport. Robin Shows with the Embassy Suites developed rapport over our mutual backgrounds enjoying the Panhandle of Florida and Cajun cuisine. When I was in the Panhandle, I sent her a picture of her high school. Donna Siegel with Marriott Clearwater always asked about my children.

I worked extensively with hotel sales managers. They were always gracious. I became friends with many and of them and looked forward to my conversations with them. So many of them focused our conversations not just on business, but also on common points of interest.

I keep track of future dates that my conversational partners discuss. If they are pregnant and have a due date, I will send a short email wishing them well as they get within a month of the due date.

If I am going into a serious meeting, I turn my cell phone off. I do not want the distractions of the spam mail vibrating and wondering if it is my wife telling me we won the lottery. Most times, it is not that important. If you are caught cheating a look at the Blackberry or iPhone, it shows disrespect to the person you are talking to. Not to mention the obnoxious ring tone of some hip hop group. If you are fortunate to have it on vibrate, everyone hearing the sound is wondering if it was a phone or an adult toy.

Absolutely no texting. Some people can multitask very efficiently. The tapping of keys draws attention away from the conversation and is a rude gesture to others. If you must return a text, pardon yourself from the conversation, take care of the text and shut down the phone. I often wonder if they are truly texting or competing for the high score in BrickBreaker.

I was attending a presentation. The presenter had started by making an admission that this was her first oral presentation. This is a daunting task in front of an audience of grizzled cops. She had everyone on the edge of their seats and scribbling away on note pads. One of the attendees answered his cell phone and began carrying on a loud intrusive conversation. Everyone was shocked and began heckling the rudeness of the interrupter. He walked out and allowed for the continuance of the presentation. Somehow, she maintained her composure. I lost all respect for the Mr. Phonecall.

I have heard some excuses that they use the phone as a watch. First, buy a watch. Second, try not to make it to obvious. Anytime you draw attention to the time, is a reflection that you have lost interest. You may have a black tie event with Elvis Presley, but avoid the jeweler's eye that is inspecting the timepiece.

I want that person to believe that they are important to me. I do not like interruptions that break up the flow. Sometimes emergencies come up that cannot be avoided. I was in a meeting and the individual had a relative that was ill. They warned me ahead of time that they might have to step out. They were considerate.

I heard of one story in which a suspect was on the precipice of confessing to a murder. They were defeated. Their body language had collapsed and they began crying. They had just started to say something, when another investigator barged into the solitude of the interview room and asked a brief question. That slight interruption was enough for the person to regain their composure and the case was never solved.

Chapter 53
Decorating and Sharing

Interior Decorating

You cannot always pick the furniture alignment. If the option is available and you can sit on the same side of the table, you eliminate the barrier of the table. Certainly, you would not want to go behind someone's desk.

If someone is at the head of the table, sit as close to the front so that you can sit more at an angle to them. If you have the opportunity to sit across from each other, it matters which sex is in front. With men, it is best to start off-center towards their right. Line up your right shoulder with theirs. As time goes on, you can skootch over to face-to-face. Face to face with men displays an unconscious hostility. With females on the other hand, you can sit directly across from them.

I have seen some studies referring to people who have preferred dominant sides. That might be true and I will not disagree. I just think it adds too much to the plate. It is like my golf game. I take so much time thinking of each part of my swing, that I am a lousy golfer.

If you are sitting across the boardroom table, this is an adversarial position. Think of negotiators battling out an agreement. Remember, to keep your hands in a natural position above the table.

It is always better to reserve a conference room that is too big than too small. I have sat there observing the anxiety of people squeezed into a conference room like a size 9 foot into a size 8 shoe. It cuts down on the creative juices as people's minds are wondering about the shoulders of others touching theirs and the poor planning of the host. They will eventually become acclimated and readjust to the matter at hand.

The more dominant seat within a conference room or boardroom setup is facing the entrance to the room with your back to a wall. A more conducive teamwork approach is the King Arthur and the Knights of the Round Table. If you watch the President in the Cabinet meetings, he sits in the middle of the long side facing the door side. His chair back is slightly higher than the cabinet members.

I was summoned to the Director's conference room to provide a short briefing on an incident that had a significant impact on our operations. I arrived early and there was only one other person in the room. I decided to assume a seat in the middle of the long conference room. The other person in the room, chuckled slightly, but did not say anything. I asked if I was in the wrong seat. He grinned and said I was sitting in the Director's chair. I then relocated to a chair against the wall where I would not infringe upon the seating protocol.

In my office, I inherited a chair with the office. The chair looked like part of someone's former living room rejects, but was comfortable. It was also low to the ground, and I had to lean forward to maintain eye contact with those that sat in the chair. It put me in a superior position, but that was not my intent. A number of visitors would come around and lean against my credenza, to face me at a forty-five degree angle, which was the more optimal position. I would swivel around so that our belly buttons were aligned.

Sharing

Do not accept your ignorance. Challenge your intellect. Seek knowledge from those around you. If you do not know something, do not bluff it and look like a fool. Most people can see through the veil. Self-disclosure can be the cement that joins two bricks. You are asking for their help. People love to talk, especially in their fields of knowledge. If they throw out a term you are not familiar with, then go ahead and ask for clarification.

Be careful when disclosing insider or fiduciary information. "Don't tell anyone, but I have a secret." It shows flaws and vulnerabilities. The person you are discussing this with will look upon you with distrust, and will always be wary of your intentions. If you are violating this trust, what else will you be willing to do?

Personal secrets are not to be confused with violating a trust as in gossip or a company secret. Disclosing an embarrassing moment or a peculiar trait can enhance bonding. In a study by N.L. Collins and L.C. Miller in 1994, they discovered those people that let you in on a little personal secret will be more admired. In turn, people who trust you will share more of their secrets. I will show you mine if you show me yours. This is one of the building blocks of building a relationship. You are sharing facets and emotions of your life that peel back the veneer and show your vulnerabilities.

One of our visiting priests is a gifted man. During one of his sermons, he was discussing being judgmental. He confessed to the congregation of being judgmental himself. He advised he had several weakness including judging the youths that allow their pants to hang down under their underwear, and public display of tattoos. His bearing his soul that he too bore weaknesses similar to everyone else, only strengthened his position. His confession of imperfection grabbed the congregation.

You do not want to share a secret that might be repulsive. I had a fellow that shared some very intimate secrets of his sex life. Let us just say he and his wife had struggled with intimacy, which lead to infidelity, which lead to an insatiable appetite for sex. TMI – Too

Much Information! This was on our first meeting. I started to feel as if I was wearing a priest's collar and we were in the confessional.

He crossed the line and made me uncomfortable. He was unleashing a burden and not developing rapport. As a side note to that story, I met this man's son ten years later. I never let on to him that I knew about his parents, but I was secretly embarrassed for him.

Think back to the courtship of a significant other. You shared information with them that perhaps you would not share with a coworker. This is information that you might not want to share with your parents. What you are saying is that I entrust you with this information. I am not talking about classified information, but sharing snippets of stories. If you are caught violating that trust by gossiping or repeating the secret, you can count on fracturing the relationship in more pieces than Humpty Dumpty.

Chapter 54
Evaluate and Analyze

Give the clients space. Do not suffocate them with attention. Have you ever made the mistake of providing your telephone number to an overzealous sales person? I appreciate someone with passion, but I do not need any stalkers in my life. An initial call to say it was nice to meet you and if I can be of assistance do not hesitate to call is acceptable. You might even forewarn them that you will call in a week to check on them. Once a week calls and I start ignoring the calls when I see the caller ID.

If you are a real estate agent and escorting clients through a house, allow them to see and feel the property. No one likes an in-depth unabridged audio book tour. Point out critical points whether they are positives or negatives. Make suggestions when necessary concerning changes to improve the property or provide options that will enhance the property. Be careful not to become too intrusive.

A quieter personality is better than a strong personality. I knew a friend who had an agent who was very abrasive and at times condescending. I am sure she felt she was doing what was in the best interest of her clients, but she landed up alienating him. He bought the house, but spoke poorly of her to other potential buyers and used someone else to sell his home.

Provide insight as to the product and alternative options. If you are asked a question that you do not know, tell them the truth and tell them you will research that and get back to them. Do not forget. People will remember you were going to get back to them. Admit your limitations and immediately seek some assistance, or you jeopardize your relationship. This is not a poker game where you can bluff your way through. You do not know what you do not know.

As a child, many of us played with the Chinese finger trap. For those forgetful people, the finger trap was the tubular bamboo braid that each person inserts a finger. As you pull on the bamboo-braided tube, it stretches and tightens the expanse clamping down on the finger making it difficult to extract the finger. As you move towards each other, the tube relaxes the grip and allows the person to extricate their finger.

The same principle holds true in interviewing. If you start in a power of will that is tugging and pulling, your progress and success will be hindered. If you work towards developing a relationship and draw the person towards you, you will have a much higher degree of success.

The University of Pennsylvania conducted a study of emergency room residents interacting with patients. A third never told the patient their name. Once they asked the opening question of the patient concerning their complaint, only twenty percent of the patients were able to complete their dissertation of their problem without interruption. The doctors on average interrupted the patient at twelve seconds. Count to twelve and see how little information you can deliver.

Wendy Levinson who was on the research team of the University of Pennsylvania recorded hundreds of interactions between physicians and their patients. She separated the doctors into two groups. One-half had never been sued. The other half had been sued at least twice. The doctors that were in the no lawsuit group spent on average more than three minutes longer with their patients than the doctors in the group that had been sued two or more times. She noted they were good at active listening and used some degree of humor. In other words, they were likeable and their patients bonded and identified with them. The extra three minutes did not add content. It was bonding and listening time.

I learned this in a sales seminar one time and employed it in numerous occasions in the police field. Feel, felt and found. I know how you must feel, I would or have felt the same way, but what I find is … You are empathizing with the person. You are displaying to them that you understand what they are going through.

I always want them to start talking about themselves. Allow them to feel comfortable in their own comfort zone. We will get to me eventually. I am looking to establish the rapport and friendship. At some point, they will let all their air out and then ask you a question. That is your opportunity to make your brief opening statement. Practice this in two sentences. Authors are taught to condense a four hundred-page manuscript down to a thirty-second commercial pitch to a perspective agent. James Cameron pitched *Titanic* with a picture of the ship and said, "Picture this boat and Romeo and Juliet." Simplicity won over complexity. The rest is history, as *Titanic* became the second highest grossing movie of all time.

When I entered an interview room with a suspect, quite often I was met with hostility. It was my goal to decrease the tension. I could not control his emotions before I entered the room, but I could control mine. The suspect's emotions were based on the fear of the situation, the fear of the future, and the fear of the moment. That fear quite often was based upon prior contact with law enforcement.

I had to identify those fears and alleviate them or at least reduce them if I had any hope of success. Many times, it took patience. My level of patience was based upon how much I needed their cooperation. I had to convince them that it was in their best interest to cooperate and they would be helping themselves.

Two of the most basic fears are the fear of losing control of the situation, and fear of being taken advantage. Everyone wants to feel in control and have the confidence that they are calling the shots.

There are not many people who enjoy the car buying experience. Why? Many customers hate the long process, the constant wrangling and worry about being ripped off. They have little control as they are shuttled along from person to person and worn down. CarMax has a nonnegotiable pricing policy. A sales person is there to offer assistance and answer questions, but the listed price is the final price. Fear is eliminated from the buying experience.

The only fear remaining is the underlying condition of the car. CarMax performs a 125-point inspection of all cars and backs that up with a five-day money back guarantee and thirty-day warranty. They will provide you with the ratings of the vehicle along with a known history. Could you find the same car at a cheaper price? Perhaps. Could I save a few hundred dollars and invest a few hours of bitter negotiating somewhere else? Probably. I am still getting a fair price and not losing control over the situation. It is one of the most pain free car buying experiences I have ever had.

We have all experienced fear of rejection or humiliation. Many people are comfortable in their own misery and are reluctant to shed the chains of their comfort zone. The first time we step into a new environment, we become uncomfortable. After having focused on investigating threat cases for eight years, I started investigating mortgage fraud. I had not investigated fraud cases in over a decade.

I will admit, I was a little uneasy as I started at a new office, with new employees and a new focus. I knew there would be a learning curve and an adjustment period. I also knew the easiest way to overcome the anxiety was to engage in action. With more practice, I became more familiar and thus more comfortable. In fact, I reached a point where my old office was no longer my comfort zone.

It is like picking up the telephone to ask for the first date or taking the training wheels off the bike. I had a coworker that was very conscientious. He also spent so much time worrying about making a mistake that at times his action was hindered. I told him that he reminded me of the baseball pitcher who stands on the mound facing a batter. He stares towards home plate and watches the signals from the catcher. Then he waves off the catchers signal and steps off the mound and picks up the resin bag. He looks at the crowd and walks to the mound. He digs his feet into the rubber and starts all over. Sometimes you just have to take a deep breath and throw the ball.

You will not be perfect all the time. We all trip and stumble. It is only a mistake if you do not learn from the error. All lapses are opportunities for learning. Inaction is no action.

As you explore the client or partners concerns, you can also zero in their personal identity and passions in life. When I speak of identity, I want to know how they see themselves. What is important to them? For some of my colleagues, they received their identity by working for the Secret Service. It sounds cool to strangers, but they had limited outside interests. For others their identity might be as a great hunter, angler, gym rat, or their position in the community or family.

Once you establish their identity, and establish why they get out of bed in the morning, you have opened the door to their passion. By exploring that passion, you are creating a bridge of friendship.

So what if you do not know anything about their passion? Ask them about their most memorable experience, how they became involved, how long they have been involved, what is their favorite aspect. Look at it as a learning experience. The day I stop learning is the day I stop living. I might not know a lot about computers, but by placing myself in the position of a student and seeking knowledge from them, they become more comfortable.

I interviewed a pilot of a small private plane one time. Due to technical difficulties, he had encroached into restricted airspace. He was a little amped up about the infraction and the possible consequences. When I found out he was a financial advisor, I asked him which was the better investment, real estate or stocks.

For several minutes, I received an interesting lesson on economics and retirement strategies. He thanked me for putting him at ease and digressing from the purpose of my visit. He was able to calmly recall the events of the incident. I ended the conversation with asking him about the prospects of the emerging company he was currently representing. I walked away from a successful interview with more knowledge than I had entered and a hot stock pick (I did not act upon the insider tip). You never know where life will take you.

You must figure out what is in it for them. For the pilot, he wanted to retain his pilot's license and avoid trouble. For many of the suspects I interviewed, they wanted to diminish their jail time, or protect their family. For others, it was to their civic duty, pursuit of justice or spirit of cooperation. Sometimes it was an opportunity to eliminate their competition. Oh yeah, sometimes they lied.

Many times people are looking to enhance their self-image. They are trophy collecting. Perhaps they want to be better than the family up the street, or they want attribution from a father that never gives praise. Some deep down inner emotions will not be uncovered in a short conversation, but it is shocking to me how quickly some people will confide if you will just listen.

Sometimes people just need to get things off their chest and are seeking peace of mind. Sometimes it is a matter of conflict or conscience. Maybe their car is no longer reliable or their neighborhood crime has made it unsafe. I met with a fellow who had a recent crime occur in his neighborhood. That became his focus and it was cathartic for him to discuss the crime. I just listened and made him more important than me.

Chapter 55
Have Fun

Humor

Use it often. People like to laugh. It releases endorphins and happy people generally do not murder other people. Humor lightens the mood and takes the edge off. Be careful, like everything, it is good in moderation. No potty humor.

You would think in this day and time people would understand that with political correctness, you could no longer make or send off color jokes. It never ceases to amaze me when I read someone has fallen from grace because of a joke that was overheard or sent in email. You have to ask, at what point did this sound like a good idea. I often receive political jokes in my personal email. Due to my position, I do not want to be attributed to some of these jokes. As a result, I delete and do not forward.

Attitude

Positive attitude is a state of mind. I have heard people advise not to read the paper or watch the news. I can see their point, but many times, it broadens your knowledge base. Many conversations are brought up from stories in the news. Stay away from politics.

Possessing confidence is not to be confused with cockiness. In the 1969 Super Bowl, Joe Namath the quarterback for the New York Jets guaranteed a victory over the heavily favored Baltimore Colts. His brashness was not well received. He delivered on his promise and won the upset victory. No one likes someone that is cocky and arrogant. If you fall into this trap, you should notice that the few friends you have are shallow straphangers.

Your bravado could incite your competition. It provides inspiration. In a college football game between Florida State and Florida, Geno Hayes a linebacker for FSU, made the pronouncement that Tim Tebow, the Florida quarterback was going down. Hayes had one lonely tackle and Tebow had a tremendous game and led his team to an easy victory. There is no doubt the press clippings of Hayes were prominently displayed inside the Florida locker room.

Be sincere in your dealings. I know one person who is in sales. The initial contact was one of being friendly and warm. As time evolved, his circle of friends deteriorated. Why? Because people discovered he was disingenuous and pretty much a snake. He hurt his referral base because of the loss of trust. I do not know if ever he figured it out. On one occasion, he stopped by a recently widowed neighbor. He never had time for her or her husband. The recently departed was not in the ground a full week, when he dropped by to offer his condolences and offer his card in case she needed his services.

It is not just cops who interview. Think about this. Every day at work, you are interviewing. This is regardless of whether it is on the phone or in person. At home when you contact a contractor, attorney, or doctor, you are interviewing them as perspective partners. All of your social interactions, from the PTA, to the community pig roast, call for interviewing skills.

I am hoping this book will provide a roadmap and the foundation to enhance these skills. This is not difficult to master. It might require some homework and plenty of practice. As it stands, unless you work alone in a cave, you are interacting with people.

Chapter 56
Developing Bonds

Many people will sit on the fence with the other boo birds and question how a cop has the ability to write about anything related to business. Good question. Now indulge me for a few moments while I explain. I always thought life insurance was the toughest sale. Real estate, cars, electronics are material items of affection and enjoyment. That is most of the time. With life insurance, you are proposing that the policyholder WILL DIE and that they will NEVER benefit from the proceeds, other than to know their beneficiaries will have one heck of a party after they are gone.

Now think about this. A person has just been caught violating the law. They immediately invoke the "not me ghost." Every cop show on TV and every defense attorney will tell them not to say a thing to the cops. Zip the zipper and throw the key away. It is against their best interest to talk. If they talk, they are guaranteed full time occupancy in a reserved 8 x 8 cell with a stainless steel toilet, noisy neighbors and the loss of all freedoms known to them.

It has been my job to convince that person he needs to empty his guilt-ridden conscience, and to cooperate, and solve this crime. I need their confession, so I can bring closure to the victim and he can go to jail. How is that for salesmanship? I listened to every sales tape that I could listen to and read many books on the subject.

This was all to help to improve my performance. The day I stop learning is the day I stop breathing.

My job for thirty years was more than interviewing suspects. I questioned witnesses, victims, or others that had some level of information. Sometimes it was business folks and sometimes it was family members or citizens. It was how I conducted those interviews that depended on the level and usefulness of the knowledge they provided. Many times, I entered the relationship in an adversarial position, but exited in a positive position. I loved taking to people and learning from them. My life and that of many others, depended on my ability to observe and react as well as to obtain information that would lead to success.

Many law enforcement agencies do not play nice in the sand box. They tend to be territorial. There has been an improvement since 2001, but fissures still exist.

In 1999, I was assigned as a liaison to FBI Headquarters and CIA Headquarters. I initially displayed a lack of interest in the opening. After two failed attempts to entice me to jump on the bait, I was told I had no choice.

Over the next two years, I embarked on one of the most interesting journeys of my career. I was treated like a valued employee and extended every courtesy possible by those two competing agencies. I never detected any animosity.

Mistakes were made by these agencies, but my handling of those only strengthened my relationships. I learned to approach the issues from their standpoint. Many of the lessons I learned during that assignment, I continued to use for the next ten years, as I was always assigned to at least one multiagency task force.

Since 2001, my primary mission was to conduct investigations of threat cases. What that translates to are all the individuals who made threats or displayed an unusual direction of interest towards persons under our protection up to and including the President. At times that leaked over into other politicians and celebrities.

It was my responsibility to investigate those individuals and conduct a complete behavioral assessment to determine the credibility of their interest and their capacity to conduct such an attack. If I failed, the consequences could be dire and I would be expected to explain my actions on Capitol Hill. I became very good at interviewing people and reading people. My life and the lives of the people I was protecting, depended on those abilities.

Everyone has seen the good cop bad cop routine. I am not a big fan. I preferred patience and spending time to develop the relationship and exploit weaknesses. I can tell you that twice I received confessions on folks that I violated one of my fundamental rules. That is that I lost patience with both suspects. Patience is one of my core beliefs when it comes to interviewing.

On one occasion it was getting late at night and the second was when I was summoned off the ladder with the paintbrush in hand on a Saturday evening. The two suspects were at the root of my frustration. I burst into the interview rooms and read them the riot act. It was something straight out of a Hollywood movie, but this was real life. I was shocked that both emptied their souls. They should have clammed up tighter than a bank vault with my approach.

That goes to show you that even bad business people get lucky sometimes. They can get by if they have a monopoly or it is a one-time sale with no expectation of repeat business. The only business that comes to mind that does not need repeat business is a coffin salesperson.

I went on a disastrous trip to the Pan Handle of Florida looking for a second home. I could not find a real estate agent willing to take my money. I went through six agents, all of which failed to deliver and left me standing by myself with my mouth wide open in disbelief. OK naysayers jump in. I must have been the client from hell. Actually, I was the client from heaven and you will see that later.

Zig Ziglar has been quoted as saying, "You can have everything in life you want if you will help other people get what they want." It is an extension of the Golden Rule. Treat others, as you would like to be treated. Try to put yourself in their flip-flops. Identify their wants and needs. Even if the timing is not right, sow the seeds for the future. I cannot tell you the number of purchases I delayed. The timing was not right. At some point later, I sought out the business or salesperson that treated me right for the sale.

Betsy Model the celebrity profile journalist said in an interview with Writer Magazine, May 2009, "I treat every interview as if it were a casual cocktail party." "I think the trick, if there is one, is to let someone know you are genuinely interested in what they have to say…"

I have had the honor of working with several real estate agents that were outstanding. They hustled and maintained communication with me. They provided their insight and expertise into the buying equation. They all followed up and kept in touch. They were all rewarded with repeat business and multiple referrals.

Unfortunately, not all agents were good. My perceived failure of real estate agents is that they failed to deliver customer service. All I ask is a little hustle and to respect me as a client. If I am buying a home, I figure the agent is good for a nice commission. Now you as an agent may go through many tire kickers that are not serious. You may have many expenses related to the business. You may have your own family obligations as well.

I was in search of investment property in the Panhandle of Florida. I had found one broker through their informative website. I sent an email conducting an inquiry. Several weeks later, I received a call from her husband who called and asked if he could be of assistance. I told him that I had sent the email a few weeks ago. He apologized and said that they had experienced some computer issues.

I had already made contact with another agent who sounded very energetic and passionate. I specifically asked her about a particular new property that was proposed. I asked several questions concerning when they were planning to break ground, the anticipated completion and occupancy dates and how far was the walk to the beach. She said these were good questions and she would check on those items and get back to me. She reminded me of a young golden retriever, who I threw the Frisbee out to fetch. She dashed off, picked up the Frisbee and kept going. I never heard from her. Several months later, I received a group email from her. I asked that she delete me from that list.

When I was left standing alone, I then called another agent. She was in a meeting and in whispered tones promised to call me back. She took my number and I am still waiting.

Upon the recommendation of a fellow who I rented a condominium from, I called his agent. I invested eight hundred bucks to travel from home. I would say that was a serious looker. I had made contact with the agent who had come recommended to me. He had initially said he might have a problem meeting me the Labor Day weekend. I assured him I only wanted to see a few preselected properties on the Friday afternoon. Period no more. He agreed on those terms and wrote down my parameters of interests.

After the agent failed to keep in contact with me, I tracked him down less than forty-eight hours prior to my arrival. I had already pulled up the MLS listings and narrowed the list to six properties. He informed me on short notice that he had a conflict. He handed me off to an associate. This is not necessarily bad, and I have had this happen before on several occasions without any worries.

When I arrived after a seven hour trip, she was thirty minutes late. I should have been suspicious when her cell phone had a different area code. Come to find out, she had just moved to the area and was still living in a RV park with out of state tags on her car. I had to direct her to the interested properties, all of which I had provided to her the day before. Needless to say, I was very annoyed.

I fired off an email upon my return to voice my displeasure. It was as diplomatic as one could expect. The lead agent never replied and the pinch hitter sent a response apologizing and promised to be better prepared. I liked her and decided that since she showed some backbone to fight for my business, I would give her a second chance. I sent a follow-up email informing her of my decision. I did not receive a response. I resent it a couple of weeks later and received a rejected notice that the email was no longer in operation.

I then made contact with another agent who promised to keep me up to date on new offerings. The next time I called him to inquire about a property, he told me they were having a lottery that day for the existing units. I asked him what it was going to take for someone to take my money. He felt bad and did show me some properties. By now, I knew I was priced out of the market and above my spending limit. For the long term, it worked out well as the market collapsed.

I was astounded that not one of six real estate agents in one small town was willing to take my money. Unfortunately, it demonstrated how bad customers could be treated and not valued. Not one of them asked me any personal questions. They did not attempt to develop any relationship. They did not ask me my occupation, why I liked the Panhandle, or anything about my family.

I can only assume that at that time, business was so good, they did not have to extend good service or develop relationships. I wonder how that is working for them now and how many of those are still making a living in sales. They failed to consider the future and lay the foundation for future long-term success.

I understand there are professional lookie loos. They are never going to buy anything. You see them at all the open houses. They are always looking for an excuse to knock down a property and come up with an excuse as why this house is not right. They might be looking for interior design opportunities.

On the other hand, you have the dreamers that keep showing up looking at the same car, or RV, or boat. You do not mind investing time, but at what expense. Time that could be spent at home or at your son's ball game, or a friends party, but do you want to waste time on someone that is not serious?

It is up to you to vet the seriousness of the purchaser. Everyone wants to scoop the cream off the surface. Remember the process to churn it into cream. Be kind and courteous to those folks. You never know when they will hit the lottery or refer one of their friends or relatives to you. Treat them with respect.

It may take a few extra minutes to display some genuine concern. Remember the Levinson study of doctors. Three extra minutes is all it took to establish the rapport with patients.

Make sure you take copious notes and file them. It is terrible when you write the notes on a napkin or scribble on one of the four hundred bright yellow post-its stuck to your desk so you will not lose it. When you return calls, you will have the file and notes in front of you for easy reference. When a person calls you, you can recall their information.

When my wife was speaking to our car salesperson months after the purchase, he inquired as to my health and said he had read up on the condition. He displayed genuine concern and empathy. He is going to have the inside track for the next vehicle purchase.

How serious are the buyers. Ask them what is their time frame? How they answer is critical to determine how much time to invest. Look them straight in the eye when you ask. If they shift their eyes away and look at their spouse while crossing their arms or bridging their fingers together and give an ahhhh answer or a nine-month pregnant pause, then they are tire kickers. An ahhh answer is instead of a definitive yes. They are delaying the falsehood and say, "Ahhhh (they are thinking and researching the creative side of the brain that comes up with fabrications) are we serious about buying, well I don't know if we are ready, but we are looking." They never answered. They have thrown up more flak than the bombers faced in the war. If the answer about their time frame starts with, "Welllll, (going into the creative side of the brain again) we are serious (about what) we haven't completely decided (nor will you ever) we were thinking in the next 6 months or so (or so? That means never) Of course if the right deal comes along we would have to jump on it (yeah right and I have some swampland for sale).

You have to jettison these folks quicker than the shuttle getting rid of a fuel cell. At some time in the future, they may become serious buyers, like if they win the lottery or Aunt Sophie dies and leaves her collection of rare china and costume jewelry. You do not want to blow out that tire they are kicking.

Get their email and forward periodic emails of interest. Put them on your newsletter and calendar distribution list. You remember what it was like to give the heave-ho to a one-date wonder. You did not want to hurt their feelings, but you needed to get back to fishing for Mister or Miss Right. They may come around some day and get serious. You do not want to alienate them, but you do not and cannot waste your precious time.

I overheard a couple walking through a model home and talking with the sales representative. Keep in mind we were in the funk of the real estate crash, but the market had stabilized and in fact sales had improved, but not the pricing. The customer threw out a Jell-O bid of fifty thousand below the sticker on a three hundred thousand dollar house. I chuckled to my wife. The sales agent diplomatically informed the buyer that the homes had been slashed a hundred thousand dollars from their peak. Were these customers serious?

Why do some people get married five or six times? Why do some people suck up to the boss? Why do some people bear their souls to a total stranger like a news reporter? It is the burning inner desire for acceptance, love, and closeness. We all want a relationship with others. Almost every person wants to develop a relationship with others. They may not know it. If you can exploit that human desire, you can start asking the bank for preferred customer status because of all your large deposits.

From the earliest days of human existence, survival was based on togetherness. You hunted, ate and gathered as a group. This is the same "herd mentality" displayed by animals. It is essential for survival. If cast as an outsider, chances of enduring and surviving through a lonely existence were greatly diminished. This is why we all crave acceptance and inclusion by the group.

In the initial conversation, you must develop a relationship with the client. When being on the receiving end of business relationships, I have found a large failure rate in this area. This will cement the loyalty of the client. God gave us one mouth and two ears for a purpose. Most people love to talk about themselves. I am not talking about you as the professional, I am talking about the client.

When you listen, be an active listener. You may not care to listen, but you had better give the impression that you do. Ask some questions that sound like you care. I do not have anything in common with them. Every time I engage someone in a conversation, I am ALWAYS looking for some commonality. This is the beginning of developing a relationship.

Use the FORM method with new clients to get to know them. FORM is Family, Occupation/Origin, Recreation/Religion, and Main Interests or money. Ask questions related to these topics and you are guaranteed to plant the initial seeds of success. You are striving for a common bond.

You want to become their friends. The Irish have a saying, "That two travelers shorten the road travelled." I know some business professionals that have no desire to be your friend. They want to maintain a business relationship. I am not talking about having them over for a barbeque. How many deals are brokered on the golf course or through networking? Seventy percent is the figure widely quoted. You have to be likeable. People are more likely to say yes to a friend then a stranger.

If you think about your arrival at the front desk of most hotels, they will greet you with a smile and friendly greeting. They are very nice and will usually call you by your name. They are creating the impression of the home away from home. Sometimes when they get busy, their brains start to short circuit and they fail to treat everyone with the empathy they deserve. It can be volatile with harried travelers anxiously waiting for their room.

I have conducted a great deal of business with the hospitality industry over my career. As a result of bringing in large groups, I dealt primarily with the sales staff. I can tell you, that their jobs are dependent on ingratiating themselves with you. They are some of the nicest people you would ever want to meet. In very few instances, did I find someone that was not competent at their job. They always expressed an interest in me and asked questions.

Everyone likes mystery movies and books. Spy novels are big hits. Why? People like to be amateur sleuths. They like to figure out what happens before the end. In the business development phase, this is your chance to play detective. Sherlock Holmes is on the case. Ask questions. Conduct the interview of the suspect. This time you are questioning a client, a future business associate or just a conversational partner.

Chapter 57
Talk!

I discussed this briefly, but it is so simple, I would like to discuss it more detail. The FORM method is a quick and easy way to remember how to engage people in conversation. I did not come up with this. I learned this at several different sales seminars over the years.

Family – Married? How many children? Ages? Spouse and children's interests/activities? How long have they been married?

Occupation – find out what they do and make their occupation sound like the most important job. This is not a lot of smoke either. I value everyone's contribution to the economy or the community. If you are not sure of what their job is, ask them a lot of open-ended questions to explain. What exactly does a real estate agent do? It must be very rewarding to help people find their dream homes. How long have you been an agent? What did you do before this job? You must be sincere in your questions, or you risk being identified as superficial.

Religion/Recreation. Religion can be a minefield. If they bring it up and they are of the same faith go ahead. If they attend the same house of worship, you have established commonality. Most times, examining religion is more dangerous than ascending Mount Everest.

What do they like to do for fun? Dancing, golf, tennis, scrapbooking, Bunco, hiking, etc. Where do they go on vacation? Ask those active listening and open-ended questions.

Main Interests/Money – This can be tricky as well. Some of this relates to the current economy and financial status. This can be like sailing on a stormy day. You are exploring the source of their income. You are also attempting to identify their passions. What makes them get out of bed in the morning.

All of these questions allow you to develop a relationship with the client and become likeable. Find something in common. Do not sound like Joe Friday interrogating a witness. Ask the questions softly and blend them into the conversation. It provides the client the sense that you are interested in them and respect them as people, not just a paycheck.

Avoid talking too much. We have all heard the "Chatty Cathy" that figures the more information they throw at you the more informed you would be. Unfortunately, people become sensory overloaded, become impatient and lose attention. You can see the drift in their eyes as they start focusing on happy hour or the steak they will enjoy later that night. Less is more. If they ask questions, respond with succinct sentences.

At Toastmasters International meetings, someone will count the space filler words. An example is ahhh or ummm. This great organization will assist you not just in public speaking, but conversational speaking as well. Sometimes we invoke these tactics to delay the answers. Quite often, they are bad speech habits that we have fallen into and we are not aware that we are saying them.

Along the same lines is the use of a pregnant pause. It helps us to gather our thoughts, but quite often, our conversational partner is wondering if we stepped out to lunch during the pause. The pregnant pause can be used quite effectively to make a point. At the end of statement that we want to emphasize, pause a moment, to let it sink into the audience.

Tom Clancy, the noted novelist, enjoys writing epic length books. I used to read them until I ran out of time. In *The Patriot*, he spent four pages describing a commercial flight from London to the U.S. I figured that as much time as he was spending on the transatlantic journey that something big was going to happen. Nothing. All souls landed safely on the ground. Four pages could have been reduced to one paragraph. As a reader, I was annoyed at the loss of time. It had limited value on the movement of the story.

Stories make excellent visual representations. Remember back to school as we listened to a teacher. The most memorable instructors were conversational in their delivery and weaved stories into the dialogue. Depending on the setting, the more relaxed your approach, the easier your message is received. Stories blended into the conversation provide some strength to the message and make it more memorable. People will often forget statistics provided by the lecturer, but they will remember the stories. The most widely read book in the world, the Bible, uses fables to deliver the message.

Do not make the stories long and boring. There was one fellow I knew that if you asked what time it was, he would tell you how the clock was built and the transition of timekeeping starting from the sundial. He had great institutional knowledge and intelligence, but people would avoid him like the swine flu. I felt sorry for him, because he was nice, but people did not want to make time. As a result, he was lonely.

Listen Listen Listen. I cannot stress this enough. Men tend to be poor listeners. When you listen, it helps to retain and absorb like a sponge. When the time comes, you can squeeze the sponge and retrieve the information. You should be listening three times more than you talk.

Do not just give that blank stare into oblivion. Nod to let them know you are alive and give an occasional verbal confirmation that you are still there. An ahah, oh really, no kidding. Every now and then, ask an inquiring question.

Remember most people are not looking out for you. They are looking at what is best for them. If they can perceive that you are interested in them, this will build trust that is paramount to success. There are only a few times that you can get by without trust. You are not going to make a major investment without the trust in the person representing the product, the company that stands behind the product and the product itself.

Most people are looking for. "What is in it for me." No matter whom I was speaking with, I always tried to present my conversation from their point of view. This was not about me, it was about them. If it was a suspect, I was trying to explain that it was in their best interest to confess. Why would they do that? I had already convinced them that I knew everything about them except the size of their prison jumpsuit. Those that cooperate would get credit by the judge for acceptance of responsibility, which could reduce their sentence.

I always stand in the flip-flops of the person standing before me. I treat them with respect. I learned this while on the police department. It did not matter if they were a witness, a victim, or a suspect, I treated them with respect. In ninety nine percent of the cases, they would reciprocate that respect back to me. This did not occur in some boardroom, but on the inner city streets of some of the most violent neighborhoods in America. People in three-piece suits all the way down to t-shirts and shorts, will respond positively if you treat them with respect.

I did not care if they were living in squalor and were junkies. They were human beings that normally would respond positively to a police officer that displayed respect and humility. I still had to maintain authority, but I could do so with humility.

Chapter 58
Stand in their Flip Flops

One evening I initiated a traffic stop. As I turned my blue lights on, the driver pulled into the parking lot of Krispy Kreme Donuts, the cops' favorite. I had hoped the driver would turn down the side street off the busy thoroughfare.

I retrieved the driver's license and returned to my squad car. The manager of the donut shop came out and asked me to move off his parking lot. I told him in clear language to go back inside and I would talk to him after I concluded the business at hand.

After I finished, I met with the manger in his office. I apologized for stopping in his lot and I told him that my initial strategy was not successful. I told him I understood that he was concerned with access to his parking lot. I then proceeded to tell him that once the driver had stopped, I was concerned with telling him to relocate because the driver could have second thoughts and flee or brandish a firearm that he had not employed, endangering everyone.

I also told him that his customers should have felt safe with my presence, and any customer that felt uncomfortable should not be the type of customer he would want. On top of that, my lights were attracting attention to his business and might actually generate some extra attention from the motoring public, who had become used to the mundane.

He was a good listener and said he had not looked at the events from that perspective and he was sorry he had interrupted and became a distraction. He offered a free donut as a peace pipe. Being a cop, I could not turn down such a peace offering of a delicious warm cream covered yeast treat.

It is not what I want. It is about what they want. If I can demonstrate to them that their need is important to me, then most times everything will fall in place. I stand in their flip-flops!

When questioning, you might ask a simple question such as, "Where are you from?" You want to avoid the tennis volley.

"I am from Boston."

"Why did you move?"

"My job."

"What kind of work are you in?"

"Sales."

Now, let us start over. "Where are you from?"

"Boston."

"Oh really, I have heard a lot about Boston, how do you like living here compared to Boston."

"How does your family like it here?"

You want to convey that you would like to know more and they are of interest to you. Really? No kidding, is that right, go on, what did they say, or you mirror the last few words.

You may be in a similar situation in which, someone is fishing in your pond. Not everyone is going to be as adept as you are at conversational skills. If they ask, "Where are you from?" Help them out. Tell them and add a sentence or two such as, "I am from New Orleans, it really has a lot of history and character to it, but I really enjoy living in Florida. How about you, where are you from, or have you ever been to New Orleans?"

Hold off on the colloquialisms. Have you heard one of your friends overuse the valley language? "Like dude, like I am the only dude that can like do this." I read an interview of Miley Cyrus in Parade Magazine. I lost count of the times she used the word dude. Perhaps she only used the word a few times in an hour-long conversation, but those few quotes suggested she overused the word dude.

Remember to maintain eye contact sixty to seventy percent of the time when listening. Do not look past the person. I have seen this quite a few times. It is what I call the "zombie look." It might be something has popped into their mind, but whatever the reason, you have lost their attention. You can choose to end the conversation or draw them back in with a question or their opinion. You do not want to quiz them if they have been listening. Help them out and throw them a life preserver. Suppose you are talking about orchids and they are drifting. "What do you think? Have you ever had an orchid get a fungus?" They can answer safely with a no. It brings their atmospheric mind back to earth.

There was one person whom I had quite a few conversations. Most of the time I could see him drift off. In his case, life was always about him. He had little concern with others input, unless he needed help. I noticed most of his conversations were one way. He controlled the floor. I kept my interactions as short as possible.

Harvard psychologists, Matthew A. Killingsworth and Daniel T. Gilbert, conducted a study on the wandering mind. Using an iPhone app, they contacted 2,250 participants concerning their level of happiness, current activity, and what they were thinking about. On average, the respondents reported that their minds were wandering 46.9 percent of time. They were focused less than 30 percent of the time during every activity, except making love. Therefore, if your partner looks like they are out to lunch and not paying attention, you are probably right.

Prepare as much as you can. Those that fail to plan, plan to fail. You must strive for success. Go back to the preparation section. If I am going into a group meeting and there was a group email, I will go back and see the list of recipients to remind me of their names, so that I can quickly recall them as we greet.

When you are speaking, try to throw some metaphors and similes. They help people visualize. It was so humid, it was like being slapped with a wet blanket across the face. You can now feel the humidity. It was hotter than the July asphalt in Las Vegas.

Novelists are taught to show, don't tell. Some writers enjoy a greater success in this department. Good writers describe a scene in such a way, so that you can feel the scene with two or more senses. The old creaky house smelled like a stale ashtray. You can picture and smell it. You do not want to salt every sentence like that. Sometimes it best to use them like pepper, sparingly. When you do use them, it adds color and interest to your story. Stay away from clichés. They are overused and boring.

Avoid the negatives. No one wants to be around a Dismal Dan. You never know when they may have a connection to the negative. The world is small and getting smaller through email and the electronic age. One of my best email buddies, who lives in Kentucky, turned out to be a student of two instructors I interacted with and a close friend to one of my former classmates and roommate. I did not learn these tidbits until months into our friendship. As time went on, we found several other mutual acquaintances.

The field goal kicker is faced with hitting the fifty-one yard field goal with five seconds on the clock to win the game. The coach can tell the kicker to not miss it. The brain might latch on to the "miss." The coach could have said, "I have confidence in your ability to be successful and win the game." Will it guarantee success? No, but it is putting on a positive spin. My oldest daughter gave me a coffee cup she made with the saying, "Life is not about waiting for the storm to pass. It is about learning to dance in the rain."

Talk of yourself succinctly. Stay away from dropping the I-Bombs. I am the greatest. Say just enough about yourself to express your credentials. It is easy to hear someone tell a story and you have one that matches that story or tops it. Think, is this really going to be that important for the success of this conversation.

I trust your mother passed along good manners. Etiquette used to be very important, but society has eased up on the social graces. Please and thank you, have not been dismissed and should be used abundantly.

If you make a mistake, say you are sorry and accept responsibility. It does not matter if it is not your fault. Step up to the plate. The buck stops here. Many people assume a, "deflect, defend, and no responsibility attitude."

A server apologizes for an undercooked meal that the cook ruined. I had the occasion once, when a server tried to tell me the ground beef was cooked thoroughly and that I was mistaken because the sauce colored the meat. Wrong answer.

Now, I always try to minimize someone's conduct to put them at ease. For example, if there is a problem with the meal and the waiter apologizes, I will usually say something about it is not their fault, they did not cook the meal. If they brought the wrong meal out, I might say, perhaps it is my fault. I may not have made it clear, which item I wanted.

You must learn to emphasize with their position. Stand in their flip-flops and look at the world from their viewpoint. This is a must. So many arguments could be avoided, if you would just look from their perspective.

One of Zig Ziglar's great quotes is, "You can have everything in life you want if you will just help other people get what they want." Put the other people first and make them feel important. So many people in today's narcissistic world only look out for themselves. You want to avoid being like the street named One-Way. Make it a two way street and stand in their flip-flops.

Chapter 59
Training & Service

The DePaul Center for Sales Leadership conducts a survey of a wide variety of businesses every two years to determine key aspects of their sales organization. The last published survey is dated 2008. The businesses fall into Professional Services, Manufacturing, Wholesale, Financial Services and Healthcare. One surprising aspect is that thirty percent of the firms provided no training to their new employees. It was left to OJT (on the job training).

Over fifty percent of the companies failed to provide follow-up training to reinforce the entry training. That is like flushing dollar bills down the drain. With computer access, there is no excuse for not providing training through online modules or DVD's. Seventy percent of the respondents reported employee turnover rates were highest in the first two years. Is this due to a lack of training and follow-up?

If you owned a sailboat, would you allow a friend to take it out for a cruise who had never been sailing? No, of course not. Every day, businesses across the country are deploying employees without the proper training or follow-up. They should all take the lead of the Ritz Carlton that provides a week of training for all employees including hourly employees. The Ritz Carlton premier name brand is synonymous with service.

Service

According to research conducted on behalf of the National Retail Foundation by BIGresearch, eighty five percent of consumers said that they spend and shop more at retailers who provide good service. Good news travels fast, as eighty two percent expressed that they are likely to recommend these retailers to friends and family. Nordstrom's is consistently one of the top retailers when it comes to satisfaction.

In the grocery market, Publix a Southeastern chain, is known for their motto, "Where shopping is a pleasure." They may not be the cheapest, but you can almost guarantee excellent service. They want the customer happy. Those happy customers return with money in their pockets.

Compare that experience with one time I was in a New York deli. The customer in front of me ordered a dozen bagels and then added a request for an additional onion bagel. The clerk placed the bag on the counter. When the customer was affirming the inclusion of the onion bagel, the clerk began to argue with her that she had not made the request. This went back and forth, as only two New Yorkers could. My thought was that in the time he took to argue with the customer, he could have apologized and placed the bagel in the bag.

It is a Wrap

You have started with making a good first impression and preparing for your interaction. Your eyes are observing and looking for common points of interest. You have avoided the I-Bombs and engaged in active listening. You have mimicked some of their actions. You have become aware of some of the body language that can convey the wrong message, for both you and your recipient. Now you know how to talk to people and ask the correct questions to obtain the information that you need to be successful. We are almost to the end, but we must put the icing on the cake and address a couple of areas that are often overlooked.

Chapter 60
Follow-up

It amazes me when I watch people who fail to utilize the resources at hand. Such as sales professionals who discard past customers like a bad habit. They spend all this money in website development, or mailers and the like. Meanwhile they could spend a portion of that staying in touch with a satisfied customer.

Most people buy a car every five to six years. With the recent economic slide, home ownership might change but most people move every five years. If you had an aunt that promised to send a few thousand dollars to you in five years, would you keep her on your Christmas card list and maybe give her a phone call once a year? Maybe you would even send a fruitcake during the holidays.

Avoid the shallow obligatory email. Think of how it will be received. Emotions are difficult to transmit through email or twitter. I was on sick leave, I received one email that made an inquiry, and the proverbial if you need anything call. This email was not from someone I considered a close friend. I responded with a thanks and some lighthearted conversation. No follow-up. That told me he felt obligated to send the message and really did not care. I recently received an email from a sales person. It was a form thank you. They attempted to make it more personable with a couple of changes. Those changes were in a different font. Oops. It was still better than no response.

After the meeting

Keep in touch with your new client. Email makes it so easy. Seek their input and feedback. Do not crowd them. After the initial nice to meet you email, give them a week or so. No more than ten days. Feel them out as to if they have any questions. If they ask a question, then respond within forty-eight hours with an answer or that you are still researching. People spend half their time in email deleting spam, you do not want to be considered a spammer.

One neighborhood organizer, who was very passionate on their mission, sent out daily emails. Sometimes there were multiple in a day. The delete key received a lot of work. I stopped reading them after awhile. Every one of the emails was marked important. Please! Delete again.

I knew of one office manager for a business that sent out copious emails to the employees. She could have consolidated the thoughts, in a single email. She was one of those that enjoys firing from the hip. As the thoughts crossed the synapses, she hit the send key. Her emails became white noise and easily ignored. Her employees quickly lost interest and hit the delete key.

Thank you cards

This is the most overlooked and cheapest investment. I cannot stress this as "The Most" overlooked aspect of the follow-up. We had purchased a vehicle for one of my children. I never received a single follow-up from the two salespersons.

A year later, I returned to Century Buick and could not remember the salesperson's name. Perhaps if they had followed-up with us, the name recognition would have been strengthened. I made contact with another salesperson, Steve Davis who did an outstanding job. We stopped in the lot several times over a three-month basis. Steve was always there to show a genuine interest in us.

After the sale, Steve called us several times to confirm our pleasure with our new vehicle. Then we received a handwritten card with a photograph of us standing in front our new vehicle. Steve's name is cemented in our mind and if I can, I will toss any business his way.

I conducted a great deal of business with the hotel industry. Most times, we would exchange business cards. I made it a point to send an email to the sales representative when I returned to the office. It allowed them to paste my contact information directly into their email contacts. It was short and sweet, but made a point to establish a personal bond.

On one occasion, Carlos Quilles of the Sheraton, responded quickly to my email. To my surprise, I received a personal handwritten note a few days later in the mail from Carlos. In this day and time, it displayed an extra effort on his part. He separated himself from the herd. I was more than happy to throw some business his direction when the opportunity came up. That card which cost less than a dollar, generated four thousand dollars in business within a month.

The handwritten card is much more personal than a preprinted or email. It takes a few minutes to write it and demonstrates your interest in them. Have a box at the ready and do it immediately. If you hit the pause button and procrastinate, it will never happen.

When we went on a tour of Florida State University, we received a handwritten thank you card from our tour guide. Considering that every day, they had at least twenty people on each tour. I was impressed. Compare that with the tour at the University in Virginia. We travelled from out of state and did not receive as much as a form email.

Stay in Touch

If the client has made an offer or made a purchase, keep in touch. Email is a great mode of communication. Leave a voicemail or talk to them. Let them know they are not forgotten. Keep them informed as to the status of negotiations or the delivery of the product. It gives them the feeling that you care and respect them.

A couple of times, I was shocked when we received a follow-up call from a surgeon or hospital. They wanted to make sure the patient was progressing and to answer any questions. It has not happened too often, but each time was memorable.

I know there are probably some clients, who hound you to death with questions. I realize that can be frustrating, but keep in mind that you will make money off this client and the next client hopefully will be different. If that client likes you, the chances are, they will refer you to someone else.

I had one friend who listed their home with a large real estate agent and team. Every time you turned around you saw their picture on billboards and ads. My friend was very disappointed with their service. They were too big and busy to follow up. Messages were left and not returned. Perhaps our friend was a nuisance. I do not know. However, because of their bad experience, I would not use that realtor.

In baseball if you fail to follow through on your swing, you may miss the ball completely or if you make contact, it could be a dribbler to the mound and an easy out at first. In golf if you fail to follow through with your swing, you will fail to achieve maximum benefit. The same holds true for the interview follow-through.

Take care of your repeat customers. It does not have to be expensive. For example: gift certificates, tickets to a ball game, a basket of fruit, flowers, etc. In one apartment, we moved into, the management gave us a basket of spaghetti, sauce, and a bottle of wine. Another time we had the listing agent, not our agent, give us a very nice basket of coffee, wine, popcorn and candy. In that case our real estate agent gave us nothing, nada, zero. When it comes time to sell my property, who do you think has the inside track? I believe gifts are tax deductible.

Here is another real estate agent tale. Follow-up with the client about a month after they move in and check on them. I had one agent at closing said she would check on us in a couple of weeks. I never heard from her again.

Give them a call. Thank them again. Ask them how everything is going. If they need any suggestions for restaurants, dry cleaners, hair stylist, lawn care, pool service etc. Send those birthday cards, Christmas cards, and calendars. I had one agent brought a Honey Baked Ham to us our first Christmas and a tin of Danish cookies the second year. The ham cost somewhere around forty dollars and the cookies were no more than ten dollars, but it was a genuine heartfelt gift. That agent made in excess of fifty thousand dollars off me from a home purchase, a home sale, as well as countless referrals. Not bad for a fifty dollar investment.

After a charity event that I organized, I would always send a thank card to each sponsor. It was personalized. I would personally drop off extra t-shirts from the event and visit with each sponsor thanking them again. I would also provide a certificate of appreciation. The next year, I walked into one of the previous year's sponsor and they had that certificate framed on the wall.

As I was retiring, a supervisor from one of the local police departments called me to wish me well. I was humbled by his generous praise. He also thanked me for a certificate of appreciation from eight years earlier that was still displayed in their squad room. As he said, it may not have cost much, but it meant a lot to him.

No matter what business you are involved in, you must be fully engaged and follow to the end. Follow-up and check back every step of the way. Never assume everyone else has done his or her job. You do not have to be a micromanager, but you had better be omniscient.

Having been in charge of a number of charity events, I had to delegate certain tasks. I always followed up and maintained occasional checks to ensure everything was on schedule. This was especially true with food vendors. There were several times, I checked back with a company that was donating food, only to find the person who had agreed to the donation had left the business, or they had no record of the request and agreement. One time, I had to replay a voicemail detailing the agreement.

After one of my trips to another field office, I sent an email to the office manager thanking her and her staff for their assistance. They were just merely doing their job, but they were very accommodating to me. After I sent the email, I received a quick response. She thanked me for the email and said it was the first one she had ever received. It made me feel good. Consider also, if I ever returned, they would probably treat me like royalty, but that was not my intent.

One of my former students had enrolled at St. Leo University in the small hamlet of San Antonio, Florida. She was from Belgium. I inquired as to why she chose this school and why she came from so far away. She told me it was due to the follow-up by the school after every step of the application process. This engagement and oversight reaffirmed to her parents that their daughter would be looked after.

If you get letters of appreciation, the first thing is to respond quickly via the same method. Email to email or mail to mail. I cannot tell you the number of times that I have sent letters of appreciation and gratitude with no response. I assume they received it, but perhaps not. One time I called Disney to see if they received a letter. They said that they received so many they did not have the staff to properly respond. In the future, I no longer bothered.

In this age of digital footprints and long lasting tails, non-professional reviewers have a huge input. According to a survey from Opinion Research Corporation, sixty one percent of respondents reported consulting online reviews, blogs, and other sources of online customer feedback before making a purchase. At least eighty-three percent of respondents reported that online product evaluations and reviews had at least some influence on their buying decision. Do not underestimate the impact of online reviews.

When purchasing textbooks through Amazon, we look closely at the reviews of the merchants. After being satisfied with one seller with a ninety-eight percent approval rate, we placed a time sensitive order. Our order was immediately confirmed and charged to our credit card. The book never showed up. Four emails to the seller were ignored and we filed a complaint with Amazon. Our credit card company promptly charged the seller back and we posted a dissatisfied approval. A subsequent buyer followed suit with a similar experience. I am sure for the near term, those two postings will hurt their future sales or at least give pause to the buyer. It could have been that the seller had some health issues or personal problems, which caused a temporary decrease in his performance.

Take care of your relationships and value everyone that enters your life. You never know where that connection will lead you. As Mitch Joel, the author of, *Six Pixels of Separation: Everyone Is Connected. Connect Your Business to Everyone* said, "If Facebook were a country, it would have the sixth largest population in the world." The world has become smaller and we are all connected by the good and the bad. Your choice is which one do you want your reputation based upon.

Chapter 61
Ethics

At a recent TEDx conference in Tampa, the noted intellectual property lawyer, Brent Britton spoke of the successful companies in today's current marketplace. He said they are focusing on making their employees and customers "delightfully happy as a business model."

Think of any business you have dealt with. You know the ones that actually enjoy their jobs and have passion. I am not talking about casual Friday. I am talking about seven days a week you treat your most valued asset with dignity and fairness. You promote the enjoyment of work that transcends to treating customers with distinction that leads to profits.

Cornell University conducted a study of 320 small businesses to determine the practice of autonomy. Half were viewed as more traditional top down closed management, while half relied on more autonomy in their management style. Those businesses that provided more autonomy to their employees grew four times faster and experienced a third of the turnover of employees.

How Full Is Your Bucket? was written by Tom Rath and Donald O. Clifton, Ph.D. They cited the number-one reason most Americans leave their jobs is they feel unappreciated. In a survey, they concluded that 65% of the workers received no recognition for good work in the last year.

People have often asked me what is the key to my success in my long-standing marriage. My answer is the three leaf Irish shamrock. Just as St. Patrick used the shamrock to teach the trinity, I use the clover to illustrate the three most important aspects of my marriage. My answer is trust, communication, and loyalty. The same principles can be applied toward the business ethics model.

How often are these key elements missing from all relationships. Often employees become afflicted with what has been coined, employee disengagement. Gallup estimates that the cost to U.S. business is $300 billion dollars in lost productivity. Disengaged employees are more willing to pick up the telephone and call in sick or take a mental health day, or lack of loyalty to the organization. This relates directly with the leadership of the organization from the top to the bottom.

Dr. Wayne Hochwarter, the Jim Moran Professor of Management in the Florida State University College of Business has studied the effects of leadership in the workplace. In a July 08, 20111 *Business News Daily* article he said, "More than 40 percent of the 400 mid-level employees surveyed said they wouldn't acknowledge their boss if they ran into each other on the street." On the good side, sixty percent would say hello. The results are still dismal. What percentage do you fall into if you saw your boss at the grocery store?

Communication is a two way street. Leaders can easily say they have an open door policy, but do little to foster and encourage that philosophy. I heard of a story of one manager who was so frustrated at his staff attempting to filter input that they removed their office door to encourage communication.

Management should be conducting regular meetings at least on a monthly basis. Informative emails should be the norm not the exception. Input should be sought and accepted from the trenches. These people are on the frontlines and the face of the business.

They will be the first to observe weaknesses and can provide problem-solving input and mitigate issues prior to hurting the bottom line. Communication is essential to developing trust with employees and clients.

Our first encounter and the determination of trust is often based on the first impression. That is until our brain has processed the initial data. That trust line will move up or down depending on the initial interaction. At church or a neighborhood gathering, your trust of another person would be high, unless you had a previous negative interaction. In a job interview, the initial meeting would have a normal trust setting. In a sales meeting, your trust setting could be lowered because of a previous bad experience, the reluctance to spend money, or concerns of being taken advantage.

When we first meet people, we want to be liked and trusted. We know not everyone is trustworthy. Trust begins with you. What are you projecting? Conscience is what you do when no one is looking.

According to a Harris Interactive Poll, trust by the American public is eroding. No shock. Only one quarter believe in the credibility of banks and a whopping ninety-six percent distrust Wall Street. The government is distrusted by seventy six percent of those polled. Compare that with 92% approval rating for supermarkets. Ethics is the basis of credibility.

The Reumedoctor.com reported that 42.7 percent of all resumes had inaccuracies. Some of these could have been honest mistakes on the dates of employment, but other errors were more egregious. The former CEO of Radio Shack was fired when discrepancies were found in his resume. He had claimed to possess two degrees when he had not earned either. Yahoo's CEO Scott Thompson, also fell victim to resume fraud.

While investigating mortgage fraud I would continue to shake my head at egregious conduct of all of those involved in the mortgage process. I will provide the caveat that the majority of those involved in the loan process performed their tasks with a true sense of fiduciary responsibility.

I found loan officers that confirmed employment through making connection with voicemails. Outrageous income and asset statements that were taken on face value. Many of the folks applying for loans were seeking wealth with the anticipation of never ending appreciation and equity stakes of real estate investments. A number of folks employed in the loan process usurped their financial responsibility for the sake of added commissions and profits.

The stories I read and heard in interviews would spin your head. Cutting and pasting of loan information, intentionally over or under evaluating property, obtaining straw buyers to perpetuate the fraud and outright falsification of loan documents.

I investigated the same occurrence in the 1990's during the savings and loan debacles. Directors and friends of these banks gave a simple wink and a nod to approval of loans on overvalued real estate. As a result, banks failed, employees were dismissed and investors lost money. It is hard for me to believe that in less than two decades the vicious cycle repeated itself.

To achieve success, you must have intelligence, common sense, determination, passion, character, and integrity. The bedrock of those ingredients is integrity. Without integrity, your character will be a façade that will crumble. No matter how smart you are, how much common sense you possess and how driven you are, without character, your success will be limited and temporary.

According to the 2009 Edelman Trust Barometer, 91% of consumers indicated they purchased a product or service from a company that you trust. While 77% refused to conduct purchases from distrusted companies.

While we watched the collapse of J.P. Morgan, Bernie Madoff, Enron etc, you have to wonder if those leeches were to use a simple gauge of conduct, would they have operated with such malice and intent while engaged in such reckless conduct. The simple barometer would be, "What would your parents think and or what would your children or grandchildren think." In law enforcement, we called it the Washington Post Rule. Would you want what you did reported above the fold on the Washington Post?

I knew of one single mother who had raised her son and worked hard to afford him the education that propelled him towards the top of the business world. He became the president of the bank and his mother beamed with pride. That is until he was convicted of bank fraud and sent off to the penitentiary. Not only was his mother humiliated, but also his kids were exposed to the embarrassment of their father being arrested and their fellow students laughing at them. As Lou Holtz said, "Do right."

Trust is not a single event. Trust is built upon a consistent delivery of services, products, and communications. McDonalds may not be considered the best culinary experience, but you know every time you pull into McDonalds, you know exactly what to expect through their consistent delivery of food and service.

Toyota built their reputation of trust by a loyal customer base, who counted on a consistent and reliable product. That trust was destroyed because of an inconsistent product and false statements. It takes a lifetime to develop trust, but it can all be lost in a moment, due to irresponsibility.

I always prided myself on being truthful. I never sold a bill of goods or made promises that I could not keep. I laugh at TV shows where the homicide detective promises the victims family they will bring the killer to justice. That is a bold statement as the homicide clearance rate stands around sixty-five percent. Never make a promise you cannot fulfill.

In dealing with informants, I was always up front with them concerning the anticipation of financial incentives. I told them their identity could not always be protected. I would try my best, but many times the criminals could figure it out and sometimes their public testimony was necessary.

I also never ever made promises concerning judicial sentences. I would tell cooperating suspects that I was willing to discuss their case and request lenience with the prosecutor. I never ever arrested a person that I was not one hundred percent convinced was guilty of committing that crime. I slept well at night. If there were doubts, I would rather a person be allowed to be free, than wrongfully arrested.

President Theodore Roosevelt was quoted as saying, "To educate a person in mind and not in morals is to educate a menace to society." In today's society, ethics is quite often shoved aside in pursuit of profits. Colleges and high schools routinely do not require ethics classes to graduate.

Chuck Colson, former Special Counsel to Richard Nixon and author of *Against the Night* wrote, "A nation ... cannot stand unless it is populated by people who will act on the motives superior to their own immediate interest." It seems that every day, somewhere in the country some businessperson is indicted for corruption after betraying their employees and investors for personal gain.

I frequented a pizzeria when I lived in Virginia. Due to his success, the owner opened a second store about five miles away. He gave it a different name. I asked him why he did not call the store number two. He told me that his name brought honor to his family. He hoped one day to hand the business off to his children. He said if the second location did not achieve the same success, he did not want his name being tarnished.

It was a good call. The other location was closer to my house. After a year, he sold the business to the manager of that location. They began to experience customer service problems and customers were treated rudely by the manager, who had become overwhelmed with his responsibilities. I returned to the original pizza man and told him he had maintained the honor of his family name.

Proverbs 22:1 – "A good name is more desirable than great riches; to be esteemed is better than silver or gold." It is amazing to watch the number of politicians and business executives who continually violate their position in pursuit of some self-adulating conduct of entitlement. My heart goes out to the devoted families of these self-absorbed individuals. The question I always ask is, at what point did this sound like a good idea?

Every employee wants to feel that they are an integral part of the business and that their input is valued. When a good performance or goal is achieved, a shout out is warranted. I am not talking about false praise over insignificant events. Folks do not need to be told everyday that they are doing a great job. One of the pitfalls to avoid is when people act like a barking puppy that jumps up and down for everything. If you praise everybody all the time, it becomes like the persistent house down the street with false alarms. The first time it goes off, it draws your attention. After awhile, you do not pay attention and you just roll over and try to go back to sleep. It takes a balance.

If you fail to distribute praise evenly and fairly, it tends to lose its luster. A good job is taken for granted and goes unnoticed. Then you witness someone else garnering all the attention for a minor accomplishment. After awhile, you become disaffected and lose the motivation to please. Why does a dog gallop after a Frisbee and run eagerly back to you? He is looking for praise. The K-9 officer trains his dog on praise and reward. Sometimes our dogs are treated better than people.

D. Michael Abrashoff was the commander of the USS Benfold, a U.S. Navy guided missile destroyer. He wrote an excellent book titled, *It's Your Ship*. He thrived on input from the sailors and developed a team effort to become the highest rated ship in efficiency. He continually brought the ship's fiscal operation under budget, while increasing the retention rate and reenlistments. One way he accomplished this was treating everyone the same way you would want your own child treated. Abrashoff said, "The more I thanked them, the harder they worked." He tried to deliver the message in person. He stepped out of the cave. It is hard for workers to have a bad attitude when the boss is spilling praise. It almost demands loyalty.

In the government or in business there will always be rules and regulations. Most were put in place for a reason. Often they exceed their usefulness and often lack updating. We often become mired in the quagmire of these institutional rules that impedes efficiency, productivity and morale. Question the rules. Why do we do it this way? Is there a better way to get the job done or is it a case of we do it this way because we have always done it this way. Does that make it the right way?

Happy employees make productive employees and lead to satisfied customers and clients. If you have a problem child and you can usually find one, then counsel that individual. I can't tell you how many times I have seen a supervisor either in a group setting or via email, in which they put out a directive attributed to the conduct of that one soiled soul.

The result is that everyone wonders whom the guilty party was that caused the entire class to be rebuked and placed in timeout. The innocents will do some soul searching wondering if they were the cause of the action and it hurts morale.

Meanwhile, the guilty offender is just as clueless and does not think they did anything wrong. The message was never delivered to the intended party. Nothing beats a one on one discussion with the offender.

Doctors have the Hippocratic Oath. Many organizations have a written set of standards of conduct to abide by. Most of the standards are common sense. It is this set of standards and the application of these documents that determine the moral compass, integrity, and ultimately the trust of the person and business.

As the pizza man said, you have to bring honor to your name.

Chapter 62
Conclusion The Tool Box

It takes various tools to complete a project. You cannot change a kitchen sink with just one wrench. The same holds true for communication. The first impression is completed in less than two seconds. You have to portray a likeability factor, and you can only deepen that through careful observation and preparation. Beware of narcissistic tendencies and learn to stand in your conversational partner's flip-flops. Approach all of your contacts with an ethical viewpoint. I hope now you can deepen not just your business relationships, but your personal relationships as well. You are now more aware of what you might be projecting and how you relate to others.

This is an integrative comprehensive approach to interpersonal communications. As we move more towards a digital world, it has become more important to make all our personal interactions count. Quite often, there is no second chance.

Thank you for allowing me to share my experience with you. I hope you find the techniques I discussed, useful to enhancing your personal enrichment and deepening the relationships in your business and personal lives.

Chapter 63
Oh I Forgot The Introduction
(you would have skipped it anyway!)

"The more elaborate our means of communications, the less we communicate."

—Joseph Preistly

Since our earliest existence of huddling in dimly lit caves and foraging for food with clubs, we have been communicating with each other. We can fly a predator drone from thousands of feet above ground. While the drone deciphers the dimples on a golf ball, the pilot sitting in a dark room several thousand miles away, can launch a precision laser guided missile into the intended target. Despite our advancement in technology, we still have troubles with interpersonal communication.

As we enter the technology driven world where our direct contact with one another is more limited, we need to hone our communication skills more. You may not have many chances to retain that client, enter into a new business relationship, or attract a new customer.

We still crave personal interaction. We might rely heavily upon email, Facebook and Twitter, but nothing beats a chat on the phone or *Face-2-Face* contact. Businesses continue to have group meetings and try to persuade prospective clients to become loyal customers. Doctors will continue to examine patients and attorneys will meet with clients. Every Friday night at clubs all around the world, partygoers practice the mating ritual in hopes of getting lucky and on Saturdays, neighbors will attend barbeques and parties.

The design of this book is to provide an insight into strengthening your integrative communication skills and understanding how people interpret your intent, as well as how to understand others through their various channels of communication.

I hope that my out of the box perspective will lend a fresh set of eyes and help you strengthen and grow your business, personal development, and communications.

Bibliography

Abrashoff, Michael. 2002. It's Your Ship: Management Techniques from the Best Damn Ship in the Navy. New York. Business Plus Publishers.

Ambady, Nalini and John Skowronski. 2008. First Impressions. New York Guilford Press.

Ambady. Nalini, Debi LaPlante, Thai Nguyen, Robert Rosenthal, Nigel Chaumeton, *and*Wendy Levinson. 2002. Surgeons' Tone of Voice: A clue to Malpractice History. *From the Department of Psychology, Harvard University, Boston, Mass; Department of Psychology, University of California-Riverside, Riverside, Calif; Legacy Good Samaritan Hospital, Portland, Ore; and University of Toronto, Toronto, Ontario, Canada.*

Ambady, Nalini and Robert Rosenthal. 1992. Thin slices of expressive behavior as predictors of interpersonal consequences: a meta-analysis. *Psychological Bulletin, Vol. 111, No. 2*: 256-74.

American Psychiatric Association. 2000. Diagnostic and Statistical Manual of Mental Disorders DSM-IV. American Psychiatric Association.

Bard, Ellen Gurman, Aylett, Matthew P., Lickley, Robin J. 2002. "Towards a Psycholinguistics of Dialogue: Defining Reaction Time and Error Rate in a Dialogue Corpus" *Bos, Foster & Matheson (eds): Proceedings of the sixth workshop on the semantics* *and pragmatics of dialogue (EDILOG 2002), 4-6 September 2002, Edinburgh, UK, Pages 29-36.*

Beach, Mary Catherine, Debra Roter, Haya Rubin, Richard Frankel, Wendy Levinson and Ford, Daniel E. 2004. "Is Physician Self-disclosure Related to Patient Evaluation of Office Visits?" Journal General Internal Medicine. 2004 September; 19(9): 905–910.

Bernieri, F. J., Davis, J., Rosenthal, R., & Knee, C. 1994. Interactional synchrony and rapport: Measuring synchrony in displays devoid of sound and facial affect. Personality and Social Psychology Bulletin, 20, 303-311.

Bernieri, F. J., & Gillis, J. S. (1995). Personality correlates of accuracy in a social perception task. Perceptual and Motor Skills, 81, 168-170.

Bernieri, F. J., Gillis, J. S., Davis, J. M., & Grahe, J. E. 1996. Dyad rapport and the accuracy of its judgment across situations: A lens model analysis. Journal of Personality and Social Psychology, 70, 110-129.

Beshera, Tony. 2008. Acing the Interview: How to Ask and Answer the Questions That Will Get You the Job. New York. AMACOM.

Boothman Nicholas. 2002. *How to Connect in Business in 90 Seconds or Less.* New York. Workman Publishing Company.

Boothman Nicholas. 2008. *How to Make People Like You in 90 Seconds or Less.* New York. Workman Publishing Company.

Boyatzis, C. et. al., 1998. "Effects of perceived attractiveness and academic success on early adolescent peer popularity." *Journal of Genetic Psychology* 159 (3): 337-44.

Brafman Ori and Rom Brafman. 2010. *Click.* New York. Broadway Books.

Cabane, Olivivia Fox. 2012. *The Charisma Myth: How Anyone Can Master the Art and Science of Personal Magnetism.* New York. Portfolio Hardcover.

Carnegie, Dale. 1936. *How to Win Friends & Influence People.* New York. Pocket Books.

Chabris Christopher and Daniel Simons, 2010. *Invisible Gorillas and Other Ways our Intuition Fail Us.* New York. Crown.

Chambliss, H, Finley, C, Blair S. 2004. *Attitudes Toward Obese Individuals Among Exercise Science Students.* Centers for Integrated Health Research, Dallas: The Cooper Institute.

Chandler, Steve. 2008 *100 Ways to Motivate Others: How Great Leaders Can Produce Insane Results Without Driving People Crazy.* Pompton Plains, NJ. Career Press.

Chartrand, Tanya L. and John Bargh. 1999. "The Chameleon Effect: The Perception–Behavior Link and Social interaction." *Journal of Personality and Social Psychology*, Vol 76(6), Jun 1999, 893-910.

Cialdini, Robert B. 1993. *Influence:The Psychology of Persuasion.* New York: William Morrow and Company, Inc.

Clever, Sarah L, Lei Jin, Wendy Levinson, and David O Meltzer. 2008. "Does Doctor–Patient Communication Affect Patient Satisfaction with Hospital Care? Results of an Analysis with a Novel Instrumental Variable." Health Services Research. 2008 October; 43(5p1): 1505–1519.

Clifford, M. and E. Walster. 1973. "Research note: The effects of physical atractiveness on teacher expectations." *Sociology of Education 46*: 248-58.

Collett, Peter. 2003. *The book of tells: from the bedroom to the boardroom – how to read other people.*

Collins NL, Miller LC. 1994 *Self-disclosure and liking: a meta-analytic review.* Ontario: HarperColins Ltd. Psychol Bull. 116(3):457-75.

Cooper, Ken. 2009. *Held Hostage: A Serial Bank Robbers's Road to Redemption.* Grand Rapid, MI: Chosen Books.

Curhan, Jared R. and Alex Pentland. 2007. "Thin Slices of Negotiation: Predicting Outcomes From Conversational Dynamics Within the First 5 Minutes." *Journal of Applied Psychology* Copyright 2007 by the American Psychological Association 2007, Vol. 92, No. 3, 802–811.

De Becker, Gavin. 1997. *The Gift of Fear.* New York: Dell Publishing.

DeGroot, T. and S. Motowidlo. 1999. "Why visual and vocal interview clues can affect interviewer's judgments and predict job performance." *Journal of Applied Psychology* 84 (6): 986-93.

Delmar, Ken. 1984. *Winning Moves: the Body Language of Selling.* New York: Warner Books.

Demarais, Ann and Valerie White. 2004. *First Impressions, What You Don't Know About How Others See You.* New York: Bantam.

Depaulo, Bella and Deborah Kashy, et al. 1996. "Lying in Everyday Life." *Journal of Personality and Social Psychology.* Vol 70, no 5, 979-99.

Dieken, Connie. 2009. *Talk Less, Say More: Three Habits to Influence Others and Make Things Happen.* Hoboken, NJ: Wiley.

Dimitrius, Jo-Ellan and Mark Mazzarela. 1998. *Reading People.* New York: Ballentine Books.

Dreeke, Robin. *2011. It's Not All About Me: The Top Ten Techniques for Building Quick Rapport with Anyone.* Washington DC. Robin Dreeke.

Driver, Janine. 2010. *You Say More Than You Think.* New York: Crown Publishing.

Duncan, Todd. 2007. High Trust Selling: Make More Money in Less Time with Less Stress. Nashville: Thomas Nelson Publishers.

Edeleman. 2009, Trust Barometer. New York.

Ekman, Paul. 2003. *Emotions Revealed: recognizing faces and feelings to improve communication and emotional life.* New York: Times Books.

Ekman, P. et. al., 1988. "Smiles when lying." *Journal of Personality and Social, Psychology* 54:414-20.

Ekman, Paul. 1985. *Telling Lies: Clues to Deceit in the Marketplace, Politics, and Marriages.* New York: W.W. Norton & Co.

Ekman, Paul. 1975. *Unmasking the Face.* New Jersey: Prentice Hall.

Elfenbein, H. A., & Ambady, N. 2002. On the universality and cultural specificity of emotion recognition: A meta-analysis. Psychological Bulletin, 128(2), 205-235.

Elfenbein, H. A., & Ambady, N. 2002b. Predicting workplace outcomes from the ability to eavesdrop on feelings. Journal of Applied Psychology, 87(5), 963-971.

Gallup Consulting. 2010. Employee Engagement: *What's Your Engagement Ratio?*

Gitomer, Jeffrey. 2008. *Sales Bible: The Ultimate Sales Resource.* New York: Harper.

Givens, David G. 2007. Crime *signals: how to spot a criminal before you become a victim.* New York: St. Martin's Press.

Givens, David G. and Joe Navarro. 2010. *Your body at work: A guide to sight-reading the body language of business, bosses, and boardrooms.* New York: St. Martin's Press.

Gladwell, Malcolm. 2005. *Blink: The Power of Thinking Without Thinking.* New York: Back Bay Books.

Gladwell, Malcolm. 2005. *Outliers: The Story of Success.* New York: Back Bay Books.

Goleman, Daniel. 1995. *Emotional Intelligence.* New York: Bantam Books.

Gordon, Jon. 2007. *The Energy Bus: 10 Rules to Fuel Your Life, Work, and Team with Positive Energy.* Hoboken: Wiley.

Gosling, Sam 2008. *Snoop What Your Stuff Says About You.* New York: Basic Books.

Gottman, J. and Levenson, R.W. 2002. A Two-Factor Model for Predicting When a Couple Will Divorce: Exploratory Analyses Using 14-Year Longitudinal Data, Family Process, 41 (1), p. 83-96.

Harris Interactive Poll. 2012. "One in Five U.S. Adults Now Has a Tattoo." *New York: Harris Interactive Poll.*

Harris Interactive Poll. 2009. Only One-Quarter of Americans Say Banks are Honest and Trustworthy :Just 4% say Wall Street is honest and trustworthy. ROCHESTER, N.Y. 06/30/09.

Harter, Jim and Sangeeta Agrawal. 2011. "Actively Disengaged Workers and Jobless in Equally Poor Health: Engaged employees report the best health" *Gallup* April 20, 2011.

Hill, Napoleon. 1937. Think and Grow Rich.

Hochwarter, W., Summers, J., Thompson, K., Perrewe, P., & Ferris, G. (2010). "Strain reactions to perceived entitlement behavior by others as a contextual stressor: Moderating role of political skill in three samples." *Journal of Occupational Health Psychology, 15,* 388-398.

Hoffmeister, David C. 2008 "Benchmarks in Sales Productivity Survey of Sales Organization Practices." *Best Practices Research Program Center For Sales Leadership.* Chicago:DePaul University.

Holtz, Lou. 2007. *Wins, Losses, and Lessons: An Autobiography.* New York. Harper.

Hoover, John. 2004. *Work for an Idiot: Survive & Thrive, Without Killing Your Boss.* Hoboken, NJ: Career Press.

Iacoboni, Marco. 2009. *Mirroring People: The Science of Empathy and How We Connect with Others.* New York: Picador.

Inbau, Fred and John Reid et al. 2001. *Criminal Interrogation and Confessions.* Gaithersburg, MD: Aspen Publishers.

Iyenga, Sheena S. r, and Mark R. Lepper, 2000. "When Choice is Demotivating: Can One Desire Too Much of a Good Thing?" *Journal of Personality and Social Psychology,* Vol. 79, No. 6, 995-1006.

Jeary, Tony. 1998. *Inspire Any Audience: Proven Secrets of the Pros for Powerful Presentations Inspire Any Audience: Proven Secrets of the Pros for Powerful Presentations.* USA: Trade Life books.

Joel, Mitch. 2009. *Six Pixels of Separation: Everyone Is Connected. Connect Your Business to Everyone.* New York: Business Plus Publishers.

Judge, T. A., & Cable, D. M. 2004. "The Effect of Physical Height on Workplace Success and Income." *Journal of Applied Psychology, 89,* 428-441.

Killingsworth, Matthew and Daniel T. Gilbert. 2010. A Wandering Mind Is an Unhappy Mind. *Science* 12 November 2010: Vol. 330 no. 6006 p. 932 DOI: 10.1126/science.1192439.

Krannich, Caryl Rae. 2004. *101 Secrets of Highly Effective Speakers: Controlling Fear, Commanding Attention.* New York: Impact Publishing.

Kushner Harold. 2004. *Why do Bad Things Happen to Good People.* New York: Anchor.

Lakhani, Dave. 2005. *Persuasion The Art of Getting What you Want,* Hoboken, NJ. Wiley.

Levinson, Wendy, Debra L. Roter, John P. Mullooly, Valerie T. Dull, Richard M. Frankel. "Physician-Patient CommunicationThe Relationship With Malpractice Claims Among Primary Care Physicians and Surgeons" *JAMA.* 1997;277(7):553-559. doi:10.1001/jama.1997.03540310051034.

Lewis, Michael. *2009. The Blind Side* New York: W. W. Norton & Company.

Lowndes, Leil 2003. *How to Talk to Anyone: 92 Little Tricks for Big Success in Relationships.* New York: McGraw Hill.

Maltz, Maxwell. 1989. *Psycho-Cybernetics, A New Way to Get More Living Out of Life.* New York: Pocket Books.

Maxwell, John C. 2005. *Developing the Leader Within You.* Nashville: Thomas Nelson Publishers.

Mehrabian, Albert. 1972. *Nonverbal Communication*. Chicago: Aldine Publishing Company.

Molloy, John T. 1975. *Dress for Success*. New York: Warner Books.

Morris, Desmond. 2010. The Naked Ape. London: Vintage Digital.

Mosscrop, Jennifer. 2005. "Nordstrom Tops Customer-Service List." *Chain Store Age News* and Analysis for Retail Executives. 11/14/2005.

Mullins, Richard. 2010. "Wikipedia Creator Had Lots of Earlier Failures." *Media General News Service*. Published: Tampa, February 19, 2010.

Naghshineh, Sheila, Janet P. Hafler, et al. 2008. "Formal Art Observation Training Improves Medical Students' Visual Diagnostic Skills." Journal of General Internal Medicine. 2008 July; 23(7): 991–997.

Navarro, Joe. 2003. A Four Domain Model of Detecting Deception. *FBI Law Enforcement Bulletin*, (June): 19-24.

Navarro, Joe. 2010. *Body Language Essentials*. Amazon Kindle.

Navarro, Joe. 2011. *Clues to Deceit: A Practical List*. Amazon Kindle.

Navarro, Joe and John R. Schafer. 2001. *Detecting Deception*. *FBI Law Enforcement Bulletin*, (July): 9-13.

Navarro, Joe. 2002. Interacting with Arabs and Muslims. *FBI Law Enforcement Bulletin*, (September): 20-23.

Navarro, Joe. 2010. *Louder than Words: Take Your Career from Average to Exceptional with the Hidden Power of Nonverbal Intelligence*. New York : Harper Collins.

Navarro, Joe. 2008. *What Every Body Is Saying*. New York: Harper Collins.

Nierenberg, Gerald I. and Henry H. Calero. 1971. *How to Read a Person like a Book*. New York: Pocket Books.

Pease, Allan and Barbara. 2004. *The Definitive Book of Body Language.* New York: Bantam Dell.

Pink, Daniel. 2011. *Drive: The Surprising Truth About What Motivates Us.* New York: Riverhead Books.

Pinsky, Drew and Mark Young. 2009 *The Mirror Effect How Celebrity Narcissim is Seducing America.* New York: Harper Collins.

Pollay, David 2010. The Law of The Garbage Truck. New York: Sterling Publishing.

Puhl Rebecca, Kelly D. Brownell. 2001 *Bias, Discrimination, and Obesity. Obes Res.*

Rath, Tom and Donald O. Clifton. 2004. *How Full Is Your Bucket? Positive Strategies for Work and Life.* New York:Gallup Press 2001;9:788–805.

Reiman, Tonya. 2007. *The Power of Body Language: How to Succeed in Every Business and Social Encounter.* New York: Pocket Books.

Reiss Steven. 2008. *The Normal Personality: A New Way of Thinking about People.* UK:Cambridge University Press.

Reynolds, Garr 2010. *PresentationZen Design.* Berkeley, CA: New Riders.

Rhodes, Karin V., Teri Vieth, Theresa He, Annette Miller, David S. Howes, Olivia Bailey, James Walter, Richard Frankel, and Wendy Levinson. 2004. "Resuscitating the Physician-Patient Relationship: Emergency Department Communication in an Academic Medical Center." *Annals of Emergency Medicine*, Volume 44, Issue 3, September 2004, pages 262-267.

Robbins, Anthony. 1997. *Unlimited Power : The New Science Of Personal Achievement.* New York: Free Press.

Schafer, John R. and Joe Navarro. 2004. *Advanced Interviewing Techniques.* Springfield, Il.: Charles C. Thomas Publisher.

Schwartz, David J. 1959. *The Magic of Thinking Big.* New York: Fireside Books.

Seuss, Dr. *Oh the Places You'll Go!*

Shea, Andy and Steve Van Aperen. 2007. *The Truth about Lies.* Australia: Bolinda Publishing.

Smith, Ned. 2011. "*Horrible Bosses* Movie Has a Ring of Reality, Professor Says." July 08, 2011. *Business News Daily.*

Snowdon DA, Kemper SJ, Mortimer JA, et al. 1996. "Linguistic Ability in Early Life and Cognitive Function and Alzheimer's Disease in Late Life: Findings from the Nun Study." *JAMA* 275: 528-32.

Sobel, Andrew. 2012. *Power Questions: Build Relationships, Win New Business, and Influence Others.* Hoboken: Wiley.

Thomason, T.C., et. al. 1980. "Test of the eye-movement hypothesis of neurolinguistic programming," *Perceptual and Motor Skills,* Vol 51, p. 230.

Thorndike, E.L . 1920. "A Constant Error in Psychological Ratings." Journal of Applied Psychology 4 (1): 25–29.

Tracy, Brian. 2010. *Goals!: How to Get Everything You Want -- Faster Than You Ever Thought Possible.* San Francisco: Berrett-Koehler Publishers.

Tracy, Brian. 1996. *Advanced Selling Strategies: The Proven System of Sales Ideas, Methods, and Techniques Used by Top Salespeople Everywhere.* New York: Simon and Schuster.

Twenge, Jean. 2007. *Generation ME: Why Today's Young Americans Are More Confident, Assertive, Entitled--and More Miserable Than Ever Before.* New York: Free Press.

Twenge, Jean M. and Keith Campbell. 2009. The *Narcissism Epidemic.* New York: Free Press.

Van Baaren, R. B., Holland, R. W., Steenaert, B., & van Knippenberg, A. 2003. Mimicry for money: Behavioral consequences of imitation. *Journal of Experimental Social Psychology, 39,* 393–398.

Vaynerchuk, Gary. 2009. *Crush It! Why NOW Is the Time to Cash In on Your Passion*. New York: Harper Collins.

Vaynerchuk, Gary. 2009. *The Thank You Economy*. New York. Harper Collins.

Vrij, Aldert. 2000. *Detecting Lies and Deceit: The Psychology of Lying and the Implications for Professional Practice*. Chichester, England: John Wiley & Sons, Ltd.

Waitley Dennis. 1986. The *Psychology of Winning*. New York: Berkeley Press.

Walker, Cami. 2010. *29 Gifts: How a Month of Giving Can Change Your Life*. Cambridge, MA: DeCapo Life Long Books.

Walters, Stan B. 2003. *Principles of Kinesic Interview and Interrogation, 2nd ed.* Boca Raton, Florida: CRC Press LLC.

Walton, Sam and John Huey .1992 *Made in America My Story. New York. Bantam Books.*

Wang, Sam and Sandra Aamodt. 2008. Welcome to Your Brain: Why You Lose Your Car Keys but Never Forget How to Drive and Other Puzzles of Everyday Life. New York: Bloomsbury. Sam Wang. (Author)

Weisfield, G. E. And J. M. Beresfor. 1982. "Erectness of posture as an indicator of dominance or success in humans." *Motivation and Emotion 6*, no. 2:113-31.

Wilder, Lilyan 1999. *7 Steps to Fearless Speaking*. Hoboken: Wiley.

Witt, Christoper. 2009. *Real Leaders Don't Do PowerPoint*. Mew York: Crown Business.

Ziglar, Zig. 1991. *Ziglar On Selling*. Nashville: Thomas Nelson Publishers.

Ziglar, Zig. 2006. *Better Than Good*. Nashville: Integrity Publishers.

Ziglar, Zig. 1985. *Zig Ziglar's Secrets of Closing the Sale*. New York: Berkley Trade.

Zuckoff, Mitchell. 2011. *Lost in Shangri-La.: A True Story of Survival, Adventure, and the Most Incredible Rescue Mission of World War II*. New York: Harper Perennial.

Zunin, L. and Zunin, N. 1972. *Contact - The First Four Minutes*. New York: Ballantine Books.

About the Author

For over 30 years, Mike Roche has used his communication skills to develop relationships from the inner city, to boardrooms, to plush hotels. His ability to develop rapport and effectively communicate depended on an integrative interpersonal communication system. Mike's ability to read people and interact with them was vital to his safety, as well as those he was charged with protecting. Mike retired after 23 years with the U.S. Secret Service. He is an adjunct college instructor and commonly shares his insights and lessons learned.

You can learn more how these skills are utilized in business, sales, human relations, job interviews and social networking. Check out his website: MikeRoche.com

Made in the USA
Lexington, KY
28 January 2013